Dear Reader: W9-CLW-425

The book you are about to read is the latest bestseller from the St. Martin's True Crime Library, the imprint *The New York Times* calls "the leader in true crime!" The True Crime Library offers fascinating accounts of the latest, most sensational crimes that have captured the national attention. St. Martin's is the publisher of John Glatt's riveting and horrifying SECRETS IN THE CELLAR, which shines a light on the man who shocked the world when it was revealed that he had kept his daughter locked in his hidden basement for 24 years. In the Edgar-nominated WRITTEN IN BLOOD, Diane Fanning looks at Michael Peterson, a Marine-turned-novelist found guilty of beating his wife to death and pushing her down the stairs of their home—only to reveal another similar death from his past. In the book you now hold, INSIDE THE MIND OF CASEY ANTHONY, *New York Times* bestselling author Keith Ablow presents a definitive look at one of the most stunning recent cases in America.

St. Martin's True Crime Library gives you the stories behind the headlines. Our authors take you right to the scene of the crime and into the minds of the most notorious murderers to show you what really makes them tick. St. Martin's True Crime Library paperbacks are better than the most terrifying thriller, because it's all true! The next time you want a crackling good read, make sure it's got the St. Martin's True Crime Library logo on the spine—you'll be up all night!

Charles E. Spicer, Jr.
Executive Editor, St. Martin's True Crime Library

Also by Keith Ablow

NONFICTION

The 7: Seven Wonders That Will Change Your Life

*Living the Truth: Transform Your Life Through the
Power of Insight and Honesty*

How to Cope with Depression

Medical School: Getting In, Staying In, Staying Human

Anatomy of a Psychiatric Illness

To Wrestle with Demons

Without Mercy

Inside the Mind of Scott Peterson

FICTION

Denial

Projection

Compulsion

Psychopath

Murder Suicide

The Architect

INSIDE THE MIND OF CASEY ANTHONY

A Psychological Portrait

Keith Ablow, M.D.

St. Martin's Paperbacks

To George Weinberg, PhD, quite possibly America's greatest living psychologist. Had Casey Anthony met a man such as he, none of this may ever have happened.

Grateful acknowledgment to the band Sevendust for the use of their lyrics on p. xi and pp. 237–238.

INSIDE THE MIND OF CASEY ANTHONY: A PSYCHOLOGICAL PORTRAIT

For information address St. Martin's Press, 175 Fifth Avenue, New York, NY 10010.

EAN: 978-1-250-03963-7

Printed in the United States of America

St. Martin's Press hardcover edition / November 2011
St. Martin's Paperbacks edition / July 2013

St. Martin's Paperbacks are published by St. Martin's Press, 175 Fifth Avenue, New York, NY 10010.

10 9 8 7 6 5 4 3 2 1

CONTENTS

The Facts   1

Suffocation   2

A Prop   5

Enabler of Death   20

Last Breaths   30

Delivery   39

My Space   52

A Brand-New Day   64

Gone   68

Lie to Live   82

Accomplices   89

Three Hundred Bucks   126

Bringing Casey Home   136

A Dizzying Romantic Time Line   142

911   148

Apartment 210   166

Reality at Universal Studios   176

Round Two   192

Round Three   198

Arrested Development   208

Night Call   214

A Real Death Amidst Fake Lives   224

Crying a River   232

Making Bail   236

Jailed and Dead, but Free   243

Identity Suppression Syndrome   249

Afterword   255

ACKNOWLEDGMENTS

Amber Roback and Jackie Hodges, my project managers, not only organized the logistics that helped me to create this book, but also contributed their own substantial research skills.

Rachel St. Pierre was an effective research assistant, on the ground in Orlando, Florida, and Warren, Ohio.

Bill Shine, senior vice president of programming for the Fox News Channel, as well as Lee Kushnir and Justin Wells or the Fox News Channel, were very helpful to me in gathering or sharing information.

Richard Pine, my literary agent, called me to suggest this book, with the simple statement, "Someone needs to explain *why* this happened." I am in his debt, yet again.

Finally, I thank Sally Richardson, the publisher at St. Martin's Press, my editor, Charles Spicer, and the team working with him. They include John Murphy, Matthew Baldacci, Paul Hockman, Stephanie Hargadon, April Osborn, Eliani Torres, Eric C. Meyer, attorney Mark Lerner, and attorney Diana Frost.

My family awakened too many nights at one and three and five A.M. while I wrote this book, turned on my office light, moved my desk chair a little too noisily over the floor, and hit keys a little too hard on my computer. To them, I officially apologize. This psychological mystery did not let me sleep.

Beneath the water . . .
I'm up,
I'm down
like a roller coaster
racing through my life
I've erased the past again

—Sevendust, "The Past"
Casey Anthony's favorite song

AUTHOR'S NOTE

The ideas and psychological theories I express in this book are based on my interviews with my sources in several states, my review of thousands of pages of legal documents and other publications, my review of videotaped testimony, and my many years of experience as a forensic psychiatrist. They are not to be taken as objective fact, but as my perspectives on how to understand the individuals involved and their behaviors. While I repeatedly sought interviews with Casey, George, and Cindy Anthony to further substantiate or refute my ideas, I was consistently refused access to them.

THE FACTS

On July 15, 2008, Cindy Marie Anthony dialed 911 to report that her granddaughter, Caylee Marie Anthony, a magnificent little girl just shy of her third birthday, was missing—and had not been seen for a month.

According to Caylee's single mother, twenty-two-year-old Casey Marie Anthony, she had dropped her daughter off at her nanny's apartment on June 16. When she'd returned there later that day, both the nanny and Caylee had vanished. Casey claimed she had then launched her own monthlong search to no avail.

The police investigation that ensued uncovered the unthinkable: Casey Anthony had invented much of her life story. She had no nanny. She didn't have the job at Universal Studios that she had been telling her parents about for years. She hadn't, as she had told her family, been traveling around the state of Florida with Caylee during the weeks between June 16 and July 15.

Casey Anthony, it turned out, was a kind of ghost—a woman with no real identity; no connection to her rageful, shattered inner *self;* and no person on this earth who really knew the truth about her.

Caylee was dead. She had been placed in a black plastic trash bag and thrown in the woods near the Anthony home at 4937 Hopespring Drive in Orlando, a cruelly ironic address for a house of horror.

SUFFOCATION

The story you are about to read is about suffocation—psychological suffocation leading to physical suffocation, leading to death.

This is a story about how toxic emotional forces in a family, unfolding over decades, slowly extinguished Casey Anthony psychologically, and then suddenly extinguished her two-year-old daughter, Caylee Anthony, physically.

Caylee Anthony was killed by a person who had never lived anything resembling a genuine life—was never really, truly alive at all—and, therefore, assigned no value to a little girl's life.

This transmutation of psychological death into physical death usually occurs without anyone taking notice. The victim's remains are buried and, with them, the true story of *why* that person was killed. The people who remain behind escape any postmortem examination. Even if one of them is tried for murder, the truth about the lethal psychological makeup of that person, or those surrounding her, may never be known. That shall not be the case here.

Does the link I suggest between psychological death and physical death surprise you? It shouldn't. One very often causes the other, though it sometimes takes two generations, or three, or even more for it to happen.

Emotional violence snaking its way through a family tree commonly snaps the newest, most innocent, most exquisitely vulnerable limb.

Looking at the corpse of a child, even combing through the physical evidence surrounding her disappearance, can't reveal her real cause of death. Hair samples, DNA, a skull left in the dirt all fail to tell the tale. But a painstaking examination of the psychological dynamics of those closest to her often will.

Few of us would deny that chronic emotional stress can eventually trigger a cardiac arrest, ending a man's life. The stress can act on blood vessels, causing them to clamp down, limiting the oxygen carried to the heart muscle, ultimately destroying that muscle. In some cases, the person doesn't survive.

Well, just as people need oxygen to feed their heart muscle, they need "emotional oxygen" to feed their souls and sustain that core identity we call the *self*.

Emotional oxygen is anything that reassures a person that she is a *real* individual, worthy of being treated as a complete human being. It includes all the times when others react to her behavior with genuine praise, concern, or even justifiable anger. It includes all those times when others honor her thoughts and feelings, listening to them with real attention, responding to them with real intention. In short, it includes all the ways she is affirmed as a person, rather than treated as a nonperson.

Emotional oxygen nurtures a person's developing humanity.

Mental, physical, or sexual abuse can suck all the emotional oxygen out of a home, psychologically suffocating one or more occupants. So, too, can subtle and toxic forms of communication that demand that one or more family members put themselves to sleep or bury themselves alive, suppressing their core identities until they are, for all intents and purposes, nonexistent. It can happen in the dark, under cover of night, as silently as carbon monoxide fills the lungs of children while they sleep.

Without enough emotional oxygen, a person can die spiritually. She can end up despising the truth because she despises the true story of her own psychological destruction.

She can become a stranger to her own feelings, then immune to those of others, then hostile to genuine human existence itself. And then she—or, more likely, someone who is dependent on her—can die physically, whether by suicide, murder, or even through carelessness that leads to an avoidable "accident."

In short, a family can be so devoid of emotional oxygen that it eventually becomes incompatible with sustaining human life.

The family in which Casey Anthony was raised, into which Caylee Anthony was born, and in which she died before her third birthday, would seem to be such a family.

A PROP

June 15, 2008, was Father's Day. Casey Anthony's mother, Cindy, who had just turned fifty, went to see her eighty-seven-year-old father, Alexander Plesea, at the Avante at Mount Dora Nursing Home in Mount Dora, Florida, a lakefront community twenty-nine miles from Orlando. She took her two-year-old granddaughter, Caylee, along.

Alexander Plesea was a first-generation Romanian-American. He had served in the United States Navy during World War II and, then, in the Korean conflict.

Alexander and his wife, Shirley, whom he met before he dropped out of high school, had had four children. Cindy was the youngest and the only girl. Her brothers Rick, Gary, and Daniel were five, ten, and eleven years older than she.

Alexander kept to himself and ran a tight ship while Cindy was growing up. He worked hard as a laborer and was bone tired when he got home. He had rigid expectations as to how his children should behave. He didn't hesitate to discipline them.

"He was a strange little man and had a hell of a temper," a close family member, who did not wish to be identified, told me.

"He didn't like us carrying on," his son Rick told me.

The Plesea family had little contact with other relatives and few, if any, friends. Their neighbor across the street, Sue Marvin, told me, "They were a very private family. They were in the neighborhood many years before we got to know them a little bit."

Maybe Alexander's own history had something to do with his tendency to isolate, and his short fuse. He, his brothers, and his sisters had reportedly grown up in an orphanage after their father placed them there following the sudden death of their mother. He was never adopted. When he finally got out, after psychological stresses one can only guess at, he went to work, then joined the navy. He got married soon after he was discharged.

The sudden severing of Alexander's bond with his mother (by death) and his father (because he felt he couldn't work and raise children at the same time), together with his being raised in an orphanage, wouldn't necessarily be enough to set dominoes falling toward a fatal catastrophe, but it could be. It is interesting to note that the same circumstances figure in multiple stories in which a family member eventually kills a child, including that of Scott Peterson—the Modesto, California, man who killed his wife, Laci, and unborn child, Conner, in 2002. Peterson's mother had been placed in an orphanage and was raised there.

Although Alexander seemed to be the disciplinarian of the family, his son Rick told me that he more commonly meted out punishments at the direction of his wife, Shirley. "She would just tell him what to do and he would listen. He was quiet around her, because he was totally controlled by her. He could be talkative and laugh one-on-one, but when he was with my mother, he was almost silent."

That doesn't seem surprising. Having lost his parents and been sent to an orphanage for his entire childhood, Alexander Plesea must have welcomed a woman who promised to make him part of a family. It makes sense that he wouldn't want to rock the boat and be thrown overboard again.

For her part, Shirley Plesea wasn't likely to yield to a man, anyhow. According to a close family member of hers, her father, Stiles, had abandoned the family when the children were quite young. Shirley herself was barely three years old.

Stiles had met another woman, taken off for Chicago, and

gone to work in a steel mill. He never paid child support, though, and had almost nothing to do with his children. He left his wife, Velma, struggling to support them as best she could. She went to work, and her own mother—Shirley's grandmother—stepped in to take care of the kids.

According to Shirley's close relative, Velma had once said, "Men are all right in their place, but I don't have any place for one."

Both Alexander and Shirley, then, were the products of fathers who turned out to be disastrously, catastrophically unreliable. They seem to have agreed that women should wield the power in a family.

"If you were just a few minutes late for dinner," one of Shirley and Alexander's children told me, "my mother would be very unhappy and very angry. If you showed up one minute late for an event, you'd hear about it. She made fun of the people she didn't like, who didn't suit her—not in front of them, but in front of us, which gave us the idea that you were supposed to fit her mold, or else. She was a control freak. That's where my sister, Cindy, learned it."

Even the Pleseas' neighbor Sue Marvin could tell that Shirley was the one pulling the strings in the family. "The mother was more in control," she said.

"Probably Shirley yelled at them a lot. They got hollered at a whole lot," Shirley's close family member told me.

Because she was the baby of the family and female, her brothers called Cindy "the Princess." They sometimes resented her because they felt she was doted upon and given material things and opportunities denied to them. Maybe she got screamed at less. It didn't help any that the family, which started out desperately poor, in a run-down neighborhood, living in a rented house in the projects, had a little more money available and was able to move to a slightly nicer area and buy a modest home when Cindy was about four. Her father eventually got steadier work, and her mother took a part-time job at Trumbull Memorial Hospital.

"My parents got by on the skimpiest budget at the beginning," one of Cindy's brothers told me. "If he had twenty or thirty cents at the end of the month, he'd take us down to the Sanitary Dairy in Warren and buy us an ice cream. A cone was a nickel. We were very, very poor for a long time. But it wasn't quite as bad as that during most of Cindy's childhood."

Maybe Cindy suffered because of her older brothers' jealousy. Maybe she resented her father's discipline or her mother's authoritarian style. Maybe she'd been called Princess, or teased in worse ways, one too many times. Maybe kids at school weren't all that kind about her living in what one of them described to me as a "ramshackle house." Maybe that explains why one of her classmates told me that she was extraordinarily quiet and shy in grade school. Maybe she did, indeed, gradually learn from her mother that a woman could achieve power by micromanaging those around her. Maybe something more unsettling happened in her family of origin—some painful chaos—when her dad lost his job and things got tougher and money got tighter and nerves were on edge.

Or, maybe, it was even worse than that. Maybe the trauma was severe. When I reached Cindy's brother Gary, who described himself as the "hermit" of the family, he told me he'd spoken to his sister only a few times over the past twenty years. "I have nothing to say to you," he told me.

"I just have one question," I said before he could hang up. "That's it. Just the one."

"Fine . . ." he said impatiently.

"A lot of people I've spoken with describe your sister, Cindy, as an extremely controlling person. In my experience, people that controlling often lived through things that were completely beyond their control. Sometimes, they suffered a lot because they couldn't protect themselves—whether emotionally or physically."

Ten seconds passed in silence—a long time without any words on a phone call between strangers. Then Gary finally spoke: "I'm not giving you that," he sputtered. He hung up.

I hung up, too, but slowly. I cannot say why, but I felt chills run up my back, as though I was at the heart of some kind of darkness.

* * *

Whatever her reasons, once she was old enough, Cindy Plesea made one decision after another that seemed designed—at least unconsciously—to make sure she was never disempowered again.

One of those decisions was to become a nurse. There are many and varied motivations for such a noble career choice, but to some who knew her well, becoming a nurse seemed like a lock-and-key fit with Cindy's thirst for control.

Nurses are very much needed by the sick patients they tend to. They are, therefore, very powerful in the lives of those individuals and their families. You might be disappointed in the care rendered by a nurse, but you're unlikely to complain a whole lot while you're lying down in a hospital bed, wearing a johnny, relying on her for pain medications or sleeping pills—or oxygen. You might think of yourself as smarter than your nurse or prettier or more fit, but you aren't going to make a point of letting her know that. You might be richer than your nurse, but you aren't going to flaunt it.

When you're in the hospital, you're vulnerable, possibly at your very worst. And you want your nurse to want to help you, certainly not hurt you. The best way to do that is to make her like you, even if that means swallowing some of your pride, turning your complaints into suggestions, smiling now and then, even when you're suffering. The best way into a nurse's heart is to give up power to her, convey how much you need her, be careful not to be an irritant, and let her take complete control.

A nurse with lots of reasons to feel weak inside can still feel very powerful working her shift at the hospital. She can certainly still look very strong in today's hospital-issue scrubs, never mind the starched white uniform—dress, apron, hat, and all—worn by Cindy Plesea at the beginning of her career.

Interestingly enough, Cindy was dressed just that way, working as a nurse, when she met her husband, George Anthony. She was taking care of his sister Ruth, who was hospitalized.

George was still legally married at the time, but Cindy would later deny that fact to her own family.

When a member of the extended family alerted Cindy's mother to George's marital status, her mother reportedly replied, "Absolutely not. Cindy told me he's divorced."

The truth was already falling victim to Cindy's habit of controlling what people knew, and when they knew it—to essentially control what they thought.

Even if Cindy hadn't been in a position of ascendance while tending to George's sister, she still would have been able to exercise a lot of power over George. He was a very flawed person, in no position to take control of any other adult. His first wife, Terri Rosenberger VanDervort, thought of him as a "mama's boy and liar." His former sister-in-law remembers him as a "pussy."

Having grown up in a family in which both her parents were completely abandoned by their unreliable fathers, Cindy apparently wasn't about to try her luck yielding any control to a man.

"Cindy sissified him," VanDervort said.

Another person who knew George well told me that when he looked in his eyes, he saw "nothing there."

"No one around him knew George that well because there was nothing to know about George," that person added. "At least there was nothing he'd let you know."

George joined the Trumbull County Sheriff's Department at age twenty-two, but, according to a source of mine, he always cared more about the uniform than he did about the work. "His entire interest in law enforcement was in wearing his uniform and driving around in his cruiser. It was like a disguise. I think it hid a lot of his weaknesses."

A nurse in starched whites. A police officer in starched blues, with a license to carry. Maybe they were both simply wearing uniforms to do their jobs. Lots of people have to. Or maybe they were, psychologically speaking, hiding behind those uniforms.

George had reportedly told his first wife, Terry, whom he married in 1972 after she became pregnant, that he wanted to move away from Ohio and live in Orlando, Florida. When she asked whether he intended to apply for a job with the Orlando Police Department, he supposedly replied, "No, I want to be a character at Disney." That never happened, but it certainly would have taken the notion of hiding behind a costume to a whole other level.

According to Terry, George once filed for divorce from her secretly, and she learned about it only when friends of hers read a report of court filings published in the local newspaper. She believes he was angry with her because her first pregnancy—which, after all, had prompted him to propose—had ended in a miscarriage, and she hadn't borne him children. They patched things up that time. But the couple did divorce after Terri came to believe that George was a compulsive liar and compulsive gambler.

"George wanted a mother figure," a source told me. "He wanted to be babied. He liked hanging around kids more than adults because they were no threat to him and no smarter."

He and Cindy really hit it off.

All that had happened long before Father's Day, June 15, 2008, when Cindy took her granddaughter, Caylee, to visit the little girl's great-grandfather at the Mount Dora Nursing Home.

Caylee had big, wide hazel eyes; straight brown hair; and a smile that could almost disguise all the pain she had already witnessed.

She had lived with her mother, grandfather, and grandmother since being born.

In a stark and chilling example of just how little Caylee's life story seemed to matter to George or Cindy—not to mention how little their daughter, Casey's, life experiences apparently mattered to them—neither pressed Casey very hard about who Caylee's father might be.

The topic didn't really come up for quite a while after Casey announced she was pregnant.

"I was just so happy of that moment, that day, that time,

to be able to look her in the eyes and tell her how happy I was," George later said.

From George's deposition with the Florida Assistant State Attorney, given years later:

Q: At that particular point was Casey involved with anyone?

A: Not that I ever knew of. I—I didn't know anything about—I mean, she had dated some different people over the—different gentlemen over the years, starting, like, her junior year of high school, but not anyone specifically, no.

Q: The who's-the-father conversation, did that occur at that time or did that occur at some later time?

A: That didn't occur specifically that day. I didn't because—I don't want to say I wasn't concerned. I was concerned—

Q: Sure.

A: —but I didn't—I was just so happy of that moment, that day, that time, to be able to look her in the eyes and tell her how happy I was.

Q: Okay.

A: You know, and I want her to take care of herself and just—you know, a lot of emotion. Just a lot of great emotion.

Q: Now, when did the—did you have a conversation with her about who the father was?

A: Oh, we had talked about it probably the next day or it could have even been later that day. I'm not really specific on that time. But she just said: Well, Dad, she says, I—she said: I believe it's this one guy I saw off and on. And I said: Well, I'd like to be able to meet the father.

Q: Sure.

A: I really would. I'd like to know—

Q: Naturally

A: —know who it is. I mean, that's—I'd like to know who Caylee's dad is.

Q: Right. And so what did she tell you about this man?

A: We would—we would eventually meet him. She says: Dad, she says, I just want to try to get through this and I want to try to just stay on track to, you know, have my daughter, your granddaughter be born. And I said: Okay. I wasn't putting any pressure on her. Because I know one thing about a pregnancy with a woman, if you put a lot of pressure on them, that can affect the child. And with Cindy being the nurse and stuff that she is and different things we talked about, we just said—

Q: Yeah.

A: —let's just get her through this thing and we'll eventually get into knowing who the father is.

Q: So initially she didn't tell you who the father was?

A: Not for the first few days. It could have been maybe a few days after that. It could have been the following week, who she thought it was. And I just said: Well, God, I'd like to meet this guy.

Q: So who did she eventually tell you she thought the father was?

A: She told me that the father, she believed, was a fellow by the name of Jesse Grund.

Q: Okay. And at this point you had not met Jesse?

A: Never had met him.

Q: And you, in fact, didn't even know he existed at this particular point?

A: Didn't know anything about him. No.

Q: How soon after that did you meet Jesse?

A: Not until Caylee was born.

Q: Did that bother you, that you didn't meet him, you know—?

A: Not specifically, no. It didn't. Because it—like I said, I was trying to honor her wishes—

Q: Sure.

A: —of being the mom that she was, the single mom she was, not trying to cause her any emotional distress, because I wanted my granddaughter to be

born healthy. And, like I said, I know that if you put
a lot of extra pressure on an expectant mother, it
can affect the child. It can affect when the child is
born, a lot of other things. So—

Q: Sure.

George was just plain thrilled that his unmarried daughter who, to his knowledge, hadn't ever been involved romanti-
cally with anyone, was pregnant. What's more, *she was seven
months pregnant*! She had ignored her growing abdomen for
thirty weeks, dismissing it as "female" problems—like
water weight gain related to erratic monthly cycles.

George was crying "tears of joy," he said. He was just "so
thankful to be a grandfather."

"That is just—you can't put a price tag on that," he said.
"You can't talk about the exact emotions. Just—to say that I
was higher than these clouds right now, I was off the charts
feeling so happy."

One thing about George: He always liked the idea of being around children.

Cindy didn't show much interest in who the father might
be, either. She would later tell investigators that a young man
named Eric could be the one—someone Cindy says "came
into town" around the time Casey was impregnated and knew
Casey from her high school years:

"Um, I believe his first name is Eric and if I heard his last
name, I would know it but I can't remember, it really didn't,
um, I really didn't stand out because from what Casey told
me he had come into town, they were old friends from school,
um, they got together, Eric was going through a tough time,
Casey was in between, um, friends, and they just had a one-
night stand."

Cindy never tried to meet Eric. She seemed to recall he
might be from Tennessee or Kentucky. What she did do was
have her attorney file paperwork stating that if anything
happened to Casey, then custody of Caylee would go to her
and George.

When the investigator asked Cindy whether she and

George wanted the father involved, she said no, noting that "he [the possible father] is not on the birth certificate" and that "the guy has no claim to [Caylee]."

That wasn't a complete answer to the question. The question invited Cindy to talk about whether she or George had reached out to the man who might have impregnated their daughter to let him know that a little girl had been born who was his child. But that kind of question goes to the issue of empathy and humanity, and it passed in one of Cindy's ears and out the other.

It so happens that neither George nor Cindy—a *registered nurse*—had suspected Casey was pregnant, either. Cindy's brother Rick had to point it out to them when the family came to attend his second wedding. At the time, she was already almost seven months along, with a round abdomen and protruding belly button. Even when Rick told them there could be no other explanation than pregnancy for Casey's appearance, they still denied it.

Cindy told Rick that Casey couldn't be pregnant, because she was a virgin.

"I just thought she was filling out," Cindy has said.

From her deposition with the Florida Assistant State Attorney:

Q: What made you suspicious that she even was pregnant?

A: I really didn't know until after she told me. I knew she wasn't feeling well. Casey had had some irregular periods for several months, and I assumed a lot of it was bloating because I would get the same way, and I went through a lot of what Casey went—you know, was going through. And I was concerned more about her having, like, uterine fibroids or something—

Q: Uh-huh.

A: —like that so—

Q: Did you ask her directly, before she ended up telling you?

A: No.

Q: You know, like—

A: No. I just asked her—

Q: —are you having female problems, stuff like that?

A: No. I just asked her to go to the doctor's office to get checked because I know she wasn't feeling good.

Q: Okay. Did some of your family members ask if Casey was pregnant and—?

A: Yeah. My brother Rick did.

Q: And what did you tell him?

A: And I said no. I said no because that was an honest anwer, was no.

Q: Okay.

A: He asked us if we had news. And I said: What are you talking about?

George never attended Rick's wedding. He stayed in the hotel room. Maybe he wasn't up for the roomful of wedding guests who kept asking Rick, "Who's the pretty pregnant girl?"

Some days later, Casey finally took a pregnancy test and drove to her mother's workplace to tell her the results. Cindy has said she was shocked, "but excited for her."

The two of them then shared the news with George.

Casey's brother, Lee, was left out of the loop—something he would later weep publicly about.

He had asked about Casey being pregnant before Casey ever attended Rick's wedding:

It would've been later at night, I was waiting for her to get out of the bathroom. When she was coming out, I could see her midsection and it was showing. It struck me as odd 'cause I guess I just hadn't noticed it prior to that. [Smirking] I believe I made some sort of comment towards Casey, like, "Excuse me, what the hell is that?" and she just kind of waved me off. The next time I would've seen my mom, I recall asking her, "Is Casey pregnant? It looks that way to me. . . ."

"That's one of the reasons I was so angry and decided not to go see my sister in the hospital [when she delivered]," he stated. "I was not included on it and when I did ask about it one time early on, it was denied to me and I was told to let it go. That's what I did. . . . It was something that was hidden from me or I felt I was not being made a part of. I'm not going to go out of my way to invite myself or know everything that's going on if I'm led to believe I shouldn't be involved in it.

"I was very angry at my mom," he cried. "I was also angry at my sister, I was angry at everyone in general that they didn't want to include me and didn't find it important enough to tell me, especially after I'd already asked. I was very hurt and I don't think I wanted to believe it."

What people in the Anthony family knew and when they were allowed to know it was up to Cindy. And being kept in the dark—when the light of your spirit was already dim—could feel like solitary confinement. It could feel like death itself.

Cindy started planning a baby shower right away.

That must have been fun—for Cindy.

For parents to focus on their own strange "happiness" and "excitement," while not attending to the obvious psychological problems of a daughter who has denied her pregnancy for seven months and is not certain who the father might be, is to essentially deny that daughter's existence.

It is as if, for both George and Cindy, their daughter, Casey, was invisible.

Casey's refusal to admit that life was stirring inside her was, then, understandable. It was not so different from her mother and father's refusal to admit that she herself was a real person, with real problems—problems that had not been addressed since she was a child.

Now, the same depersonalizing, dehumanizing, psychologically suffocating forces—multiplied by two generations—would be focused on Caylee.

Just think about bringing Caylee to the nursing home that Father's Day. It had to be a frightening place for a little girl just two years old. Mount Dora is a facility that houses 114 elderly individuals, with 57 on each of two units. There were frail strangers in wheelchairs, some with oxygen tanks nearby. There were elderly people with Alzheimer's dementia, others with bipolar disorder, a few with psychotic symptoms. Patients with schizophrenia are sometimes accepted as residents. The place was of good quality, but even the best nursing home doesn't smell great. Yet Cindy thought that her father, Alexander—though he wasn't thinking all that clearly and had suffered a stroke that severely limited his ability to speak—would enjoy seeing his great-granddaughter. That, or *Cindy* wanted to see him with his great-granddaughter.

Maybe the picture-perfect notion of a great-grandfather snuggling his great-granddaughter was more compelling to Cindy than the reality of a vulnerable little girl confined to a traumatizing environment. Maybe she thought of Caylee more like a therapy dog.

Or maybe Cindy was replaying something that had happened in her own life. "There was something very wrong with Cindy's father," one of my sources, who had gotten to know many family members, told me. It was simply his impression of Alexander Plesea. "I ended up especially friendly with one of Cindy's brothers," he told me. "And I asked him at one point, 'Why is Cindy the way she is?' You know, because I got such a bad feeling when I met her father. Well, I never saw him again after asking that."

Certainly, little Caylee couldn't benefit very much from spending part of the day at Mount Dora. She wasn't using words well enough yet to communicate a whole lot with her great-grandfather, even if he could have held an intelligible conversation (which he couldn't). She was as much a hostage to the scene being directed by Cindy Anthony as her great-grandfather was.

Marc Siegel, MD, Associate Professor of Medicine at NYU Langone Medical Center, who works with elderly patients in institutional settings on a daily basis, said that bringing a two-year-old into a nursing facility like the one that held Alexander Plesea would be "sadistic, barbaric, and assaultive to a young child's sensibilities."

Perhaps that explains why Caylee was so much in need of comfort that day. A woman named Karen Angel, who worked at Mount Dora, noticed her and stopped to play with her.

"I was playing with her," Angel later told Detective Kevin Kraubetz. "I ask[ed] her what's her name. I was like, 'Hey, cutie. Tell me your name.' And, uhm, she kind of blushed. And then I said, 'Can I have a hug?' And I picked her up and she laid on my shoulder."

When I shared that scene with one of my sources and asked whether it seemed like a good idea or a bad idea to bring Caylee to Mount Dora, he said, "It had nothing to do with Caylee. Caylee was nothing more than a prop that day. Maybe most people are props to Cindy Anthony."

Maybe so. Indeed, in a videotape shot by Cindy Anthony that day, Caylee looks paralyzed with fear as she sits on her great-grandfather's lap while he sings—though unintelligibly—the song, "You Are My Sunshine." It seems he is singing this at Cindy's suggestion. He is seated in a wheelchair, with other residents of Mount Dora in wheelchairs around him. Several seconds later, Cindy tells Caylee, "Give Papa a hug and kiss." The little girl does not comply. By all accounts, she has, after all, rarely seen her great-grandfather. Hugging and kissing a very elderly man with dementia, seated in a wheelchair after suffering a stroke, struggling through a song he once knew, as he looks off into space, may not be something she wants to do. Cindy waits a few moments, then repeats, "Give Papa a hug and kiss, Cay." Again, the little girl does not perform. Then Cindy says, more forcefully this time, "Cay, give him a kiss." Finally, Caylee does as she has been told, then pushes her great-grandfather's arm away from her and struggles off his lap.

I showed the videotape to a few children who, without prompting, said, nearly in unison, "She's really scared."

ENABLER OF DEATH

After Cindy Anthony visited her father at the Mount Dora Nursing Home, she drove back to have some chili for dinner at her mother, Shirley's, house, just a few blocks away.

Cindy and her mother had had to deal with some trouble over the past few months. During April, Casey—Caylee's mother—had stolen $354 from her grandfather Alex's account, where his Social Security checks were routinely deposited. She had used the money to pay an AT&T bill.

Shirley had found out during May, once she received her bank statement and got around to reviewing it. She'd been livid. After all, it wasn't the first time Casey had stolen from her. Back in August 2007, at Caylee's second birthday party, Casey had taken a blank check from her grandmother's purse, made it out to Publix for fifty-four dollars and supposedly used it to pay for some of the party supplies (although the money might have been spent on other things). Shirley found out, but she let it go. "I was mad, but I forgave her," she later told investigators. "She apologized, and I told her, 'Don't let it happen again.'"

But it had happened again, and this time Shirley suggested to the Bank of America that they have Casey arrested and press charges against her. Instead, the bank simply reimbursed Shirley her money and left it at that.

Shirley hadn't called the police or the district attorney's office to press charges, either.

Shirley had called Cindy, though, and told her what had happened.

Cindy was no stranger to Casey's stealing. Casey had not only stolen money from her purse on many occasions, had not only forged checks from her account to buy merchandise from stores like Target, but had also stolen tens of thousands of dollars from her by using her credit cards without permission. Cindy had had to use funds from her retirement account to pay down the balances.

Covering up had become a habit for Cindy. At the end of Casey's senior year of high school, Cindy learned that Casey hadn't graduated. But that didn't stop her from sending out a high school graduation picture of her daughter to relatives and hosting a graduation party. She invited her mother and father, who actually went to the high school graduation ceremony expecting to see their granddaughter walking with her class. Of course, she never did. So they headed over to Cindy's house for the festivities.

Cindy never returned gifts sent by out-of-town relatives, or told them that Casey didn't get her diploma.

According to one family member who lives out of state, "I got a graduation announcement and I sent a gift, then I found out six years later or so that she didn't even graduate. Cindy never told me. She never called me and said, 'I'm sending your gift back. She didn't graduate.' She never even told her own mother. Shirley knew that Casey didn't go to her graduation ceremony, but she didn't know why."

"Cindy didn't want any negative news to come out of her house," Cindy's brother Rick told me.

Even George had learned not to make waves and bring up inconvenient facts around Cindy. After Caylee was born, Casey had told her father that she was working at the Sports Authority store in Westford Lakes, Florida, in addition to her job at Universal Studios as an "event planner." George went to the store one day, purportedly to bring her lunch, but also because he had a hunch she might not actually be working there at all.

When George got to Sports Authority, he asked for Casey, but learned that she, indeed, was not working there and never had. He called Cindy and told her, "Well, she's not here."

"What are you doing? What are you doing checking up on our daughter?" Cindy demanded.

"Because I need to," George said. "I need to find out where she's at. I need to find out what's going on, why she's supposed to be somewhere, specifically, and why she's not there."

Cindy was extremely upset with him. "Well, why are you following your daughter around?" she demanded. "You know what this is going to do to her? She'll be irritated."

George brought up the issue timidly with Casey, who did, indeed, get irritated with him. Then he let it drop. He later said he hadn't "wanted to upset my wife . . . that I'm trying to stay with . . ."

He also had his suspicions about whether Casey's job at Universal Studios was real, but he let that go, too. "I didn't bother with any more because, number one," he said much later, "is it would have upset my wife. . . . [I] decided to swallow it and let it go. . . . Even though, you know, it could have—it bothers me. It bothered me inside and it still does a little bit to this day. But, then again, I've got to think about my marriage and some other stuff."

Yes, well, a father can't allow himself to be too bothered by stark evidence that his daughter is living a fraudulent, make-believe life, can he? Not when his wife might get upset with him for bringing it up.

Life is all about positives and negatives. Things happen to real, live people that are regrettable or painful or even embarrassing. In order to have no negative news come out of a house, the truth must be given no quarter. All must be micromanaged.

Fake. There can be no chink in the armor. People living in such circumstances cannot be real. They cannot be, for all intents and purposes, alive.

Maybe that's why Casey had such an affinity for social networking sites like MySpace and Facebook. She could re-create herself by creating a profile. She could pick and choose which photographs her mask would comprise. She could permanently block unwanted feedback. She could pretend to have an identity when she was suppressing hers almost entirely.

Cindy wasn't just covering Casey's debts and covering up her foibles and failures, she was also covering her husband, George's, debts from online gambling. He had reportedly been ordering up credit cards under Cindy's name, using them, and leaving her on the hook for the charges. He had cashed in his retirement account, leaving her to pay the taxes due. And he had reportedly taken his sixty-thousand-dollar cash settlement from a workers' compensation claim and thrown that into the online gambling kitty, too.

On June 5, 2008, Cindy's mother, Shirley Plesea, wrote to her sister Marylou Lillicotch:

> I called Cindy. She doesn't sound good, sounds depressed. . . . Cindy was doing fine, supporting the house, saving etc. till George got them into debt, with the online gambling.

Shirley went on to write that she believed George might suffer with bipolar disorder, implying that his overspending could be characteristic of the euphoric, disinhibited high phase of bipolar disorder, called mania. She added that Casey was afflicted, too.

Perhaps. What was certain is this: When you try to control everyone and everything in a family, you end up having to control lots of loose ends, too.

Sometimes, those loose ends are more unwieldy than you ever bargained for—especially when one of the ways you've controlled people is by breaking them psychologically, or enabling them to remain broken.

People deprived of emotional oxygen will often flail about—and sometimes strike out. After all, they're dying, both spiritually and psychologically.

As Cindy's brother Rick put it, "Casey and George were both prisoners in that house."

Even Cindy's son Lee had suffered with major depression. He'd struggled with it for over a year, starting at age fifteen, according to Cindy. Cindy considered it a side effect of the acne medicine Accutane. But every one of the people who lived with her—her husband, her son, and her daughter—had gotten sick or stayed sick psychologically.

Her granddaughter, though, would be the first not to survive.

As I wrote above: *A family can be so devoid of emotional oxygen that it eventually becomes incompatible with sustaining human life.*

Enablers are power hungry and addicted to control. They make excuses for the damaging or self-destructive behavior of those close to them because it increases their importance as the seemingly "stable" center around which chaos and depravity swirl. Without sick people depending on them to stay afloat, enablers wouldn't be distracted from their own, internal psychological turmoil. They would have to focus on it and, therefore, feel it. And they will do almost anything to avoid that.

Cindy had medical patients to tend to at work and the equivalent of psychiatric patients to tend to at home. She had lots of ways of not looking in the mirror and seeing the truth about her own psyche.

What was she running from? What darkness made her close her eyes so tightly? What could her brother Gary have been telegraphing when I told him that in my experience, people as controlling as Cindy have all suffered greatly at some point during their lives, and he replied, "I'm not giving you that," then hung up?

Why was that source I interviewed shunned by one of Cindy's brothers, from the moment he asked what had happened to her?

I remember meeting with a married couple and their son in my psychiatry office near Boston several years ago. The wife had made the appointment by phone, explaining that her husband was an alcoholic who couldn't hold a job anymore and that her son was suffering from depression, had maxed out his credit cards, and had recently been arrested for cocaine possession. She was seated between them, wearing a pristine Chanel jacket, a sparkly diamond cuff bracelet, and perfectly pleated pants. Her husband was so drunk, he could barely keep himself from tumbling out of his chair. Her son was emaciated, fighting back tears.

As their story unfolded, I realized that the woman in my office had been keeping herself very busy picking her husband up from bars or picking him up off the floor, paying off her son's debts and hiring lawyers for him. But she'd also been careful to keep either of them from taking responsibility for himself or getting real help. She paid all the family's bills. She routinely called her husband's work and son's school to make excuses for their absences—before they'd finally get fired or thrown out. And she'd told each of them that twelve-step groups like AA were for "losers and deadbeats."

"What brings you three here today?" I asked her. "If I understand correctly, I'm the first psychiatrist you've ever visited with."

"I haven't been able to get my life started, really," her son began earnestly. "I—"

"I just can't handle it anymore," his mother cut in. "It's overwhelming. Just *look* at them." She motioned at her husband and son. "I don't know if they need antidepressants or maybe they both have attention deficit disorder and should be on Ritalin or something. I mean, these things run in families, right?"

Depression and attention deficit disorder do tend to run in families, but not always because they're encoded in a family's genes. Sometimes, they're the result of psychological dynamics alive in those families. "Do you need help with anything yourself?" I asked the woman.

She smiled. "My problems are to my right and to my left," she said. "Help them, and I'll be fine."

It took me only a few months to help this woman's husband

and son see that they were part of a family architecture that relied on them being sick, in order to maintain this woman's mask of normality.

As her husband and son started to feel better, she threatened to stop their treatment, arguing my fees were too high.

"Why stop now?" I asked her. "We're making progress. I wasn't aware you were having financial difficulties."

"The well does run dry," she said. "I can't be expected to—"

"I'll pay," her husband interjected. He was on to her. His son glanced over at him with admiration, something I hadn't seen him show for his dad before. "I start working again next week," the husband went on. "I'll have the money, if you can wait a month or so for me to get it to you," he told me.

He was finally seeing that his recovery and his son's were actually threatening to his wife. I nodded at him. "No problem," I said. "I'm sure you're good for it."

I have never forgotten that case. I've told psychiatry residents and medical students who were learning to treat families to remember my patient in that pristine Chanel jacket of hers—to remember that the person in a family who looks the healthiest may be the sickest one of all.

Here's another case to consider: A young woman I once treated had come to me for a very specific and very ominous symptom. She had gone away to college for the first time. Having had her life micromanaged by her mother, to the extent that she had run every single decision by her, she felt confused, despondent, and off balance. She tried to settle her nerves by drinking. She slept with a few male students indiscriminately—just to feel *something, anything*. Then, about six weeks into the school year, she called home with a peculiar observation, which she shared with her mother without any particular emotion. Her hands, she told her, didn't feel like hers anymore. They seemed like they must belong to someone else. She wasn't sure if she should keep them, or somehow get rid of them.

Her mother got my name from a friend and called me late that night on my cell phone, panicked. I called her daughter.

When I spoke with her in her college dorm room, she promised me she wouldn't do anything to "get rid of" her hands, but did admit that she had thought of cutting them off, just to "be freer."

She was pondering amputating her own hands—her own flesh and blood—in order to restore herself.

I hospitalized her.

When you take over another person's life, sometimes that person is left so disconnected from anything like an inner self, so enraged by her psychological rape, that she can perpetrate horrific acts of violence—destroying herself or others—and feel nothing save for, perhaps, freedom.

That day on the phone, Cindy Anthony immediately offered to pay her mother, Shirley, back for the check Casey had forged. It appeared that burying the truth had become her habit—one that kept her daughter and husband weak and dependent on her. But Shirley explained that the bank had already refunded her money.

When Casey overheard the conversation between her mother and her grandmother, she asked to get on the phone. Shirley refused to speak to her. That was understandable, but it was also consistent with the idea that Cindy was Casey's keeper—despite Casey being of age.

Shirley e-mailed Casey instead, telling her she knew exactly what Casey had done. By Shirley's recollection, Casey replied with an e-mail that said, *Dear Grandma, I'm so sorry. I apologize. I'll come down and do some cleaning for you.*

Shirley wrote back, *Casey, I don't want you up here.*

Casey stealing from her grandmother a second time was enough to finally send Cindy to a therapist. But when the therapist suggested drawing a line in the sand and making Casey leave home, Cindy balked. She worried that that could mean losing access to her granddaughter, Caylee.

Enablers fear being alone with their demons—unable to feast on the life force of others—more than they fear anything else.

"I did speak to the therapist that I was going to back in

April/May of 2008 of possibly bringing Casey in for counseling with me," Cindy later said. "Because part of it was for
me handling the financial aspect with Casey. So at some
point I did consider having her come in to counseling, but
then I nixed that because I wasn't happy with the counselor
that I had. She was telling me to abandon my daughter and
to make her and Caylee move out of the house, and that was
not going to happen. So I just quit her."

Casey didn't need couples counseling with her mother.
She needed counseling of her own. But Cindy apparently
didn't consider that. Even Casey's lies—and the underlying
psychopathology fueling them—couldn't be hers, alone, to
deal with.

She wasn't allowed to exist as an individual.

Though being thrown out of the house with her daughter
might have been terrifying for Casey initially, it would at
least in my opinion have gotten her outside her suffocating
family for a much-needed breath of emotional oxygen. It
could have ultimately ended the vicious cycle that was crip-
pling her psychologically and draining away her capacity to
care about her life, or anyone else's. It might have saved her
daughter's life.

It didn't happen.

Cindy never returned for another session with that therapist. Instead, she again enabled her daughter's behavior. "You
know, I just told her I was disappointed in her," she said
later. "And I was upset that she—you know, she didn't come
to me if she needed it [the money she had stolen]."

That wasn't the end of it, though. Cindy's therapist had
apparently planted another seed in Cindy's mind. And that
one began to grow. According to Cindy's brother Rick, the
therapist suggested Cindy could force Casey to leave, but
keep Caylee at home—as her own child—by filing for legal
custody of the little girl.

According to Cindy's mother, Shirley, Cindy was seriously
considering that idea.

Rick later told authorities that when he inquired with his
mother how many times Cindy had threatened to take Cay-

lee away, he was told that it was at least two or three times "that she definitely got in fights with . . . Casey . . . about . . . taking Caylee off of her."

In fact, a lot of what Cindy and her mother reportedly spoke about that Father's Day, June 15, 2008, over bowls of chili, was how to handle Casey and finally put an end to her lying and stealing.

Caylee was playing nearby, very possibly able to hear her grandmother and great-grandmother discussing how inadequate her mother was.

"They discussed it that evening . . . ," Cindy's brother Rick told me. "They discussed what to do about Casey. So Cindy, according to my mom, left there with a head of steam to confront her."

LAST BREATHS

Cindy Anthony returned that night to her home at 4937 Hopespring Drive in Orlando, Florida, a pleasant street in a middle-class neighborhood. The house was four bedrooms and two baths, a modest 1,472 square feet, with an above-ground pool and a little playhouse for Caylee out back.

The Anthonys had moved to Orlando in 1989 from Niles, Ohio, where they had fallen on hard times financially, filed for bankruptcy, and had their home taken by the bank.

The family's financial problems had started back in 1985, when Cindy convinced George to leave his job after ten years as a deputy in the Trumbull County Sheriff's Office and go to work with his father, who owned Anthony's Auto Sales and Service. Several sources told me that Cindy's motivation was jealousy. She had grown up poor—and self-conscious about it. Her sister-in-law Kathy was married to Chuck Eddy, who was earning a very good living working with his own father in a successful car dealership in Austintown, Ohio. Why shouldn't her husband do the same for her, even if he was happy in his position as a deputy sheriff?

To Cindy, after all, people seemed to be characters or props in a story she was intent on writing for her own purposes—apparently to distance herself from her own inner turmoil. What people wanted for themselves, what they needed to feel whole and truly alive, didn't seem to matter much to her.

The couple had one child at the time. Lee Anthony, named for his grandfather, had been born on November 20, 1982.

George switching careers meant him stepping out from behind his uniform and abandoning the other kind of police work he liked—"undercover" (using his own word) investigating. In a uniform or not, he still seemed to gravitate toward secrecy and pretending.

Even once he transitioned to the car business, people who knew him or worked around him found him hard to connect with in any genuine way.

"George wasn't interested in dealing with customers. He didn't want to talk to people. He thought of them as dirty. He's very obsessive," one source told me. "George's father even enrolled him in a Dale Carnegie course and paid for it to try to help him warm up, but he just couldn't."

Tim Given, who owns a business nearby and got to know George and his father, Lee, told me, "George's hair was like a mannequin's—not a hair out of place. He wore his clothes like a uniform. Everything perfectly pressed."

George just couldn't seem to pull off a convincing façade when he wasn't in disguise. Maybe that's why he had told his first wife, Terri, that he longed to be a character like Mickey Mouse or Pluto at Disney World and why he was always volunteering to play Santa Claus for children at Christmas.

George and Cindy had their second child soon after George went to work in the car business. Casey Marie Anthony, who shared her mother's middle name and her intials, *CMA* (lest she be allowed, even for an instant, an identity wholly her own), was born on March 19, 1986.

Cindy had apparently never stopped to wonder why George was so secretive and why he liked being around children so much. She had never sought out Terri to ask her why her marriage to George ultimately fell apart. Had she, she would have learned that Terri believed it was because she wasn't producing children "at a fast enough pace." For some reason, George wanted kids around the house—and quickly.

George needed Cindy, and it seems he was too weak and troubled to resist her demands. That was apparently good enough for her.

George and his father, Lee, argued frequently during the nearly three years they worked together. Part of it was supposedly Lee's dictatorial style. But there was also lingering ill will between the two from long ago, when Lee had had to get George out of trouble of one kind or another.

George later told law enforcement officials that the reason he had moved on from Anthony's Auto Sales and Service was because his father "had a chance to sell the business": "Oh, my father made me an offer to go back in the family business, which was a good offer. He was getting ready to retire, or at least step back, and he wanted to keep it in the family. . . . I was considered the general manager of the business, overseeing the sales and service department of our business, of our family-owned business."

The Florida Assistant State Attorney questioning George seemed understandably confused whether George was his father's business partner (as he seemed to want to imply) or his father's employee.

Q: . . . So you went to work as—now, at that point working for your father, were you working just as a salaried employee, or were you given profit sharing or something like that?

A: Basically salaried. I mean, when the business did better each month, or a quarter, something like that, yeah, I would get an extra maybe two or three percent or whatever it might be. I mean, it's—it's like anything else. Business is doing well, you make more, and when it's not doing well, you don't do as well, so—

Uh, that's called being salaried, with a bonus at the discretion of your boss. It isn't "like anything else." It's *precisely* that.

Q . . . And so you kept working for—how long did you work as the general manager for your father's business?

A: Just about—about three and a half, maybe four years. And we decided to part because he had a chance to sell the business.

Q: Okay.

A: And I went out on my own and started my own, George Anthony's Auto Sales, so—

Q: Okay. So it—had it been your impression that he was going to sort of turn the business over to you?

A: That was my—

Q: Okay.

A: —feelings back in—when I left the sheriff's department; yes.

Q: Okay. But that didn't turn out—didn't turn out that way?

A: Not fully, no.

Q: Okay.

A: No.

Q: So he sold the business. Did you get—did he give you any sort of part of the business or anything like that, or was it just he sold the business and you started out on your own?

A: He sold the business and I went out on my own.

George was dancing around the truth, or just plain lying. Not only had his father Lee "not fully" turned the business over to him; his father had fired him after George attacked him.

According to multiple sources, the two men were arguing at the dealership one day when Lee shoved George. George then pushed his father with so much force that the older man crashed through a plate glass window, got cut up, and reportedly had to go to the hospital.

Cindy later denied the whole story, telling her brother Rick it had never happened.

George did wrestle with his dad and put him through the window, Rick later emailed his sister. *Don't lie to me about it.* In a subsequent email, he added, *I see how Casey is so screwed up between you and George as role models.*

Being fired by his father, after trying to satisfy Cindy by leaving his police work behind, reportedly left George feeling intensely depressed. According to Rick, that was the first time George tried to kill himself. "He took a whole bottle of aspirin. He had to have his stomach pumped out."

"We knew George was weak and weak minded," Rick said. "He was being molded by Cindy into doing things he didn't want to do. She took his life."

After getting back on his feet emotionally, George tried again to deliver the wealth Cindy thirsted for. He took out a second mortgage on the family home to finance his own car business, a used car lot called George Anthony's Auto Sales during 1987.

But he couldn't keep it afloat. It isn't clear if the lot itself was a bust or whether George gambled away his working capital on other risky ventures. Whatever the case, by 1989, the place was out of business, and George had lost his and Cindy's house in the bargain. Cindy supposedly knew nothing about her husband's financial problems, until he told her one day, out of the blue, that they were broke.

When you marry a man who is psychologically fractured, when you derive power from how much he needs you to cover up his weaknesses, and when you then send him out to try to make his way in the world without wearing one disguise or another, you should expect some unpleasant surprises.

Apparently, when family members couldn't deliver for Cindy, they hid the facts as long as possible. Not giving Cindy what she wanted could make her withhold her false but well-staged affection toward you. And if you had been selected as her mate because you had nothing else to sustain you (like George), or raised as her child to have no accessible, strong, internal self to steady you, that could throw you into serious withdrawal. It could feel like the end of the world.

Maybe George hadn't told Cindy about their looming financial problems because he was too afraid of pulling the needle filled with Cindy's special brew of neediness, sex, criticism, control, and contrived compassion out of his arm. That would have been the same as him not getting high by gambling, the same as a heroin addict quitting heroin cold turkey. It would have brought on terrifying feelings of anxiety and paralyzing despondency connected to all the suffering he had been trying to keep a lid on by trying to keep his hair perfectly in place and his uniforms perfectly pressed and his luck alive on Internet gaming sites and his mind focused on female body parts. It also would have been his only chance to save himself from a life spent not truly alive, enslaved by his fear and self-loathing to a woman who behaved as though she embraced both those qualities in him.

There was nothing to keep the couple in Ohio anymore, and lots of bad memories to run from.

Cindy's parents had recently moved to Mount Dora, Florida, so Cindy decided to follow them. She was hired as a nurse by an orthopedic surgeon named David Osteen, MD. She managed to buy another home by assuming a high-interest loan held by the family that had been living at 4937 Hopespring Drive.

Hopespring Drive. Irony of ironies. She and George closed on the place for ninety thousand dollars on October 4, 1989.

Casey was just three and a half years old. Lee was almost seven.

George never did get to work as a character at Disney World—the dream his first wife said he had shared with her. Instead, he found a job at the Orlando Centroplex as a security officer, then went to work for Snappy Car Rental as a sales representative, then moved onto the *Orlando Sentinel* as a security officer again, then landed at a pest-control company called Falcon Termite and Pest Control. Even if he didn't earn much money during those ten years or so, at least he'd had plenty of different uniforms to wear.

All that must have seemed like very long ago when Cindy returned home after dinner with her mother, Shirley, that

Father's Day, June 15, 2008, with "a head of steam" to confront Casey about her lying and stealing.

George Anthony was not at home and would not return until after his 3-to-11 P.M. shift.

Cindy's head of steam turned into an explosion.

According to Cindy's brother Rick, Cindy again threatened Casey with making her leave the house and leave Caylee behind. "I believe she made it plain that evening that she was going to file for legal custody of Caylee," he told me.

Casey wouldn't have been able to dismiss her mother's threat as a bluff. About three years before, when Cindy had had enough of George's lies about finances or other matters, Cindy made him move out.

According to George, however, Cindy's motivation for making him leave the house seems to square more with the allegation of abuse Casey's attorney eventually laid out at trial.

"I think maybe she [Cindy] was worried about maybe both of them [Casey and Caylee] leaving or something like that because of me," George later told authorities, "and I just said: Okay. We'll handle it your way, then. You know, we'll just—because I didn't want to see Casey or Caylee leave. I didn't want to do that."

Cindy had only taken George back once he got a lawyer, preemptively filed for divorce, and made it plain that she would end up owing him half the equity in the family's house, not to mention possible alimony, since he hadn't kept a steady job.

Perhaps Cindy's mother put it most clearly: "Oh, Cindy had told me a couple of times that one of these times she was going to get it [custody]. . . . Cindy would have took that kid in a minute," she told law enforcement officials. "She would. . . . She wanted to be in charge of Caylee."

On the night of June 15, neighbors heard shouting from the Anthonys' home. Cindy apparently had printed photographs off one of the social networking sites Casey was addicted to. They showed Casey clad in only an American flag, at an "Anything but Clothes" party she had attended on a recent night when she told Cindy she was at work and needed her to babysit. She confronted Casey with those images, railed about her stealing, and called her an unfit mother.

Casey wasn't backing down. Not this time. I believe that inside her was a cauldron of rage and despair stoked for decades by Cindy—rage at having been spiritually annihilated in a house airless and without exit. A neighbor across the street named Jean Couty later told Corporal Yuri Melich of the Orlando Police Department that she had heard heated arguments between Casey and Cindy more than once. Casey would scream at her mother, tell her to shut up, and even shout, "Fuck you!"

But Casey's brother, Lee, told a friend that this time it was worse—far worse. This time Cindy lurched at her daughter, grabbed her neck with both hands, and tried to choke her.

"It got into a very heated argument, which turned physical and Cindy started choking Casey," Jesse Grund, who had been engaged to Casey and once believed he might be Caylee's father, later told sheriff's investigators. He claimed he had been told about the scene by someone at home that night.

If these events actually took place, perhaps Casey had a moment of clarity while gasping for air. Maybe she saw, for an instant, that she'd been born into a life-and-death struggle with the woman choking her. Now, at least, all pretense of love was gone, all the phony trappings of family stripped away.

Maybe Caylee Anthony was mercifully asleep. Or maybe she got a glimpse of reality. Maybe that would have been better. Maybe she could at least take the truth—however ugly—to heaven with her.

I can imagine Casey smiling, maybe even laughing, as her mother's hands tightened around her neck. And I am reminded of Charles Manson's testimony in court:

I am only what you made me. I am only a reflection of you. You want to kill me? Ha! I'm already dead, have been my whole life. I've spent twenty-three years in tombs that you built . . . You expect to break me? Impossible. You broke me years ago. You killed me years ago . . . I don't think like you people. You people put importance on your lives. Well, my life has never been important to anyone . . .

Cindy Anthony was face-to-face with the terrifying woman she had created. As Cindy's brother Rick once told her: "You created her, now deal with her."

The emotional oxygen in the Anthony family had run out, leaving behind a fatal psychological vacuum.

DELIVERY

To fully understand how seriously Casey may have taken her mother's threat to jettison her and take legal custody of her daughter—and how ominous she may have considered that possibility—one need only bear witness to the scene in the delivery suite the day Caylee was born, August 9, 2005. That scene will prove that living alone with Cindy and George Anthony meant being suffocated psychologically. And the same would be true for any child—including Caylee.

Actually, one fact may suffice: George Anthony stood with his lovely wife near the foot of the bed, watching his daughter give birth. That's right: Casey's father, who was so deliriously happy about a granddaughter being delivered to him that he took almost no interest in who the baby's father might be, was free to look as long as he liked at his daughter's vagina as she lay in stirrups.

It must be said that there are those who believe that George Anthony had impregnated Casey himself. The defense had even attempted to question his paternity at trial. If true, that would mean George was in the delivery room when Caylee was born as the father, not the grandfather.

Those who support this theory contend that it would explain why he would not have been angered upon learning that his daughter was pregnant (since he was responsible) and why he expressed no particular interest in who the baby's father might be (since he knew that he was the father). They assert it also explains why Casey seemed to have hidden the pregnancy from family and friends (since it was the result of incest). They also point to the striking resemblance between Caylee and George, who look even more alike than Casey and he.

Proponents of this idea point out that, even with the mountain of evidence that was later assembled after Caylee's death, no one presented credible genetic data at trial that ruled out George as Caylee's father. Of course, jurors weren't presented with any data that would have identified him as the father either, and according to some reports online, he was ruled out.

Does that sound too much like a psychological thriller and not enough like real life?

Maybe, after all, it was simpler than that. Maybe George was just too lost in the wonderful possibilities of another vulnerable little girl living under the same roof with him to focus on Casey's anatomy in the delivery suite. Or maybe he didn't really think of her vagina as her property, anyway. Or, maybe, both.

In any case, George Anthony, would-be Mickey Mouse or Pluto at Disney World, the man so excited to dress as Santa and entertain the kids at family parties, the undercover cop turned insect exterminator, was at the foot of the bed, with his daughter's pubic area shaved clean and her legs spread.

Is that scene painful for you to imagine? Imagine Casey Anthony living it. It's almost unthinkable, right? Well, it happened. And if you don't believe that that would be enough to lead a young woman to continue hating reality and preferring lies to the truth, then nothing could ever convince you.

It would be enough to make a young woman want to disappear from all genuine thought and feeling.

Why say it more gently? Why mince words? Why not just say it the way it seems to have happened? Why not let the truth, however stark, take you inside the split and shattered mind of Casey Anthony, where words, actions, and even thoughts were designed to convey her away from reality, not closer to it? For what woman who remained alive at all in her self, at one in any way with her mind or soul or body, would allow such a dehumanizing invasion by her lying, manipulative, gambling father?

What kind of mother could Cindy Anthony have been to permit such a violation of her daughter? What other assaults might such a mother have tacitly condoned or pretended not to see?

According to Casey, after all, she had told her mother that her older brother, Lee, had fondled her breasts, beginning when she was age eleven, until she was fifteen. That would correspond, roughly, with Lee's depression. "It started just before I turned twelve," Casey wrote as an adult, in a jailhouse note later released by authorities. "When I told my mom about it two years ago, she made excuses, saying that he was sleepwalking. Not only did she say I was lying, but when I explained everything her reaction was literally like a knife in my chest—'So that's why you're a whore?'"

Well, if Casey had grown up to be sexually promiscuous, having been sexually abused could certainly be part of the reason. After all, if a child feels special (in a tragic way) because she is commanding the sexual interest of males—especially powerful ones, like an older brother and father—she can become addicted to that pathological dynamic.

"Yes, Mom," Casey might have thought to say, "You're right. The reason I have sex a lot is because it's one of the only ways I've *ever* felt valued. At least when I was being assaulted, I felt a tiny bit alive. I felt *something*. Even my pain and humiliation were better than being entirely anonymous, in that airless, anonymous space you allowed me. And sadly, the fact that my developing body meant I could compete with you for attention—and win—is something etched very deeply into my cortex. You're very, very hard to compete with."

Of course, Casey never said that. As revealed by documents made public by the state, she wrote that she couldn't quite believe she was being held responsible for her own brother "walking into [her] room at night and feeling [her] breasts while [she] slept." She couldn't quite believe that she was being held responsible for awakening night after night to notice her bra unhooked or her sports bra lifted up.

"I woke up many times," she wrote in these notes, "to a flashlight on my face, and he [Lee] would be sitting on my floor, in front of the bed, staring at me."

All that, if true, certainly wasn't the façade of domestic tranquillity Cindy seemed intent on forcing upon her family and projecting to other people. And even if all of it was happening, so what, Cindy might have thought—if only unconsciously—it wasn't happening *to her*. It was happening to another person—which was akin to it not happening at all.

What Cindy Anthony apparently lacked—a startling possibility, considering her profession—was empathy. It would have gotten in the way of her enabling everyone around her to get psychologically sick or stay psychologically sick or both.

When a real enabler is faced with an ugly truth that threatens the pathological architecture of the family she has created, she will bury that truth. She is an expert at denying her own suffering, after all. So she instinctively turns a blind eye to that of others.

Remember what Cindy's brother Gary told me when I asked him what might have happened to turn Cindy into the controlling person she had become: *I'm not giving you that.*

In her writings released by the State of Florida, Casey went on to describe "really vivid dreams" she had begun to have, dreams she considered to reveal "things that have already happened."

"I think my Dad used to do the same exact thing to me [as she alleged her brother, Lee, had done] but when I was much younger," she wrote. She said she could see him in her room, back when she was in elementary school, but the images in her dreams would get fuzzy from that point on.

"But I wake up feeling both sore and sick to my stomach," she wrote, "the way I used to feel growing up."

Casey's criminal attorney, Jose Baez, would later contend that George went further than Lee, touching her between her legs and putting his penis in Casey's mouth repeatedly.

"It all began when Casey was eight years old, and her father came into her room and began to touch her inappropriately," Baez would tell a jury. "She could be thirteen years old, have her father's penis in her mouth, and then go to school and play with the other kids as if nothing ever happened."

Casey wrote that she wondered why this would all be surfacing in adulthood. And, while she was no friend of the truth—quite the opposite—she wrote quite convincingly, "If there's more to this, is it possible that I purposely tried to forget? I grew up trying to be everything to everyone and trying to please everybody. I put on a good front, but inside, I was constantly falling apart."

In my experience as a forensic psychiatrist over the past decade and a half, girls (and boys) do, indeed, sometimes suppress memories of sexual trauma and recover them only as adults. In fact, some individuals I have treated have actually gotten confirmation—from other victims or even from their abusers—that the memories they recovered were, indeed, based in reality. Several have reached out to attorneys and been compensated for their pain and suffering.

One of the reasons memories of sexual trauma get buried is that bringing the events to consciousness sooner—while still exposed to the assaults being perpetrated—would be too terrifying. Imagine, after all, being fully aware as a child that you are entirely dependent on adults who are raping you psychologically or physically or both. It could literally precipitate paralyzing and even permanent psychotic symptoms.

Experiments on primates, in fact, demonstrate the power of denial. When young monkeys are given electrical shocks whenever they cuddle with their parents, they don't learn to avoid them. They cling more tightly, even though it means more shocks—as if it is unthinkable to them that their mothers or fathers are, in any way, associated with their suffering. Their minds insulate them from that horrifying reality.

Perhaps the same dynamic explains why I have observed that some abuse victims remain especially close with their parents, even living at home for extended periods of time.

With space and time outside the family architecture in which they suffered, they would be more likely to come face-to-face with the pain they endured—and they unconsciously choose to avoid that reckoning.

Of course, only *with* that reckoning—only once coming into possession of the truth—is there any hope for real self-possession and healing.

If Casey really had been abused by her father, she was still lost in denial on August 9, 2005. Otherwise, she would never have invited him into the delivery suite, to watch her drugged, supine, and naked, with her legs spread.

He thought being there was just wonderful.

George testified later:

> I was in the delivery room for my own two children, but also being in there also for Caylee, which was amazing but also embarrassing to a point. If I might say there are some things in your life as a father that you don't want to see again, grown up [meaning Casey's vagina]. But you know something, it's just an experience that's hard to put into words just how elated you are and how happy you are to see your own child give birth to another child. It's amazing.

It isn't clear why George personifies Casey's genitals. Taken literally, though, his statement means that he considers her vagina to have been a separate, living being, which has now "grown up." It is also possible, from a psychodynamic standpoint, that he essentially considers *Casey* to *be* her vagina, and nothing else.

He was certainly focused on vaginal anatomy. George also stated, "From the time that we found out that we were gonna be grandparents . . . we started going with our daughter to the doctor. To get sonograms, different things like that. Get a chance to see, what they called it, the hamburger of the . . . the birth. And you know that was exciting. That was, wow, emotions are just terrific. . . ."

The memory that had stuck in George's mind wasn't the

way the fetus seems to be at peace, floating in fluid. It wasn't hearing the baby's heartbeat. It wasn't seeing the baby move. It wasn't the awe-inspiring sight of the baby's developing fingers—already so profoundly human that you can imagine reaching out to hold her hand. It wasn't her forehead, hinting at a developing intelligence that is nothing short of miraculous. No, what stuck in George's mind was what some ultrasound technicians call the "hamburger sign," a rather crass way of referring to the fetus's labia and clitoris, which some technicians feel look oddly like the buns and patty of a hamburger.

Why was that what George remembered as exciting, as *wow*, as *terrific*? Why was his attention rigidly riveted *there*?

Cindy must have been elated to witness the birth of her granddaughter, too. Maybe she had even chosen the name Caylee. After all, it was a contraction of her two children's names—Casey and Lee. It was as if Caylee were not the offspring of Casey at all, but a kind of second-generation product of George and Cindy—a sequel by the same executive producers. And—no surprise—their granddaughter's initials were the same as Cindy's: *CMA*.

Had she done it again? Had she stolen the potential for individuality and autonomy from another human being, from her first breath. CMA, RN: Harvester of Souls?

On August 9, 2005, from a psychological standpoint, Casey Anthony may as well have been a steel pipe through which a baby was delivered to Cindy and George Anthony. That's how nonexistent to them she had become, in that crescendo moment of horrifying depersonalization that should have been the moment she felt most alive and capable of creating life.

Everyone in the delivery suite seemed to understand that Caylee was the property of Cindy and George.

George's words capture the scene:

Oh, just that—the day Caylee was born, when Caylee was—first came out of Casey and she was placed and getting cleaned up and stuff like that, the very first person that the aide or whatever it was, the nursing assistant, was going to give Caylee to Casey, but because Casey was getting stitched up and stuff like that, the doctor said, no, that wasn't appropriate at the moment because she needed to be still and stuff like that. She handed her—Caylee was handed to Cindy. . . .

That was not true. In most situations despite the woman being cared for by the obstetrician, the baby is given to the mother first—even if a little time has to elapse.

Maybe Cindy had made a point of telling those in the delivery room that she was a nurse and could be a real part of the team.

George went on:

Naturally, Cindy is not going to turn the child away. Neither am I. And she opened up her arms. She says: Oh my gosh, yeah. I'll hold my granddaughter.

And I remember Casey did say: Well, geez, you get a chance to hold my daughter before I do.

Imagine a new mother not given a single instant to enjoy the presence of her baby—her joy replaced, instead, by understandable disappointment, jealousy, and anger. She should have been holding Caylee, looking into her eyes, feeling the warmth of her body against her chest. Instead, she was looking at Cindy as she smiled, wide-eyed at the infant whom she would refer to again and again and again as her own child.

Casey never forgot what her parents did to her that day.

At least she wasn't in complete, utter denial, anymore.

"And she's thrown it up to my wife a few different times," George said.

Even Lee Anthony, Casey's brother, had heard from his sister that she'd been mortified by Cindy's willingness to replace her in the delivery suite and take Caylee into her own arms.

Of course, the further depersonalization of Casey and the

commandeering of Caylee would not end in the delivery suite. In fact, it had just begun.

Casey eventually became engaged to Jesse Grund, the young man who believed for a time that he was Caylee's father but, ultimately, learned from a paternity test that he was not. Not surprisingly, when Casey met him, he was working as an undercover security officer at Universal Studios. She was powerfully attracted to anyone "in disguise," who pretended to be one thing, but was another—just like her dad, the undercover cop.

Yet, despite the couple being engaged, and despite the fact that her daughter obviously had been sexually active enough to have a baby without knowing the father's identity, Cindy and George became enraged when they saw Jesse, Casey, and Caylee lounging on Casey's bed together. They were all fully clothed. Caylee was asleep, and Jesse and Casey were watching television.

Cindy seethed and said that the rule of the house was that there would never be a man in Casey's bed while she lived at home and that Jesse should leave.

It was as though she didn't want anyone even *looking* the part of Caylee's father.

Jesse told her she was being unreasonable and a shouting match ensued—a challenge to her steely authority, which she never forgave him for.

What Jesse may not have thought of was the theory that Casey wasn't allowed real warmth, or a real relationship. He probably hadn't considered whether it might have suited Cindy better to have a daughter who didn't know who impregnated her and didn't even know that a human being was developing inside her for thirty weeks. He might never have stumbled on the notion that Cindy wanted her, spiritually speaking (at least), buried six feet underground, with just enough oxygen to keep her in suspended animation.

The Reaper does not rest.

Cindy would later state, in referring to Caylee's developing language skills: "Once in a great while I might have to ask what she was talking about, but you learn your child's speech."

Your child?

When asked whether Casey ever considered not raising Caylee and, instead, putting her up for adoption, Cindy said, "There was never a doubt we'd keep that child."

We?

In George's words: "And I—and to go forward just a little bit, I know a couple different occasions that when Caylee would come to Cindy or I, she'd always say: Well, she always goes to you first. You're like—you're like her mom or her dad."

On another occasion, he told investigators: "You know, we loved that child like—I mean, she is ours. She's part of us. And I think that just got to be—maybe just Casey took it to a point and she just said: Well, you know, she comes to you more than she does to me."

And, on yet another occasion, he stated:

> I don't know if you have more than one child or not, but sometimes you slip. Sometimes I would start to call Casey "Lee" and went through this with my mom. I have three brothers, but I would be Rick, Dan, would be Gary, sometimes. And it's hard when you're holding a new baby. And I had never said "grandma" before. And the first time—one of the first times at the house, I think I said something like: "Let Mommy pick you up" [meaning Cindy]. And I picked her up and said that and Casey heard me. And I said, "Oh, I mean Grandma."

Maybe when Casey heard what George had said, she had the faintest realization of why Cindy and George didn't seem to care who the father of Caylee really was: Because Caylee was *theirs*. That would explain why they didn't voice much worry over the fact that their daughter was obviously already psychiatrically decimated enough to deny her own pregnancy for seven months: Maybe they wanted her baby for themselves. The carrier—the steel pipe called Casey, who stayed like an anesthetized surrogate in a little room at home—wasn't even clearly a living being to them.

What's worse, Cindy really didn't need Casey for anything at all anymore—not even to control into oblivion. Casey didn't even merit negative attention any longer.

Cindy had a new daughter to work her magic on—little Caylee. And George had a new little girl in the house.

By that point, Casey may only have had three choices—all of them unconscious.

First, she could strike out at her assailants (as some theorists believe she may have once planned to do—by doing away with Cindy and George).

Second, she could entirely disown her real thoughts and emotions, then experience them only as seemingly insane perceptions or thoughts—perhaps hearing voices telling her to kill herself or experiencing psychotic delusions that she was being stalked by murderers. In this case, only a skilled psychiatrist would have been able to posit a theory of what might lay behind her symptoms: parents who indeed, wanted her spiritually dead, needed her spiritually dead, and metaphorically speaking, had been trying to kill her for two decades.

I recall a patient of mine, in her late twenties, who visited my office. From the beginning of her first session, she spoke just above a whisper.

"Why are you talking so quietly?" I asked her.

She nodded at the wall. "My parents . . . ," she said softly. "They have listening devices in the walls. They put them wherever I go. That way, they know whatever I'm thinking—if I say it too loudly."

That was a terrifying, paranoid delusion. Of course, on the face of it, it would seem to be entirely irrational. But as I got to know this woman, I was able to understand. I learned that her parents had micromanaged her entire existence, second-guessing every decision she made, instilling fear of their disapproval deep in her marrow, making her question her thoughts and intentions to such an extent that it must have seemed as though they were not her own.

After several meetings, I told my patient that her fear that her parents had listening devices in the wall actually *under-estimated* the problem.

"What do you mean?" she asked. "No one has even been willing to agree with me that they're bugging every room I'm in. What could be worse than that?"

"If they were bugging this room," I said, "the solution would be simple. We'd take down the drywall and find the listening devices. Then we'd be done with their eavesdropping." I leaned a little closer to her. "But here's the thing: They don't need listening devices, because they already know what you would think and what you would say about almost anything. That's because they've convinced you what thoughts and actions are allowed—only the ones that please them."

"How do I get them out of my head?" she asked.

"For starters, by telling me the first time you decided it was too much trouble to resist them."

She did. She shared an early memory from when she was about eight. She'd chosen her clothes to wear that day and remembers her mother looking at her dismissively, laughing, then shaking her head. "Oh my God, you look absurd. Go upstairs and put on the clothes I left on your chair for you to wear before you embarrass yourself in front of other people."

"I'm sorry she was so cruel," I said.

"Was she?" my patient asked. "I don't remember what I felt." She looked confused for a few moments; then her eyes filled up. She hugged herself. "This hurts," she said. "I don't like doing this."

It does hurt to remember one's spiritual annihilation. But it was the only way that she could be restored to a genuine life and a world free of paranoid delusions.

Eventually, slowly, painfully, she took that journey.

If Casey Anthony had ever done so, Caylee Anthony would probably be alive today.

But there was a third "choice" for Casey, given her traumatic life experiences. She could buy more time by continuing to deny her ongoing spiritual and psychological rape. This option would require her to distract herself from reality as completely as possible and keep people away from her genuine thoughts and feelings. She would have to live a dissociated existence—essentially leaving her *self* buried and reinventing herself, almost as a fictional character. Otherwise, she would come perilously close to that cauldron of grief and rage churning inside her.

The third option seems to have won out. Casey apparently suppressed her identity until her real thoughts and feelings were contained behind nearly impregnable walls of denial. But they were still there, and they would not be denied forever.

I have said it many times elsewhere, and will do so here again: *You can't outdistance the past. The truth always wins.*

MY SPACE

Long before any memory of being sexually abused surfaced, Casey had become addicted to online social networks.

Perhaps unwilling or unable to draw upon her genuine, internal self to interact with others—it having been rendered a dark and forbidding space—Casey posted profiles on MySpace.com, Cupid.com and Facebook.com. All of them helped her to keep her exquisite psychological pain repressed and her traumatic memories out of consciousness. She published lighthearted profiles of herself that camouflaged what she has since described as her real, true identity—a victim of psychological suffocation and (according to her) sexual abuse, with tremendous stores of rage built up inside her.

She also shared photos and videos on slide.com, stumbleupon.com, webshots.com, youtube.com, picturetrail.com, nutsie.com, and photobucket.com.

Online, she could reach out to hundreds of people, yet stay at a distance from any of them who might try to connect more deeply than sending pithy lines her way, sharing cool photos, or posting invitations to parties.

Looking for romance on Cupid.com, she shared that her most prominent memory was the moment she found out she was going to be a mother, which she described as an unexpected one that horrified her, in a way, but made her feel that she "was going to become the happiest [she had] ever been."

She described herself as "extremely outspoken," and a

"mom" to everyone, said that she had "the coolest daughter in the world," loved "to laugh with friends," and that her best physical feature was her eyes.

Yet she hinted at how important it was for her to keep her memories from surfacing. Under a section titled, "My motto . . . ," she wrote, "Live for the future, forget the past."

It turned out to be a fatally flawed philosophy.

On MySpace, she could keep it short and simple:

I fucking love you mark . . .
It's been ages ☹
Hey girl . . . you should check out Fusion ultra lounge.
I miss your happy ass, plus, you need to join me for a few beverages . . .
We need to get drinks & listen to some crazy music.
You are the man alex.
So, seriously, we have to get together.
It's been over a week ☹ i miss ya kid!
Seriously can't wait for Wednesday it's my new favorite day of the week!
Hope you're doing well! We miss the hell out of ya, weirdo ☺

On Facebook, she could literally block unwelcome feedback or delete unwanted messages or change her status from "Single" to "It's Complicated" to "In a Relationship," then back again, with the click of a mouse.

"She . . . lived by the MySpace and the Facebook," Jesse Grund, Casey's onetime fiancé said. "Her life was reported on there."

Wouldn't it have been nice, after all, to be able to click a mouse and have grown up with a normal, loving mother instead of an enabler? Wouldn't it have been nice to be able to click a mouse and not be vulnerable (as she later claimed to have been) to sexual predators? Wouldn't it have been nice to edit out her brother's major depression and her father's gambling habit and even her grandfather's allegedly unwieldy temper? Wouldn't it have been nice if her two great-grandfathers hadn't abandoned their children and set dominoes falling through the generations that would, ultimately, crush a little girl to death? Wouldn't it have been nice to delete from her real-life profile that revolting scene in the delivery suite with her father at the foot of her bed, and her baby getting handed over to her insatiable mother?

Social networks are psychologically toxic for the very reason that Casey was so drawn to them: They permit people to turn themselves from genuine, living, breathing human beings with complex emotions and behavior patterns into mini reality TV–like presentations of themselves that obscure their real thoughts and emotions. They encourage people to fictionalize themselves and project a synthetic "front" to the world. They give everyone the tools to live life the way Cindy Anthony had lived hers: On the run from reality, suppressing her own truth and that of those around her, putting on a false front for family and friends, as though enough fiction could keep facts from surfacing forever.

It's a bankrupt strategy. It was Casey's motto on Cupid .com: *Live for the future, forget the past.* And it never, ever works. The truth always wins.

Casey's use of social networking wasn't her only way of suppressing her real thoughts and feelings and keeping painful memories at bay. Her choice of jobs reflected that strategy, too. On June 24, 2004, she had been hired by Event Imaging Consultants, a concession stand owned by Kodak, located at Universal Studios. What could be more fitting for a woman trying to avoid anything deeper than sharing one-liners and snapshots than a position selling photographs of people taking rides at a theme park?

She had kept the job until 2006.

She also loved reality TV shows themselves, especially *Survivor.* That's no surprise: Reality TV is all about staging dramas and passing them off for real life when they aren't real at all. They're fabricated scenarios in which people are trying to act as though they are not acting—a double denial of reality, like the Escher drawing of the hand drawing the hand—that reduces the actual joy and pathos of human existence to a contrivance. Wouldn't it have been wonderful, after all, if Casey's only concern were whether or not she would be jettisoned from a fictional island, inhabited by people pretending to be marooned, rather than being jettisoned from her own reality, left so completely without emotional nurturance as to risk spiritual death at 4937 Hopespring Drive?

Not surprisingly, Casey also used instant messaging as a tool to communicate with people. She could reach out to them, after all, without really connecting with them. In a single two-month period, she sent her friend Amy Huizenga 553 text messages.

Casey routinely communicated with the men in her life through texts, as well. She sometimes sent them thousands of messages in a single month, some of them graphic in content, but all of them delivered through the depersonalizing interface of a cell phone keyboard. She could use that filter in order to filter out her facial expressions, tone of voice, and any other telltale sign of her real feelings.

She had gotten to be an expert at seducing men via text, without getting too close to them emotionally.

She sent Orlando police officer Anthony Rusciano—whom she had sex with a few times—many instant messages per minute, lying compulsively to keep him "connected" with her yet at a distance.

In one exchange released by authorities, Rusciano essentially pleads with her to come see him again:

> nyitaliano3 [Rusciano]: and as for the sex thing lets clear this up right now, when its as good as it has been, i need it, I told you me and routine, but its not my main concern for seeing you, but once in 3 weeks is a tease, plus again, you're pretty damn good in bed sex is good with us, really good . . .

One source explained to me that Casey was "good in bed" because she was so willing to please. She didn't voice her own impulses as much as she responded to and served those of others. Whatever her deepest desires may have been, she either didn't know what they were or kept them to herself.

What would she have wanted, had she let herself get in touch with her erotic needs? Almost certainly, her sexual appetite would have been either to be controlled completely or to exercise complete control over another person. The developing sex drive is like a locomotive steaming through one's developmental years, being filled up with the most powerful emotional forces that are operating during those formative stages. For Casey, those forces were all about submitting to her controlling mother and her fractured father.

Allowing herself to be tied up naked and given no choice as to what would be done to her—or demanding that level of submission from a lover—would likely have come as close to tapping her pent-up sexual urges as anything.

Something about being choked—literally, struggling to breathe—may have proved highly erotic to her. During adolescence, after all, when her sexual desires were taking shape in an accelerated way, was also likely a time when Cindy exerted especially powerful efforts to prevent her from achieving autonomy.

Yet, Casey very likely had no conscious fantasies, because she would not let herself be so intimate with herself, let alone another person, as to get in touch with them.

In instant message exchanges with Rusciano that Florida state made public, Casey keeps him at bay, while also keeping him very interested:

nyitaliano3 (2:25:27 p.m.): well you can stay then

casey o. marie (2:56:42 p.m.): i'll see how that works. . . . Possibly

casey o. marie (2:56:50 p.m.): if not tonight, maybe this weekend

nyitaliano3 (2:57:07 p.m.): i won't push my luck tonight just get here

casey o. marie (2:57:22 p.m.): i am . . . i am

casey o. marie (2:57:31 p.m.): what the hell are we doing for your birthday?!

nyitaliano3 (2:58:00 p.m.): lets not push it thats 3 weeks away

nyitaliano3 (2:58:03 p.m.): haaha

casey o. marie (2:58:09 p.m.): serious . . . jerk

casey o. marie (2:58:52 p.m.): well, don't hold your breath or anything, but i'm cooking up a surprise for you.

nyitaliano3 (2:59:10 p.m.): not getting exited [sic] cause after that or after today . . . i won't see you till august

casey o. marie (3:00:01 p.m.): shutup.

Rusciano later told investigators that Casey had other ways of keeping him at a distance, too:

Corporal Yuri Melich: Did you, uh, did she spend the night afterwards [after having sex]?

Anthony Rusciano: No. Never spent the night. Always left five minutes after we were, it was over.

YM: Okay.

AR: I kind of, that's when you kind of feel like the girl. You're like damn man, I just got used. You know what I'm saying? I always felt hosed after, like just sort of, that's, I definitely remember that. Because every time it was over I was like, she's putting her clothes on, phew, right out the door.

Right out the door. Lingering after sex might be a time when a man expected her to share her real thoughts or feelings, or listen to his. Casey was impossible to coax into a genuine relationship. Judging from her own statements and all available data, she'd been hurt enough, growing up. She'd learned to bury her real "self," in hopes of keeping the tiniest glimmer of her soul still glowing. She couldn't access it to resonate with the inner selves of others.

She reportedly had other strategies to keep herself "safe" from truly being known, knowing others, or knowing herself. One of them—contrary to her Cupid.com profile—was to voice no strong opinion about much of anything and never be pinned down.

According to Casey's friend Michelle Murphy, "[Casey's] just a very agreeable person. There's no conflict, no contentiousness, no approaching her with an issue and getting her to argue about it. She would simply not engage."

Another of Casey's friends named Iassen Donovan told me, "She was not aggressive and not opinionated. She was very pleasant. People would be hard-pressed not to like her."

"If you were going to confront her on an issue, she would already be gone," Michelle Murphy told me. "If you wanted to call her on something she had done, or be angry with her, she would sense it and be nowhere to be found."

That, or she would disappear in another way. "She could diffuse things or push them away and make you feel like maybe you had misunderstood her," Murphy said. "I remember talking to her about some guy that I thought maybe she had showed an interest in, when I was still with him, and she made me feel badly for even thinking that. She was, like, 'I would *never*. You have to believe me.'"

Murphy added that Casey's brother, Lee, helped Casey remain at a safe distance from everything and everyone. "We were all very familiar with her pattern," she said, "and Lee was a very good big brother. You didn't want him holding a grudge. So nobody was going to say to Casey, 'We've got to talk!' You wouldn't want to offend Lee by pressing his little sister. He'd get up in your face and be, like, 'You know how she is! Really, are you surprised about this? You can't just let her be? You *know* her!'"

No one was eager to mess with Lee. According to Mark Fuhrman, a former LAPD detective who worked on the O.J. Simpson case and is now a contributor to the Fox News Channel, "Lee is very aggressive and has a bad temper."

Richard Grund, Jesse Grund's father, put it this way: "He is very detached. He made my skin crawl. George has it to a degree, but Lee . . . *wow*."

Murphy said she got along well with Casey, partly because both of them had "an emotional on/off switch. Either one of us could get to a stage where we would be, like, that's enough worrying or being upset, so I'm over it, let's go out. Flip a switch. It's over. Forgotten. Time to move on. In high-stress situations I think we both could dissociate. Just shut off. Period."

Perhaps because of their similarities, Murphy knew that Casey wasn't about to get really close. "She never really had long-term, intimate friendships," she said. "They were all short and passionate, just like her romantic relationships—where she'd be very observant and affectionate and offer lots of words of affirmation—and then she'd move on. We've known of each other a very long time, all through school, and we became friends, but it's like a butterfly. You see her, and then she's gone."

Murphy also observed that Casey didn't like to drink much alcohol or ever use illicit drugs. "She was not one to not be in control of herself," she said. "She did *not* like losing control and being in a situation where she would end up talking more deeply than a casual conversation."

Perhaps Casey's best defense against intimacy and reality—including all the negative, powerful feelings of betrayal, grief, and rage swirling inside her—was to lie. She'd had excellent role models in that regard, after all.

Casey had been lying for years about having a job—ever since 2006, when she'd lost hers at that Kodak/Event Imaging Solutions kiosk at Universal Studios and ended up unemployed. She'd been lying about having a nanny to take care of Caylee. She'd been lying about anything and everything she could to try to avoid the disdain of her parents—especially Cindy—and win their approval. They had suffocated the rest of her; that's all she would have left.

According to Melissa England, an acquaintance of Casey's, she was once driving in a car with her while Casey was on her cell phone. "When Casey hung up," England said, "she threw her phone onto the dashboard and said, 'Oh my God, I am such a good liar.'"

Her friends all knew she was lying. Her parents were too self-focused to notice or to care.

"We all knew she had no job," Michelle Murphy told me.

But what would confronting her on it do? It would piss her off and piss Lee off. And what business was it of ours, anyhow? She was doing it out of pride—to keep up appearances. And she'd been going with it a long time.

She didn't bother telling us she had a nanny, because we'd never have believed that, and she knew it. We always saw Caylee with her, and we knew she didn't have money for a nanny, anyways. With people who she *knew* knew her, she couldn't get away with as much. People who didn't know her as well [like her parents]—it was a blank slate.

Even her social networking profiles seemed to have lots of lies designed to please others.

Casey's Cupid.com profile wasn't exactly the place she was going to admit to being ambivalent about having had a baby—or about having kept her. But according to her friend Kiomarie Cruz (who told authorities that Cindy had reportedly refused to let her inside the Anthony home because Cruz was Hispanic), Casey had informed her (contrary to Cindy Anthony's assertion) that she wanted to give Caylee up for adoption.

Kiomarie—who couldn't have children of her own—had even entertained the idea of adopting Caylee herself, but Cindy had nixed that.

". . . I'd been told about the doctor, the doctor told us years ago I gone to go get an exam [sic] and the doctor said unfortunately because of my condition. That I was not suppose to have children," Cruz later told investigators.

So, when Casey found out she was pregnant I asked her what are you gonna do about it? And she's like, well I really want to give it up for adoption. And so I figure you know it's a good idea [to adopt Caylee], 'cause I can't have kids and I know Casey's a cute girl and you know it's a baby you know and it's perfect and I had money at the time and I was doing pretty good. So, I said if you are going to give it up for adoption then you know I'm strongly considering adopting the baby from you. She said that's a good idea. But then she called me back saying that her mom pretty much told her that no she needs to keep the baby and that she's not giving it up for adoption. Even though she really did not want to have the baby.

What Casey wanted had never really mattered, because Casey had never really existed for those closest to her—her parents. Her own feelings and thoughts were irrelevant. Like Charles Manson, she was already psychologically dead, and had been her whole life.

During the first part of 2007, Casey, like her brother and father before her, seemed to be feeling especially lifeless, especially depressed. She told Michelle Murphy she felt "crazy." She sought out her friend Annie Downing and told her that she needed to go to a psychiatric hospital because she felt like she was "having a breakdown." She said her mother could take care of Caylee.

Within a day, however, Casey reassured Annie that she would be all right. She said she had spoken with her mother and that everything was "okay."

Cindy had apparently worked some sort of magic to convince Casey there was no need for any hospital.

But everything was not okay. Casey was a very ill young woman. She really did need intensive psychiatric care. Her mother had simply, however, seemingly refused to accept it and help her deal with it. Instead, she had apparently helped her bury it—just like her failing to graduate high school, her stealing, and the psychopathology reflected by her being seven months pregnant without ever mentioning it, or maybe without even knowing it. Because to Cindy, Casey may not have existed as a separate human being. She may have been a prop in her fake, fictionalized world—just like Caylee. Props don't need help. They need touching up and propping up.

The great psychologist Arno Gruen wrote eloquently about the potential dire consequences of a person betraying her own self and attempting to appease those who withhold any genuine love from her and demand she essentially disappear spiritually, in order to win their praise:

> Developing in this way, a person begins to fear [her] own impulses, and thus the need for approval and acceptance becomes of central concern. The struggle to be accepted for doing and being what is expected becomes a mechanism for evading inner anxiety. By locating life's meaning in approval, one renounces the possibility of being loved for the sake of one's true self. The very desire to be loved in this way becomes a source of self-contempt because wishing to be loved for one's own sensitivity would designate one as weak. Under such circumstances . . . children learn that love can be won only through docile maneuvering [by submitting, i.e. giving up one's true self]. But coming to terms with this situation leads to a secret contempt for the parents. In order to go on living with oneself and one's need for love, one must hate oneself, as well as everything reminiscent of authentic love. Neal Ascherson (1983) reports that Klaus Barbie, the Gestapo chief of Lyon, who tortured Jean Moulin [a high-profile member of the French Resistance to Hitler during World War II] to death, once said in an interview, "As I interrogated Jean Moulin, I felt he was myself." In other words, the more he saw himself, that is, that part of himself he had rejected, in Moulin, the more he had to hate and kill himself/Moulin.

When Cindy Anthony reportedly attempted to strangle her daughter, Casey, it may have finally become apparent to Casey that even completely annihilating her *self* had failed to win over her mother. That may have signaled—in the most ominous sense imaginable—the very end of her attempts to do so.

As Gruen has also written, "To the extent which our true self is lost and our human sympathies and the responsibility for them disappear, we become vengeful without even being able to realize it."

Again, the trial testimony of Charles Manson seems relevant:

> We're all in our own prisons, we are each all our own wardens and we do our own time. I can't judge anyone else. What other people do is not really my affair unless they approach me with it. Prison's in your mind. Can't you see I'm free?

A BRAND-NEW DAY

The sun was shining the next morning, June 16, 2008.

George Anthony got up at six thirty or 7 A.M.

Cindy Anthony was getting ready for work at Gentiva Health Services.

Around seven thirty, just before Cindy left, little Caylee woke up and wandered out to say good-bye. She had slept in Casey's bed with her, which was her routine five or six nights a week.

"I know that her and I went out and gave her some cereal, some juice, and made some more coffee . . . ," George later told authorities.

Caylee settled into a lounge chair to eat and watch a video, and George sat down on the couch.

"I can't remember which video exactly she was watching that morning," George told authorities. "I know [I] was sitting on the couch, which is really close to the lounge chair, having some coffee and a bagel. [I] remember her getting up and coming over and taking a bite of my bagel and, you know, just spending a routine morning with her, you know, playing with her, coloring, just doing a bunch of little things. . . . We talked and we laughed."

Around nine or ten o'clock, Casey got up. She packed the bag she usually brought with her whenever she claimed to be leaving for work. She packed a change of clothes for her and Casey, too.

According to the deposition George gave later in the Circuit Court of the Ninth Judicial Circuit, for Orange County, Florida, he and Casey didn't discuss the violent argument she had had with her mother the night before. If his report is to be believed, then their silence on the matter was deafening—dramatic testimony to the possibility that neither one of them was connected to the other in any genuine, emotional, positive way. Perhaps, by that point, they were living only to transfuse Cindy with their pathologies—in order to distract her from her own. If so, they were no different from Jeffrey Dahmer's victims—zombies Dahmer created by injecting hydrochloric acid into the frontal lobes of their brains.

Wouldn't that explain why neither one of them—not George, not Cindy—had even noticed Casey's pregnancy until her uncle Rick pointed out her rotund belly, at seven months?

> **Q:** And when Casey got up, anything—did you have conversations with her? Anything out of the ordinary?
>
> **A:** Oh, you know, just good morning, how you doing—stuff like that. Let her know that I had gave Casey—I mean, Caylee some breakfast and that was pretty much it.
>
> **Q:** Did you have any conversations about, you know, what she had been up to, what's going on, anything like that?
>
> **A:** I don't remember anything specifically at all. We just—my whole concentration was just on Caylee. It was not too much of my daughter. It was just about Caylee—
>
> **Q:** Okay.
>
> **A:** —spending time with her.
>
> **Q:** Did you at that initial stage have any conversations with Casey about the plans of the day, what was going on that day?
>
> **A:** We just talked about work. She knew that I was going to be going to work that day, that afternoon.

That was just in the normal conversation of days. That was nothing specifically at all; no.

Q: Did she indicate what she was doing that day?

A: Just going to work. Had a work meeting and she was going to work.

Q: Did she give you any other details about what this work meeting might be or what it was about or—?

A: No. Just that she and Caylee were going to be leaving and they were going to be leaving probably, you know, in a few hours. And I said: Okay. And that's about it.

Q: Anything else out of the ordinary happen the rest of that morning?

A: No. Definitely not.

George testified in court that Casey got Caylee dressed. Then Caylee came back out and announced, "I'm going to see Zanny."

Zanny was the woman whom Casey had spoken of so many times as Caylee's nanny.

But neither George Anthony nor Cindy Anthony had ever bothered to meet her. Why would they if their daughter wasn't a real person to them, anyhow? Why should they care if the nanny she talked about was real?

"I'm going to work," Casey told him. She implied she might be working quite late. "I may be staying over at Zanny's house."

"She had—she was going for a meeting at work, and if it lasted a little bit longer, she was going to stay over, and Caylee would be staying at the babysitter's," George later told the Florida Assistant State Attorney, "and Casey would also stay there because she didn't want to come in late to wake us up."

Q: I know you relayed a number of times you were watching a show on the Food Network, the last thing you did before—

A: As a matter of fact, I remember that specifically at that time. It was about ten minutes to one that day on the sixteenth of June. I was watching one of my favorite shows on TV, and it's called *Drive-Up Diners and Dives*. And to say I'm sort of hooked on it, I guess I am. I was watching it and I remember Casey and Caylee, you know, leaving. . . .

Q: Were you outside the house when they actually left or were you inside?

A: I walked with Caylee and Casey out when they left to get in their car and go.

While many people have cast doubt on whether Casey even left the house that morning, according to George, he recalled—very definitively and specifically (despite over a year having elapsed by the time he was questioned) all the details of their departure. He remembered that Caylee had been wearing a pink top, with a slight sleeve to it, blue jean shorts, white sandals and white sunglasses, and that she'd been carrying a small, off-white backpack with monkeys printed on it. He'd always been very attuned to the costume/ clothing thing, after all—not so much the human being thing. He'd held the back door to Casey's car open while she buckled Caylee into her car seat. Then, he'd said good-bye, blown her a kiss, and told her that he loved her.

Oh, really? What was that again about being in the delivery room and seeing his daughter's vagina all "grown up"? What was that about remembering the ultrasound of Caylee mostly because the technician had pointed out her labia and clitoris?

According to George and Cindy Anthony, they were never to see their granddaughter alive again.

Their daughter, of course, was already dead.

GONE

On June 16, George Anthony has said he left for work in plenty of time to make his three o'clock shift working security for what he called a "movie premiere" at the Fashion Square Mall.

Beginning at 3:03 P.M., Casey made six calls to her parents. The first was to her father and the last, at 4:24, was to her mother. She also tried her mother at work.

During that time period, Casey also called Tony Lazzaro, her current boyfriend, twice. She called and spoke with her ex-fiancé, Jesse Grund, for eleven minutes. Jesse has said that he could hear Caylee in the background, but many people question his credibility on that matter.

Casey had been telling Jesse for months that her mother and father were planning to divorce and that her mother would be getting a condominium where she would live alone. Her father would reside elsewhere. The Anthony home would be turned over legally to her, and she would continue living there with Caylee.

Casey had been telling the same story to her friend Amy Huizenga and had even invited Amy to be her housemate. Amy had gone so far as to have her mail forwarded to the Anthony residence.

Now, everything had changed, according to Casey. Her parents *were* divorcing, but she wouldn't be able to stay at home, after all. She was going to need a new place to live.

Casey was leaving. Something had happened to put an end to her life at 4937 Hopespring Drive. Unable to contact her parents, Casey was reaching out to the man who had offered to marry her despite the fact that he knew he was not the father of her child, a man who had honestly loved her at one time—and probably still did.

"Jesse was her knight in shining armor," Richard Grund told me. "Even to this day, I have always believed that she will reach out to him again. Even though he is over it, there is something about it. Something about Jesse always wanted to save her."

There was another reason why Casey may have been reaching out to Jesse. While they were engaged, she had come to believe that he loved Caylee more than he loved her. It was the reason she had broken off the engagement.

If Casey now intended to move on from Hopespring Drive—and move on alone—maybe she consciously or unconsciously believed there was a chance to reunite with Jesse and be the undisputed center of his universe.

Moving on, after all, was almost unimaginably, unfathomably easy for Casey. The "self" is like an anchor that holds people to their morals, opinions, relationships, and memories. It also grounds people in the greater ocean of humanity, where one can imagine the horror of being submerged by an undertow because one feels the tides pulling and pushing. It allows for empathy. When a person's tethers to the self are severed as a defensive measure in response to a mother who commandeers her, or a father who emotionally or physically abuses her, or a sibling who preys upon her, or, God forbid, all three, then that person can pick up a new role in life as easily as picking up a new script and stepping out onstage in a new costume. The self has retreated to an internal fortress for safekeeping. But mind this well: Inside that fortress, the self can be growing into something deformed by ferocious rage at its fate and disgust at its own willingness to accept that fate. And it can make a grotesque, destructive appearance in the world without notice, then creep back into its fortress, horrified by the deformed shadow it has cast in the world, by the evidence of what it has become.

I believe Casey Anthony was at that great a distance from her*self.* She was, essentially, Camus's Meursault, in *The Stranger.* Condemned to die after committing murder following the death of his mother, Camus visits with a chaplain. But the chaplain's words of redemption fall on deaf ears. Mersault opines:

> But I was sure about me, about everything, surer than he could ever be, sure of my life and sure of the death I had waiting for me. Yes, that was all I had. But at least I had as much of a hold on it as it had on me. I had been right, I was still right, I was always right. I had lived my life one way and I could just as well have lived it another. I had done this and I hadn't done that. I hadn't done this thing but I had done another. And so? It was as if I had waited all this time for this moment and for the first light of this dawn to be vindicated. Nothing, nothing mattered, and I knew why. So did he. Throughout the whole absurd life I'd lived, a dark wind had been rising toward me from somewhere deep in my future, across years that were still to come, and as it passed, this wind leveled whatever was offered to me at the time, in years no more real than the ones I was living. What did other people's deaths or a mother's love matter to me? . . .

My sources propose five main theories to explain why Casey was temporarily shaken enough to reach out to her parents; her boyfriend, Tony; and her ex-fiancé, Jesse. While no one of these theories was ever proved in a court of law, and keeping in mind that Casey Anthony was found not guilty of killing her daughter, all five theories assert that Caylee was dead by the time Casey called Jesse, or that she died very shortly thereafter.

THEORY #1

The first theory was eventually put forward by the State of Florida when Casey Anthony stood trial for capital murder, facing the death penalty. According to this theory, Casey was so enraged and horrified by her mother's threat to jettison her from the family home and take custody of Caylee that she (after doubling back to the house after her father left for work, if she, in fact, ever left the house at all) used homemade chloroform or another drug to put Caylee to sleep, placed a heart-shaped sticker on her lips, then wrapped duct tape around her nose and mouth—depriving her of all oxygen and ending her life. She then wrapped Caylee's lifeless body in her Winnie-the-Pooh blanket and put her in a black plastic trash bag.

THEORY #2

The second theory, embraced by many sources I interviewed, including some of Casey's friends, is that Casey may have known how to drug Caylee with the antianxiety, sedating medicine Xanax. Without that medication on hand, they reason, she used instructions readily available on the Web to make chloroform. Approximately three months prior to Caylee's death, in fact, someone used a computer in the Anthonys' home to search how to make chloroform.

Inexperienced with how to make chloroform safely, however, Casey gave Caylee too high a dose, asphyxiating her. While this may have happened in the house, proponents of this theory claim it could also have happened if Casey carelessly left a rag soaked in chloroform anywhere in her closed vehicle. Chloroform will absorb oxygen around it and can turn the interior of a vehicle into a death chamber.

Understanding that she would be held responsible for her actions (which would constitute second-degree murder),

Casey covered them up by using the sticker and duct tape and disposing of Caylee's body.

THEORY #3

The third theory, which is far-fetched, was shared with me by several people I interviewed (and was considered credible by an alternate juror in the case). This theory is that Caylee was already dead when George Anthony went to work on June 16, 2008. In fact, the defense suggested at trial that George Anthony actually played a role in Caylee's disappearance.

Proponents of Theory #3 point to the fact that Casey, if she was being honest about her own reputed abuse at her father's hand—part of the defense's theory in its opening statement—would have had a long history of covering up for him—no matter what.

THEORY #4

The fourth theory, presented by Casey Anthony's defense team, including Attorney Jose Baez, also places George Anthony at home when Caylee Anthony died. That theory is that Caylee accidentally drowned in the family pool the morning of June 16, 2008, panicking Casey and her father, who couldn't fathom the consequences of not protecting the little girl, and tried to hide the tragedy from their metaphorical jailer and spiritual executioner, Cindy.

Some of those who espouse Theory #4 suggest George Anthony would have been motivated to help hide Caylee's body if an autopsy would have revealed she had been sexually abused and/or genetic testing could reveal her to have been the offspring of Casey and George (a notion never definitively ruled out—or proven—at Casey's trial).

THEORY #5

The fifth theory is that the drowning took place, but that Casey was alone at the house when it happened. For one reason or another, the theory goes, she let the little girl swim unattended or didn't keep an eye on her whereabouts, only to find her dead in the pool. Admitting to the accident, and facing her mother's wrath, was unthinkable. The death would have had to be covered up.

Each set of tragic events is actually consistent, from a psychological perspective, with Casey's bizarre, detached odyssey during the thirty-one days following June 16, which finally ended with Cindy Anthony calling 911 to report Caylee missing. But the first theory—while not embraced beyond a reasonable doubt by the jury at her capital murder trial—is the one that would actually line up every cylinder of the lock on the door to those dark, forbidden catacombs of her mind into which her *self* had retreated.

In saying this, I am not asserting that events unfolded as outlined in Theory #1, nor am I second-guessing the jury's verdict. I am only observing, as a forensic psychiatrist, that this theory—when analyzed carefully—leaves no psychological question unanswered.

It is Theory #1 that pays full homage to the weight of five generations of abandonment, denial, and toxic enabling that began with Shirley Plesea's father running off to Chicago with another woman, and Alexander Plesea's father dumping him at an orphanage. It is consistent with the way that Shirley Plesea's authoritarian style seemed to crystallize in her daughter, Cindy, who acted as though she believed that controlling everything and everyone around her, by any means possible, was the safest way to live. It embraces Cindy's apparent strategy—whether conscious or unconscious—to marry a weak, broken, man who would not abandon her, with whom she raised children who grew up deprived of emotional oxygen, constantly fighting to keep their heads above water psychologically, and, therefore, in no position to challenge her authority.

It is Theory #1 that is consistent with the notion of Cindy Anthony giving birth to Casey, yet being unable or unwilling to let her breathe, lest she develop into a full human being able to challenge her—or remind her of the fuller life she had sacrificed in favor of one spent controlling others.

We should not forget, after all, that the life lived by Cindy Anthony would not be one chosen by any innocent little girl looking forward to growing up. She was not born evil. At no time did Cindy Anthony crouch in some corner, rub her hands together, and scheme about how to undermine and absorb her children and contribute to the downward spiral of her husband. Her failings were wrought of emotional injuries, too. In my opinion, Cindy Anthony sacrificed *herself* by failing to face, feel, and understand her pain long before she sacrificed others to that lethal dynamic.

It is Theory #1 that is consistent with Cindy treating Casey as nonexistent, as a nonperson, driving Casey's real feelings and thoughts—including her grief and primitive rage—deep into a fortress with walls built of denial, duplicity, and all manner of distraction.

With enough time and resolve, in fact, we could add more than five generations of Plesea–Anthony family history to support Theory #1. We could learn what had damaged each of Caylee's great-great-grandfathers so badly that they would callously abandon their own children. We could wonder together at the missed opportunities for light to enter a family tree of life histories that, for more than a hundred years, had been tending, nearly unavoidably, toward the complete darkness of June 16, 2008.

In the words of Mersault:

Throughout the whole absurd life I'd lived, a dark wind had been rising toward me from somewhere deep in my future, across years that were still to come. . . .

If only Shirley Plesea had married a man as strong as she—a man who was fair and compassionate, but did not so readily defer to her, a man who would have stepped in to defend his children when she screamed at them for being a minute late to dinner. Yet, how could she? How could she take the risk of joining hands with someone capable of standing up to her? Wouldn't such a man also be capable of walking away from her, as her father had? And how could she ever have imagined that the disequilibrium in her own marriage would be reproduced—but hyperbolically—in her daughter, Cindy's, marriage? How could she know that time does nothing by itself to dilute toxic dynamics in a family, that absent a stroke of luck or the rare determination to gain deep insight into one's life, dominoes of destiny fall by their own weight, accumulating momentum and force, ultimately crushing the innocent?

Caylee Marie Anthony was one of those innocent victims.

It is Theory #1—rejected by a jury and, therefore, not to be considered historical fact—that, nonetheless, opens the door to a seamless psychological narrative.

Mind you, there are those who would reject the psychological lens as itself flawed, challenging how accurate any view of events can be, if they are not physically witnessed or captured on video. There are those who would argue—and correctly so—that the psychological realities in this case can fit more than one of the five theories closely enough to make them possible.

Make of this particular vision, then, what you will. Think of it as pure fiction, if you like.

Theory #1 has Casey's mother, Cindy, coming home from having visited her father, Alex Plesea, at the Avante at Mount Dora Nursing Home and having had dinner with her mother, Shirley, and little Caylee. She arrives home intent on finally putting an end to her daughter's lying and stealing. Casey's theft of Cindy's own checks or credit cards could be largely ignored in service to keeping her weak and dependent. But the leakage of Casey's pathology outside the immediate family cannot be tolerated. It has again alerted outsiders to something amiss in Cindy's household. It has created a chink in her armor and made her seem less perfect in her mother's eyes—and anyone her mother might tell, like Cindy's brother Rick or her aunt Marylou. In Cindy's psychological world, a mere pinhole threatens to unleash a tsunami of truth—a sea of crushing realities held back for a lifetime.

She presents Casey with photographs from her MySpace page, showing her naked but wrapped in an American flag, at an Anything but Clothes party, when Cindy believed she was at work. She demands to see Casey's pay stub or any evidence that she is working at all. When she meets with Casey's trademark evasiveness or hostility or both, she becomes furious. A shouting match erupts, during which Cindy seeks the control she has always ultimately exercised—but this time by actually reaching out with both hands, grabbing Casey's neck, and choking her. It is a stark, physical translation of the suffocation of Casey's self that has been going on for twenty-some years. It is, essentially, the disowned rage and destructiveness of Cindy Anthony, the fatal enabler, unleashed from within, no longer disguised by a nurse's uniform or a pretty smile. It is the real mother of Casey Anthony stepping out from behind her mask of sanity.

When Cindy bears witness to her own shadow—perhaps even sees its reflection in the wide eyes of a terrified Caylee standing at the door to her bedroom, awakened from sleep, witness to a horrifying bit of truth—she backs away from Casey, but is still seething. She has been stripped monstrously naked, psychologically, in front of her granddaughter. She yells that she will finally make good on her threats to take custody of Caylee and force Casey to leave the house. She yells this in front of Caylee, in order that the girl may know once and for all that her mother is really no mother at all—that she is reprehensible, unreliable, unworthy. She has never sounded more determined to take the little girl, and Casey is conveyed back to the moment when an obstetrical nurse handed a newborn Caylee over to her grandmother in the delivery suite, before Casey could touch her.

Casey again feels the humiliation of lying with her legs spread, and her father looking at her nakedness while her mother cuddles her infant daughter. She may not even be able to consciously link those events with the terrible shame now bringing tears to her eyes, but she *feels* it. She feels completely and utterly violated and worthless. Worse than dead. And the specter of leaving Caylee alone in the house where she herself was spiritually and psychologically raped and (by her report) sexually abused literally takes her breath away. She sees clearly, for a fraction of a fraction of an instant—what amounts to a single frame of a motion picture—that Caylee is doomed to suffocate just as she did. She looks at her mother and smiles knowingly, watches her turn a hellish shade of red.

Casey's brother, Lee, has to hold his mother back from unleashing another physical assault.

Casey retreats to her bedroom with her weeping daughter. She gets into bed with her and holds her until the two of them fall, mercifully, asleep. But it is a restless night for Casey, who awakens more than once with a strangely familiar feeling from childhood—feeling sore between her legs and sick to her stomach. The feelings are there, then they are gone, but they cannot be dismissed entirely. They bring back the choking sensation from earlier that night, with her mother's hands tight around her neck. Or is that the only time she has felt that choking sensation in this house? Another single frame of a motion picture flashes into her mind's eye. It registers as something short of a memory. A grotesque intuition.

She looks at Caylee and thinks only of her *self*, sees her *self*. Her daughter reminds her of everything she has lost, every seed of autonomy that was never allowed sunlight, everything once innocent inside her, all of it now shriveled and ugly, behind thick walls that were once a fortress, but are now a prison.

If only she could sleep, but now she is awake, thinking. She feels like a prisoner in her little room. She is a prisoner. She has always been a prisoner. She glances at the clock. 3 A.M.

F. Scott Fitzgerald once wrote:

In a really dark night of the soul, it is always three
o'clock in the morning.

She wills herself asleep, then awakens hours later to hear
her mother and father moving about. She realizes she dreamed
they were dead, and that she was a little girl, again, before . . .
before. . . . Before *what,* exactly? There are tears in her eyes,
but she has no idea why.

She doesn't feel sad, after all. She feels anger and resolve.

The soreness between her legs is there again, then gone
again.

Would it not have been better, she thinks, to have ended
her days filled with potential, instead of regret and pain and
rage? Would it not *be* better. She is anchored so tenuously to
her *self* that she floats freely from her wish never to have
lived to imagining the very same thoughts filling Caylee's
mind. It is easy to slip the binding of her own existence and
enter Caylee's because, in a real way, she has never moved
past the trauma of her own childhood.

From the beginning, Casey had known this would turn
out badly, had hidden the reality of her pregnancy from
everyone, maybe even from herself, at least not speaking of
it, not acknowledging it, until it could be denied no longer. It
would turn out badly because it was part of her, and she was
dead inside. How can a living baby be delivered of a corpse?
What evil trick of destiny was being played on her, Casey,
her, Caylee, then back again, to keep her from unconditional
love, from the love of a healing God? Let those who would
keep her in suspended animation grieve over her corpse. So
much better to be held in God's love than to die slowly in an
airless home with no exit. So much better to go home to
Him. So much better to sleep forever than to be awake for
one's own suffocation.

Death made its home at 4937 Hopespring Drive. Eternal
life was in heaven.

Casey feels Caylee stir, then wake up. She closes her eyes,

not wanting to have to look into those of her daughter—eyes that have seen her attacked and humiliated, eyes now reflecting the glare of Cindy Anthony's hatred of her own daughter.

She feels Caylee sit up, then leave the bed and walk out to the living room. She hears her father say, "Let's go freshen you up, Caylee." He says it every morning. She pictures him walking with Caylee to the bathroom. He does that every morning. He is all about being neat and clean, true, but, still . . . Still.

A disembodied voice: "Be still."

She shakes the words out of her head.

An hour later, she hears her mother leave the house for work. After a bit, she gets up herself and walks out to see her father serving Caylee breakfast. The three of them sit watching television for a while, as if nothing has happened the night before, as if nothing has changed this morning.

But everything has changed. Because Casey can *see*. She can really *see* that she is sleepwalking through a nightmare while awake—a nightmare of suspended animation. Slow, creeping death.

She feels the rank self-loathing and rage leaking from the fortress inside her. She looks at her father and feels only disgust, looks at her child and feels only regret. She is poison and poisonous, and nothing good could ever have come from her.

Remember the words of psychologist Arno Gruen:

"Under such circumstances children learn that love can only be won through docile maneuvering [by submitting, i.e. giving up one's true self]. In order to go on living with oneself and one's need for love, one must hate oneself, as well as everything reminiscent of authentic love." Neal Ascherson (1983) reports that Klaus Barbie, the Gestapo chief of Lyon, who tortured Jean Moulin [a high profile member of the French Resistance to Hitler during World War II] to death, once said in an interview, "As I interrogated Jean Moulin, I felt he was myself." In other words, the more he saw himself, that is, that part of himself he had rejected, in Moulin, the more he had to hate and kill himself/Moulin.

Everything alive in Caylee would remind Casey of what she had lost.

"She always said she wanted to grow up and be like me," Cindy Anthony later told investigators.

When her father leaves, Casey goes back to her room. She has what she needs there. It is enough to make a little girl sleep for a while, or the kindest way to help her sleep forever. She thinks how much better it would have been had she herself never awakened, sore and sick to her stomach, pretending to be loved by her father or her mother. After all, she was never allowed to truly come to life. Such a cruel trick played for so long. The pain had no purpose. How much better to be truly loved by God, the perfect Father?

Dismiss Theory #1, if you will. It is only this: A theory held by a number of my sources, consistent with psychological insight.

It may very well be pure fiction.

Maybe Caylee drowned when she was ignored and allowed to wander into deep water, where she suffocated. Accidents certainly happen out of the blue, but they also happen when others are just props, when their inner lives are disregarded, when they are—after all is said and done—expendable.

A child at the bottom of a pool can be a powerful, unconsciously staged metaphor for one's own drowning.

Shirley Plesea had, after all, drowned emotionally when her father, Styles, abandoned her, her siblings, and her mother for another woman and work in the steel mills of Chicago. Cindy had, after all, drowned emotionally when she grew up in poverty, amidst brothers who disliked and taunted her, with a mother who took complete control of the family, cementing her authority with verbal abuse and with physical violence dispensed by her husband. Casey had drowned emotionally when she was exposed to a spiritually lethal combination of having her humanity denied, her strengths ignored, and her weaknesses enabled and exploited—by her account, in every way imaginable.

If Caylee Anthony drowned, the weight of at least five generations (counting Shirley's mother) held her underwater.

Or maybe Caylee died when a hand was placed over her mouth to prevent her from screaming while she was touched. The struggle for oxygen is all the same. One of these horrors is really no better than another.

Caylee was not yet three. Her decomposed body parts were found sealed in a trash bag tossed in the woods. She was placed in that trash bag because she was considered disposable, perhaps by someone who also felt disposable and projected his or her self-hatred upon her. Now, if part of you wants to close your eyes and try to forget about what you have just read, then you already understand one one-millionth of how much Casey would have wanted to close her eyes and forget about what she had lived through for over two decades. But she could sleepwalk—eyes open, heart and mind closed—through life. She had been trained to, from the very beginning.

What was it again that Casey accused Cindy Anthony of saying when Casey supposedly complained that she was being sexually assaulted by her brother? *When I told my mom about it two years ago, she made excuses, saying that he was sleepwalking.*

Struggle, please, not to forget anything you have read here. Don't strangle your sadness or anger. They are gifts. They mean you are alive, that you possess the miracle of human empathy. Count yourself lucky. Many people have had that miraculous element of self entirely extinguished.

Believe one theory. Believe another. No matter. Each of the five, after all, seeks to explain *how* Caylee died. Others will continue to ponder and debate that question. My interest in this book is *why* she died and *why* her mother did not grieve in any way that seemed human. And fully answering those questions will require that we continue looking, with open eyes, at evidence of the spiritual and emotional death of her mother, Casey Marie Anthony, branded at birth with her mother's initials.

LIE TO LIVE

The night of June 16, with Caylee Anthony missing (per Casey's report) and quite likely dead, Casey drove over to her most recent boyfriend, Tony Lazzaro's, house, went to a Blockbuster video store with him, and rented two movies, *Untraceable* and *Jumper.*

Untraceable is about an FBI agent tracking down a seemingly uncatchable serial killer. *Jumper* is about a young man with a genetic anomaly that allows him to teleport himself anywhere in time or space.

Maybe Casey fantasized about being entirely untraceable, completely free of time and place herself. She had spent her whole life in hiding, after all—untouchable, undefined, invisible. It was the only way she could survive at all in the presence of parents who wanted to either devour or dissolve every last bit of her. And it must have seemed possible to her that she could travel the final distance away from all reality, by cutting all tethers to her real life story.

She was already an expert at burying reality, pain, and trauma, after all. She was "good" enough at it to celebrate graduating high school when she hadn't, good enough at it to deny a pregnancy for thirty weeks (and turn up at a wedding expecting everyone else in attendance to deny it, too), good enough at it to leave unanswered and largely unexplored the question of who her daughter's father might be, good enough at it to pretend to be working more than one job when she wasn't working at all, good enough at it to shrug off the protests of her mother and grandmother when she stole from them, good enough at it to pretend to have a nanny when she had none, good enough at it to pretend to be in love again and again when she knew nothing of it and had never taken the risk herself to truly experience it. She could slip the binding of her own existence so readily because she had suppressed her real identity so completely that she was almost entirely free of the God-given gifts of spirit and self that anchor the more fortunate among us who value truth, feel empathy, experience guilt, and know fear.

She had surrounded herself with "friends" who didn't challenge her alternative versions of reality, because they enjoyed her warm smile, her pretty face, and her bubbly energy. Just talking to her must have felt like a little vacation from the stresses of real life. She had, in her brother, Lee, a kind of "bodyguard" to push back against anyone who might try to hold her to her word or take offense at her lying.

And she had, of course, from birth, an enabler of the most potent variety in her mother, Cindy, who acted as though she had a natural aversion to anything genuine about her daughter, anything truly alive, and nursed along her abdication of self every step of the way.

Casey's friend Michelle Murphy felt that the two of them had the same sort of internal circuitry—an emotional on/off switch that flipped whenever they felt too much sadness or anger, and allowed them to say, "That's it. I'm over it. Let's just go out." But if Michelle's on/off switch was like a light switch with a dimmer; Casey's was more like an industrial circuit breaker. She could almost cut the electrical lines themselves.

Remember, if her own statements about her childhood—presented at trial and contained in documents released by the State of Florida—are to be believed, she had gone to grade school after having her breasts fondled by her brother and repeatedly taking her father's penis in her mouth—unless that sore feeling and nausea she felt were hinting at something even more grave.

Grave is an apt word. You can be buried alive in your

own home and swear you are aboveground and loved, because to admit otherwise is to invite panic of a kind that threatens to shatter your mind into pieces too tiny ever to gather again.

If a girl in the third grade learns to go to school and successfully repress the image of her father's erect penis freed from his pants, so she can smile at her teachers and play four-square with her friends, then that girl can grow up able to move on from almost anything—even the loss of her child—and feel almost nothing. The death of her child is no more or less momentous than that of a character in a novel, not much more momentous than "de-friending" someone on Facebook, no more traumatic than losing cell phone reception and being unable to send instant messages, no more a real good-bye than breaking up with a man she describes as the love of her life, who is really just an acquaintance, if not a complete and utter stranger.

If a girl in the seventh grade is agonizing over which boy to go to a dance with, sending notes back and forth across a classroom, blushing in school hallways, while being penetrated psychologically by her mother and physically by her father at home (not that we know this to be fact at all), then the adolescent drama of boy–girl crushes can be a shield against reality that lasts a lifetime, grows hyperbolically, and blocks her even from the grief of losing her daughter or the reflexive horror of having killed her.

Casey spent the night of June 16, 2008, at Tony's watching movies. But maybe it was also a night when he took total control sexually and let her disappear into his needs, just do the things he asked and not have to think, not even feel. *Be* untraceable. *Jump.*

Maybe she asked to be tied up, unable to move even a little, the way she had perhaps lain stiff under an adult man as a little girl. Maybe she asked to be choked, to feel herself leaving the earth, to feel something erotically connected with having left this world psychologically if in fact that man had been on top of her making it hard to breathe.

Dissociation is a well-known psychological phenomenon

wherein a person, sometimes while undergoing acute trauma, but sometimes long after the trauma has passed, loses her *self* and experiences disruptions of memory, perception, consciousness, or identity.

According to psychiatry's official diagnostic compendium, called the *Diagnostic and Statistical Manual of Mental Disorders* (DSM), one example of a dissociative disorder is dissociative amnesia, "characterized by an inability to recall important personal information, usually of a traumatic or stressful nature, that is too extensive to be explained by ordinary forgetfulness."

Another example of a dissociative disorder is depersonalization disorder, "characterized by a persistent or recurrent feeling of being detached from one's mental processes or body."

The labels are really irrelevant. The point is that psychiatry has long understood that acute or chronic stress can cleave a person from her *self* so dramatically that memory, perception, consciousness, and even her identity can be destabilized to the point of crumbling.

While the disturbance can be fleeting, it can also be chronic.

For Casey Anthony, her memory for traumatic events may well have been impaired, but her sense of self—her identity—had been in my opinion effectively buried. To keep it underground took all the texting and sexting and Internet surfing and Facebook photos and MySpace entries and sex and drama and lying that she could manage to fit into each day and night.

If Casey is to be believed in stating that she eventually began to have nightmares about being abused, and if those nightmares did indeed have roots in real trauma, and if they did not plague her until her twenty-fifth year, when she was no longer living at home, then her defenses against reality—including dissociation—had been operating for decades, even as she slept.

The next day, June 17, Tony skipped classes at Full Sail University to spend the day with Casey.

According to Brian Burner, who lived next door to the

Anthonys on Hopespring Drive, Casey returned to the Anthony residence briefly that day. He has stated that she seemed to be alone and that he did not believe her parents were at home. She backed her white Pontiac Sunfire into the garage. That was unusual for her. She always pulled straight into the driveway. After a short period of time, she left.

"The child was in that trunk, most likely, from that point on," former LAPD Detective Mark Fuhrman told me. His statement parallels the theory prosecutors presented in court. Others have agreed.

Casey returned to Tony's apartment.

Casey and Tony had first connected—no surprise—on Facebook on May 21. According to Tony, he had "hit her up" on the site because she was "a good-looking girl" who had listed herself—apparently erroneously—as a Valencia Community College student. He was familiar with that school. The two of them decided to meet up at a party on May 24. Tony was one of the disc jockeys that night. When he wasn't playing songs, he and Casey played beer pong.

At the time, Casey was already dating a man named Ricardo Morales. But Ricardo was out of town on May 24, so after Tony and she said good-bye that night, Casey slept with her sometimes-lover, Orlando police officer Anthony Rusciano.

Yet, according to Casey's friend Annie Downing, who attended the Anything but Clothes party with Casey on May 25, Casey ran into a man named Brandon Snow that evening and became extremely upset. She disappeared with him for an hour and a half, then reemerged in hysterics, saying she wanted to leave the party immediately. She confessed to Annie that she had gotten pregnant by Brandon in the recent past, had kept the pregnancy secret from her parents, and had then miscarried on Valentine's Day. She said she was still in love with Brandon and wanted to reunite with him. Annie doubted the story about the pregnancy, but didn't challenge Casey.

That makes four men in Casey's life at the same time:

Ricardo Morales, Tony Lazzaro, Anthony Rusciano, and Brandon Snow.

Casey and Caylee stayed the night with Ricardo on May 29 and May 30.

On May 31, Casey attended a pool party at her ex-fiancé's house, Jesse Grund. She introduced Tony to Jesse. Jesse, of course, still had feelings for Casey, so there was probably more than a bit of tension in the air.

The next day, on June 1, Casey and Tony began sleeping together.

On June 2, Casey supposedly broke up with Ricardo, explaining that she and Tony had "kissed." But by June 9, according to trial transcripts and documents from Casey released by the State of Florida, she was having sex with both men.

Some sources have stated that Casey began essentially living with Tony Lazzaro starting on June 9.

On June 10, she texted her friend Amy Huizenga:

[Ricardo] finally decided to tell me he loves me . . .
and unfortunately i'm not there with him anymore.
I waited months for this and now . . . i can't say that
he is the only guy i have feelings for. . . . . Ugh.

On June 11, she changed her Facebook profile to reflect that she was "in a relationship" with Tony.

If all that sounds confusing, that's because it is. One of the ways Casey had stayed at a distance from the remnants of her *self*—keeping her real identity under wraps and avoiding real intimacy—was by drugging herself with chaotic, short romances fueled by sex and drama.

She kept these romances alive while lying to all the men about having a job and having a nanny to take care of Caylee. None of them really knew her at all. She was using them to get high, like a junkie uses heroin.

Indeed, one could almost forget while reading about Casey Anthony's dalliances that the State of Florida later alleged that the body of Caylee Marie Anthony was in the trunk of Casey's car on the seventeenth of June, when she returned to Tony Lazzaro's apartment. The whirlwind existence Casey Anthony had created for herself could submerge almost any fact. That was the purpose of it.

She needed to be a stranger to herself and to everyone else, lest she feel all the pain of the past. She needed to be able to flip the circuit breaker of her own identity and completely shut down her emotions and, perhaps, even her memory.

Remember Casey's motto on Cupid.com: *Live for the future, forget the past.*

Casey returned to the Anthony residence on Hopespring Drive again the afternoon of the eighteenth or the nineteenth, at approximately one thirty, according to Mr. Burner. He was outside doing yard work when she walked over and asked to borrow a shovel to dig up a bamboo root in the yard that she had been tripping over. He gave her one, and she walked back over to her house and into the garage.

Again, no Caylee.

Mr. Burner has stated he finished the yard work he was doing and took a shower before Casey returned with his shovel, around two thirty. He remembers that she was "calm, just normal." From the looks of the shovel, it didn't really seem she had used it.

ACCOMPLICES

Although there certainly are those who theorize that George and Cindy Anthony knew about the death of their granddaughter and might have helped orchestrate an elaborate ruse to keep the facts about it secret—because they can't quite fathom how they could have ignored the warning signs—a more ominous possible explanation exists for their extraordinarily peculiar behavior in the days and weeks following June 16, one more in line with themes I have developed in this book: They may not have been connected to Casey or Caylee in any genuine, human way.

The same parents who could deny their daughter's pregnancy and show almost no interest in who their granddaughter's father might be, then host a baby shower, might actually have been blind to the tragedy that was unfolding in their midst. They may have been that detached, that focused on serving their own needs for distraction.

The end of Caylee's life would then be the final chapter of a story about how a toxic enabler, surrounded by the broken people she needed to keep her from looking at herself, can suck all the emotional oxygen in a home into her own lungs and turn it into a death trap for the weakest, most vulnerable member of the family.

Accomplices need not plot or plan a killing or fatal "accident." They need not even dispose of the body or the murder weapon. They can just keep sleepwalking as the storm clouds gather and evidence of a calamity mounts.

According to what he told investigators, George Anthony didn't speak with Casey on June 17 or June 18 or June 19 or June 20. He has said it was up to a week after he saw her leave with Caylee, on the morning of the sixteenth, before he had a brief cell phone conversation with her.

He was questioned about this by Florida's Assistant State Attorneys:

Q: Prior to this period in June, starting on the sixteenth, what is the longest period of time that Caylee had ever not been in your house, consecutive nights?

A: Maybe just one—just one night.

Q: One night.

A: I never knew of her gone for any longer than that.

Q: Now, when Casey did not come home on—on June 17, did you and your wife have a conversation about that?

A: Cindy and I just talked briefly about it. And Cindy just says that Caylee—Casey and Caylee were staying at a friend's house or the babysitter's house. I—I don't remember the exact conversation, but I remember she just says that she had talked to Casey and everything was fine.

Q: Did you recall making any comments that, that— of finding that odd or being concerned about that?

A: No. I didn't. Because I trusted Cindy's judgment. I trusted Casey. I had never seen any reason to be alerted to anything at all. I just—just did.

Q: How about on the eighteenth? Same question. Any discussions about—?

A: Well, I just wondered where they were at for a couple of days and, you know, I said how much I missed her. And I know how much Cindy missed her also. And Cindy said, well, she's been talking to her and everything's okay.

Q: Did you attempt to contact Casey any time up to that brief cell phone conversation you talked about?

A: I probably did. I don't remember exactly. I—I'm not really sure. I possibly did. I mean, I'm sure I maybe called out to her. I really can't remember. But basically Cindy was the one talking to her more than I.

Q: By the twenty-third, which is a week later, were you starting to become concerned about where they were and why you had not seen them?

A: Absolutely. I mean, I talked to Cindy about it. I mean, because, like I said, her and Casey were extremely close and just concerned about, you know, where she might be and how she's doing. And if I'm not mistaken, Cindy says: Well, she's with a friend. She's been working a lot. I think she was thinking about going—doing some traveling or something like that. And I said: Well, you know, it would be nice to have—I used to call—refer to Caylee as our little girl. And I says: Well, I wonder how our little girl is doing. God, I'd sure love to hear her voice. I haven't heard it for a week.

Our little girl. Gotcha.

And what was that about George having "trusted Casey"? Why would he trust someone who had lied and stolen for years, who he knew wasn't even working at the Sports Authority store she had told him she worked at? He was a retired undercover cop, after all.

Maybe, like Lee, George had simply decided on a hands-off approach where the bizarre relationship between Cindy and Casey was concerned. He wasn't about to push his luck with Cindy and end up getting thrown out of the house again.

Where would he go, anyhow? How would he live? He had shared his life long enough with Cindy to be left without any real way to earn a living and without the self-esteem to figure one out. That's probably the real reason he had lawyered up and threatened to take half the house when she told him she was done with him: He was like one of Jeffrey Dahmer's victims, most of his thinking capacity destroyed already, wandering the streets like a vagrant.

As for Cindy, she told investigators that Casey had indeed called her on Tuesday, June 16, to tell her that she had too much on her schedule to get back to Hopespring Drive and that, as expected, she and Caylee would stay over with Zanny, the name by which she had called her fictional nanny for about two and a half years.

That's right: For two and a half years, Casey had been talking about a nanny who did not exist.

Cindy's brother Rick would later write to his sister, out of sheer exasperation, "No grandparent that I know doesn't know who is babysitting their grandchild. . . . Your ignorance is intolerable. You need to get some psychiatric help."

Keep in mind, when pondering the nonexistent nanny, that Casey herself did not exist, thanks to her childhood on Hopespring Drive. She didn't just have an imaginary nanny and imaginary friends. She was her own imaginary friend.

Casey gave Cindy the same explanation about being deluged with work for not coming home on Wednesday, the seventeenth.

On the eighteenth (perhaps after borrowing and returning Brian Burner's shovel), Casey called her mother and told her that she was going to the Hard Rock Hotel at the Universal Orlando Resort for a (nonexistent) convention related to her (nonexistent) event-planning work for Universal Studios.

She supposedly stayed at the Hard Rock until Friday, the twentieth, when Casey said she was being transferred to Busch Gardens, to do event-planning work for Universal Studios at a hotel there—maybe a Marriott. (Cindy wasn't certain.)

Casey then explained to her mother that, since she was lucky enough to be enjoying the company of her coworker Juliette Lewis and Juliette's little girl Annabel, they intended to stay at Busch Gardens and have some fun together at the park. They were all enjoying one another's company so much, in fact, that they decided to stay the weekend, June 21 and 22.

At no time did Cindy speak directly with Caylee.

Maybe Cindy thought that she was being punished for

confronting Casey about her stealing and lying. But that would completely miss the gravity and depth of the rift between the two women. For if Cindy had presided over the psychological strangulation of Casey, if she had upped the ante by, for all intents and purposes, stealing her child, then a cold war between mother and daughter had been under way for many years. And it had just gone nuclear.

Shirley Plesea, Cindy's mother, eventually put it this way, ". . . I don't want to think, uh, I don't not want to think that Casey, or that Caylee isn't alive, but I just wondered if she hated her mom more than she loved Caylee."

Shirley's slip of the tongue even got to the heart of the matter regarding Casey being spiritually dead: *I don't not want to think that Casey . . . . . . isn't alive.*

Removing the double negative leaves: *I want to think that Casey . . . isn't alive.*

Well, consider it done, Shirley. Mission accomplished. Think back to all that yelling at Cindy and whatever else set up your daughter to enable others all the way to their psychological graves. Casey was not alive, and had not been alive, in any sense beyond the strictest biological one, for quite a long time.

On June 22, Casey told her mother that Zanny's roommate Raquel was coming to join them.

On Monday, the twenty-third, Casey supposedly called her mother and told her that the group was returning to Orlando. But, at 5:30 P.M., Casey spoke with Cindy again and told her that Zanny and Raquel had been in a car accident. Zanny had suffered a concussion. Juliette, Raquel, Annabel, and Caylee had gone back to the hotel at Busch Gardens and checked in again. Casey, the dutiful friend and employer, had stayed by her nanny's side at the local hospital.

Cindy apparently never checked whether anyone named Zaneida Gonzalez (Zanny's full name, according to Casey) was being treated at that hospital.

Keep in mind that neither Cindy nor George Anthony had ever met anyone named Zanny and had never been introduced to anyone claiming to be Caylee's nanny. They had never seen a check made out by Casey to any babysitter. They hadn't seen a pay stub from Casey for years. Yet, despite these rather glaring problems with Casey's credibility, Cindy apparently chose to believe her.

That doesn't seem to make sense, until you think about the consequences for Cindy of *not* believing Casey, of doubting her. Being skeptical, and acting on that skepticism, would have led Cindy to evidence that Casey was inventing many aspects of her existence. Her problems would have then been obvious and severe enough that Cindy might be forced to acknowledge them and get her some kind of help. And she was not about to do that. She had already told George, in no uncertain terms, that he was not to check up on his daughter, even though he had already learned that she was not working at the Sports Authority store where she claimed to be employed.

Getting Casey help, after all, might end up making her strong enough to stand on her own two feet and leave Cindy, rather than making her feel as though Cindy were the only force holding her up and keeping her together.

What sort of mother learns that her daughter is inventing a job—lying about where she is going and what she is doing— and takes no action? Only a mother in my opinion who consciously or unconsciously wants a daughter who is perpetually mentally disordered could do such a thing.

Think of the power Cindy must have felt, convinced that she was the glue holding together the shattered pieces of Casey. It had to be intoxicating—intoxicating enough, at least, to obscure the reality that Cindy was the one who had shattered her to begin with (with some help from her fractured husband and her troubled son). And she just wasn't going to detox from that drug.

"And you know it's . . . I don't really . . . you know a lot of people say, well you're Grandma you're supposed to be concerned, why don't you know?" Cindy told law enforcement officials later. "Well, you know what? I trust my daughter. I still trust my daughter. I mean, they lived with us. She was a loving mother. And you know, I hope that the apple doesn't fall far from the tree."

Well, she was right about that part. The apple hadn't fallen far from the tree at all. Casey was no more able to keep her daughter alive than Cindy had been.

Alas, poor Zanny, Casey said, suffered more complications from the car accident—a punctured lung, Cindy seemed to recall—so the hospital had to keep her until late on Thursday, the twenty-sixth.

It was too late to drive home. So Casey, Zanny, Juliet, Caylee, and Annabel stayed over again at the hotel at Busch Gardens.

Cindy apparently didn't bother to check to see if any of them were actually registered there.

On Friday, the twenty-seventh, Casey told Cindy she was finally back in Orlando, but would be staying over again at the Hard Rock Hotel to work more on event planning for Universal.

From the twenty-seventh to the thirtieth, Casey told her mother she was hanging out with a man named Jeffrey Hopkins, whose child was also cared for at times by Zanny, the nanny. Jeffrey and Casey had known each other since middle school, but now, according to Casey, they were really hitting it off.

Then, from the thirtieth until July 3, Casey's story was that she couldn't come home, because she was working late every evening, making Zanny's apartment the best place for Caylee to sleep over.

On July 3, Casey told her mother she was finally back in Orlando and back at work at Universal. Caylee had come with her and was having lots of fun attending character breakfasts, where actors dressed up as cartoon characters and mingled with the children in attendance. That would have been a perfect metaphor for the way Caylee had spent her whole life—with people in disguises, behind masks—but it wasn't even true. Casey wasn't at Universal that day, and so far as anyone can tell, Caylee was dead.

Casey later told her mother that she had decided to travel to Jacksonville, Florida, to spend more time with Jeffrey Hopkins, but Cindy had already driven to Universal Studios in hopes of seeing Caylee. Of course, neither Casey nor Caylee were there when Cindy arrived.

Here's what Cindy later told investigators:

> Earlier that day I had some issues and I really wanted to talk to Casey about those issues and I really wanted to see Caylee. I wanted to spend at least one day with her. . . . I decided when I left the bank to go ahead and drive to Universal Studios. I didn't buy a ticket. I just figured she would meet me down at guest services and I would be able to talk to her and pick up Caylee from that point, I didn't tell her I was coming. . . . . I called Casey and told her I was there and said, "Can I talk to you?" and she told me she was not there. She told me she was in Jacksonville, Florida. She told me that she took Caylee back to Jeff's condo in Jacksonville and was going to try to rekindle more, that their friendship because it had gone very well those days that he was in town. She didn't want me to know that she had left town without me seeing her and Caylee. It was a shock and I was upset.

But Cindy apparently wasn't all that "shocked" and "upset" about the fact that her granddaughter, who hadn't slept more than one night outside her home since being born, had been gone for weeks, supposedly staying at a variety of hotels, with people Cindy had never met, while Casey worked. What seemed to bother her at least as much, in fact, was that she had spent money and time looking for the little girl on July 3. "So, I wasted ten dollars to go up there [to get into Universal], which is no big deal," she said. "But you know it was in the afternoon."

Cindy had wasted ten dollars. For the record, she remembered this devastating financial loss and shared it with law enforcement officers on April 21, 2009, ten months later. The remains of her granddaughter had already been found in a trash bag in the woods.

Ten dollars.

Cindy was motivated enough, however, to go home and hop on MySpace. She knew if she really wanted to reach out to her daughter, she had better abandon reality and sign on to a social networking site. Casey's friends knew that about her, too.

Cindy didn't call the police. She didn't demand to know the exact location of her granddaughter from Casey. She created a little docudrama of her plight for public consumption.

Her later interview with law enforcement personnel about her online activity that day is worth lingering over:

Q: All right. What made you decide to create a MySpace account?

A: Because I wanted to talk to Casey in a way—I had told her on the phone I was upset with her that she didn't let me see Caylee. And I pretty much—Casey, and I, and Lee, when we are upset, we tend to write. So this was my way of getting my feelings out. And I wanted her—I asked her to be my friend. And I really didn't know how MySpace worked at that time. I didn't realize that it was a public thing.

Q: Uh-huh.

A: I figured if you clicked on someone's profile, then that's who you were—and allowed them to be your friend, then they could see your site.

Q: Who helped you create that?

A: I did. I figured it out the best that I could.

Q: Okay. You had some prior knowledge that Casey communicated with her friends via MySpace?

A: Oh, yeah. MySpace and Facebook.

Q: Okay. So did you feel that on July 3, by writing that, that you could get a reaction—?

A: I figured. . . .

Q: . . . Did you tell Lee that you had created or were going to create a message on MySpace for Casey?

A: I can't remember if I told him or not. I really
    can't. . . .

Q: . . . Okay. You put a title on your message?

A: I think: "My Caylee Is Missing."

My Caylee. Cindy seemed utterly unable to stop herself
from claiming the little girl as her own. Even while knowing
that using language like "my Caylee" might well cause resent-
ment in her daughter, Casey, she did so anyhow. *My Caylee.*
Those were the first two words of a MySpace entry she
thought would bring Casey home.

She could not have been more wrong.

But that's no surprise. Those intent on overcoming another person—taking that person's emotional oxygen and
sucking it deep into their own lungs—have a habit of continuing to exploit the other person's emotional triggers. They
can't help themselves. It's like an addiction.

The interview continued:

Q: Why did you select that as your title ["My Caylee
    Is Missing"]?

A: Because she was missing in my heart at that point.
    I mean, she was not in my life at that point, so
    that's the aspect that I was referring to, not physi-
    cally missing. . . .

Q: . . . It also has a section on there for the mood, and
    you put what, do you remember?

A: Probably "distraught."

Q: Did that give you options or is that something that
    you wrote yourself?

A: I think it gives you options.

Q: All right. And you selected "distraught"?

A: Yeah.

Q: All right. [Examining] Now, your first sentence:
    "She came into my life unexpectedly, just as she
    has left me."

A: Correct.

Q: What did you mean?

A: You know, Caylee came in. She wasn't planned. And again, Lee and Casey and I are writers. So we—

Q: Sure.

A: —write kind of metaphorically. So—

Q: Certainly.

A: —it's not always exactly what it means.

Q: Which is why I'm asking you.

A: But Lee and Casey and I understand that. We kind of have that same mentality, I guess. So it just meant that she suddenly—you know, she was there and then she wasn't there physically, you know, in my heart. . . . .

Q: . . . [Examining] The second line: "This precious little angel from above gave me strength and unconditional love." Okay. You're referring to Caylee—

A: Correct.

Q: —as giving you those things. . . .

Children are not household pets one procures in order to feel unconditional love. Many people raising children, in fact, are focused on *providing* unconditional love to them so that their sons and daughters can develop individuality and autonomy. When the emotional current runs in reverse, and is limitless, children can end up serving their parents' needs and losing their true selves. They empty themselves out trying to fill up their needy parents. And they always, always fail at it. Because the parents who set up these toxic dynamics are bottomless pits. They are trying to transfuse themselves with the life forces of others, instead of trying to find out when and where their own life forces were extinguished. If that sounds like something you've read in this book before, you have. It is Casey Anthony's story.

More of the interview:

Q: [Examining] Okay. "All I am guilty of is loving her and providing her a safe home." Okay. You use the word *guilty*. Did—was there some suggestion

> that somebody felt—that you felt somebody was
> thinking you were guilty of something else?
>
> **A:** No.
>
> **Q:** Why did you choose those words?
>
> **A:** I don't know. I seriously don't know.

Here, Cindy may as well have been in Sigmund Freud's office as that of the Florida Assistant State Attorney. The attorney clearly was on to something that the good doctor would
have appreciated. He was addressing Cindy's sense that she
has done something wrong that had led to the disappearance
of her granddaughter.

Here's one possibility Freud might have suggested Cindy
consider as the source of her guilty feelings: stealing Caylee
away from Casey, who was already psychologically decimated, leading Casey to feel that anything exquisitely alive
(like her little girl) was an intolerable reminder of what was
dead inside her and, therefore, must also cease to exist.

That could really spark some unconscious feelings of guilt,
don't you think?

Cindy was being honest, though. She was completely baf-
fled by why she had chosen the words, "All I am guilty of is
loving her. . . ." In my opinion, she had no insight whatsoever
into her own destructiveness. I don't think she was conscious
of the fact that the true nature of what she called love was
more like emotional bloodletting. It was, in my opinion, one
of the reasons—perhaps the chief reason—that her daughter
was no longer at home, and her granddaughter could not be
found. And, no big surprise, Cindy Anthony felt guilty, unconsciously, about that.

The attorney continued on an illuminating path:

> **Q:** [Examining] And then you wrote: "Jealousy has
> taken her away."
>
> **A:** You know, you start thinking of things. And I didn't
> know if Casey was jealous of the fact that I was off
> that week and I was going to spend time with her.

Because the week in June when I had taken off, over my birthday—

Q: Uh-huh.

A: —Caylee and I spent the entire time together that week. It was, you know, pretty much her and I bonding and, you know, having, you know—

Q: Fun.

A: —fun.

Q: Why would that make Casey jealous?

A: Because—in my mind, it was because she was working and not being able to spend time with her. So that's my perspective. And this is what she said, she wanted to have time to re-bond with Casey—I mean, to Caylee during this week, that she was not going to be working and she'd actually have those days to spend with her. But I kind of was jealous of Casey, too, because I figured the three of us could do something together. We usually did.

Cindy was getting to the heart of the matter—again, unconsciously. It's too bad she couldn't integrate such thoughts into her conscious mind and allow them to influence her behavior. It was a slip of the tongue, but a profoundly meaningful one, that *Casey needed time "to re-bond with Casey."* Exactly. Yes. Correct. Casey had been cleaved from her true inner thoughts and feelings nearly completely, and she desperately needed to re-bond with her *self.*

It is also poignant that Casey may have hoped to spend a week re-bonding with her self (as well as bonding with Caylee) while she was "not going to be working." That would have meant that, for one week, at least, she wouldn't have to be inventing lies about where she was going.

It could have been a life-affirming, maybe even lifesaving week.

Of course, Cindy couldn't stomach any of that. She must have had a knee-jerk reaction against Casey reconnecting with her self or with her daughter. It seems that she felt excluded, vulnerable, and empty anytime someone showed autonomy or sought to forge a real and genuine bond that didn't include her. That's why she felt "jealous" and apparently suggested it would be best were she present with her daughter and granddaughter.

The Reaper could not risk losing two souls who might find each other and, in so doing, discover a reservoir of emotional oxygen that could sustain them both as independent, though connected, human beings. She could not risk two souls finding each other and casting her aside.

The psychological revelations flowing from Cindy didn't end there:

Q: Okay. [Examining] Then you wrote: "Jealousy from the one person that should have been thankful for all of the love and support given to her." Who are you referring to?

A: Casey.

Q: Okay. So you're speaking to Casey in this?

A: Correct.

Q: Basically saying, you know—

A: Hey, what's up.

Q: —you're jealous of—

A: Yeah. Why can't I spend time with you? I would have gone to Jacksonville. I would have gone wherever. I—you know, if I would have been off when she would have been in Tampa, I would have gone there. But I had to work. So this week I was off and I felt like I didn't have my girls.

Cindy sounded like a jilted lover or a famished emotional vampire begging for blood: *Why can't I spend time with you? I would have gone to Jacksonville. I would have gone wherever.*

She would have gone anywhere on earth to make sure that Casey didn't have alone-time with her daughter, yet she had never gone down to the Sports Authority store to find out if Casey really worked there, had never gone to Universal Studios to find out if Casey *still* worked there, and had never gone to pick Caylee up from her nanny to see what sort of woman she was and find out for sure whether she really existed at all.

To top it all off, when she referred to Casey and Caylee as *my girls,* Cindy made it sound like they were her two daughters. She didn't say, "I felt like I didn't have my daughter and granddaughter." She didn't say, "I felt like I was without my family." She didn't say, "I felt lonely."

The Assistant State Attorney pressed on:

Q: Okay. But instead of saying that directly, you decided to say it indirectly by—

A: Again, when we write—

Q: —accusing Casey of being jealous?

A: Yeah. When we write, we kind of—we write your deepest feelings. You write it in a way it's going to grab the other person's attention.

Q: Okay. [Examining] You wrote: "A mother's love is deep." Are you referring to you?

A: To both of ours.

Every attempt by the attorney to determine whether Cindy was referring to herself or to Casey was blocked by Cindy. Her lack of boundaries couldn't be written more compellingly for a textbook of psychiatry seeking to illustrate such a problem. Cindy believed that Casey and she thought precisely the same way, wrote precisely the same way and loved children precisely the same way. (The latter, tragically, may have been dead-on.)

It isn't clear from reading Cindy's interview, in fact, whether she even understood Casey to be a separate person from her. And if she didn't understand that, then it follows logically that Casey's baby was hers from inception. A father in the picture would have been an unwelcome intrusion.

Maybe that explains why Cindy was so hostile to Jesse Grund lounging, fully clothed, on Casey's bed with her and Caylee. It could have gotten her very worried about Casey having a real family of her own one day. Lord knows, she could have ended up living a block away, or across town, instead of in her little bedroom.

Maybe it was Cindy who planted in Casey's mind the notion that Jesse wasn't the man for her because he supposedly seemed overly connected to Caylee—as though he loved her more than he loved Casey. Maybe she was the one whispering in Casey's ear to break off her engagement to a fundamentally decent fellow who loved her and was willing to help her parent a daughter not biologically his own. Maybe it was Cindy who lobbied Casey not to get married and instead to stay at home, fighting for whiffs of emotional oxygen.

Cindy had apparently tried the reverse strategy of attempting to get Jesse to bail out of the relationship. According to Jesse Grund's later testimony,

> Uhm, were were laying on the couch. Her and Casey started having an argument about something and I, I stuck up for Casey. And I said, ". . . Please don't do this while I'm here. Don't talk to her like that. You know I love your daughter." And then she immediately just throws Casey under the bus. A proverbial turn, just lays her out there. "How do you want to be with somebody who's got no future? She didn't even go back to get her high school education. You know she's got a, she's got a job [at] a place where she doesn't really even make enough money to support Caylee. I'm . . . the one supporting Caylee." And [Cindy] just basically just threw her out there. Totally.

It's interesting to note that when Caylee was a baby, both Cindy and Casey had audio monitors in their rooms to listen in on the nursery. That's right: *They both did.* Cindy got up every time that Caylee awakened and brought her to Casey to be fed. Even in the middle of the night, Cindy wanted to be included in Casey and Caylee's mother–daughter time. She needed Casey's breast, in order to breast-feed (if Caylee was, in fact, breast-fed), but it was essentially a surrogate breast, a donor breast.

Cindy would also testify in court that some days after Casey and Caylee left home on June 16, she "went and grabbed Caylee's favorite teddy bear."

"We call him Teddy," Cindy stated, "and I would cuddle with it at night. I was used to cuddling with Caylee, Caylee and or Casey, the three of us would usually cuddle at night if she was home, if not it would be me and Caylee before I went to bed. . . ."

CMA, CMA, CMA. The initials of Cindy Marie Anthony, Casey Marie Anthony and Caylee Marie Anthony told the whole story: No one was going to get very far away from Cindy Anthony. No one was ever going to truly get his or her own life.

You will remember that in the Old Testament, God sends one plague after another to convince Pharaoh to let His people leave slavery in Egypt. The last of those plagues is the death of the firstborn. Only that—not turning rivers to blood, nor smiting the land with frogs or lice or flies, nor epidemic disease among livestock, nor boils, nor thunder, nor hail, nor locusts—snaps Pharaoh's will and melts his heart. Only death of the firstborn achieves that, because the suffering in his house and throughout the land is so great.

"There was never a doubt we'd keep that child," George Anthony once said, of Caylee. He added, "I never wanted her to grow up anywhere else except our home."

Huh? Why would a grandfather say such a thing? Wouldn't he want his daughter to find a life partner who adored her and her child? Wouldn't he want his granddaughter to have a chance at having siblings? Or did he figure at the back of his mind that Casey would probably end up pregnant again by some anonymous lover, and his own multigenerational immediate family would grow?

He did adore kids, after all.

Casey and Caylee even had the same room décor as

two-year-olds—Winnie-the-Pooh. There was a Winnie-the-Pooh blanket, in fact, found near Caylee's remains.

The symbolism in that element of this tragic tale is nearly merciless. Caylee ended up dying physically in childhood, just as Casey had died psychologically in childhood. And she was found amidst the same memorabilia.

The items placed into evidence from Caylee's "crime scene"—where her bones were strewn—could, it seems, be placed as easily into evidence in a case that will never come to trial, but deserves investigation: the case of the psychological murder of Casey Anthony.

The Florida Assistant State Attorney kept delving into Cindy's writings and thought patterns:

Q: Okay. [Examining] "A mother will look for the good in her child." You're referring to yourself looking for the positives in Casey?

A: Correct.

Q: Okay. [Examining] "And give them a chance to change."

A: Correct.

Q: Again, you're referring to your giving Casey—

A: Casey a chance to—like, to make up for when she took money and, you know, giving her that opportunity to make good. I mean, it's—it's difficult to be a young adult. And I know, you know, you can make mistakes. And parents should give their children opportunity to—

Q: Second or third or even—

A: Absolutely

Q: —fourth chance?

A: Absolutely. You never want to give up on your child.

Q: Okay.

A: At least I would never give up on my children.

Q: All right. [Examining] "This mother gave chance after chance for her daughter to change, but, instead, more lies and betrayal." So that's your referring to—

A: The last few days.

Q: The last few days, not the past year?

A: Pretty much pinpointing it down to the event of that day. I mean, that's what—you know, over the last year, but, you know, to this point.

Q: Okay. [Examining] "What does the mother get for giving her daughter all of these chances?" That's— you're referring to you—

A: Uh-huh.

Q: —as the mother; Casey as daughter?

A: Correct. Correct. I mean, I felt like Casey was my best friend, my confidante. And then I found out she had been lying about where she was at and I didn't understand it, because that wasn't Casey. We talked about everything.

Not true. Cindy and Casey Anthony had never in my opinion talked about anything—not really. Casey had been lying to her about nearly everything for years: her having finished up high school in good standing; her job; her romantic and sexual relationships with men; her having a nanny; her supposed love for Cindy, which was actually, according to Casey's own grandmother Shirley, hatred; her being Cindy's best friend, when she had seemingly long ago retreated so deeply inside herself—to those confining, disfiguring catacombs of her mind—as to be unable to have a single true friend.

Casey Anthony had recoiled reflexively from a mother who would have absorbed her completely, leaving her empty and choked for air—a mother who would have taken every thought and emotion of Casey's and made it "theirs," not hers, because anything that belonged to Casey alone was an affront to Cindy's insatiable need to dominate others.

All those "chances" Cindy Anthony talks about having given Casey weren't expressions of love; they were ways of avoiding the truth that Casey was sick, keeping her from getting the help she needed, and thereby, keeping her dependent. That's what enablers do to achieve power. The more toxic the enabler, the more it happens.

Yet, life is forgiving. There had been many opportunities for Casey and Cindy to actually achieve a degree of genuine human connectedness. One of those moments—if Casey's words can be believed at all (we are, after all, in a hall of mirrors, or more accurately, a tomb of mirrors)—would have been when Casey supposedly complained she was being sexually abused. Her mother could have listened to her and protected her, rather than asserting (as Casey recalled) that the events never took place, or took place while Casey's purported assailant was sleepwalking. Another of those moments, if Casey's criminal defense attorney Jose Baez's words can be believed at all (and every individual must decide that independently), would have been coming to Casey's rescue when she was being forced to perform oral sex on her father.

Even if you reject both those scenarios as wholly fabricated by Casey, there were other moments. Cindy could have brought her daughter to a talented, insight-oriented psychiatrist right after learning that Casey had hidden her pregnancy for seven months—or, even more alarming, had been unaware of the pregnancy entirely. She could have brought her for help when it became clear she was compulsively lying or when it became clear she was stealing repeatedly. She could have brought her for help when she complained that she was having a nervous breakdown and needed to be hospitalized.

How does a young, single mother who feels so completely overwhelmed that she admits she would be better off in a hospital not end up even seeing an outpatient therapist? What would a young woman like Casey, who takes the chance to admit she is suffering to that extent, and is provided no real support or solution in return, conclude about whether her pain has any significance, or whether she will ever be allowed an exit from it? A breath of air.

It is an important moment when a woman declares that she will breathe easier on a locked psychiatric unit than at home.

No one paid any attention.

What if the reason that Casey felt like someone else should take care of Caylee and that she should head to a locked psychiatric unit was that she was hearing voices telling her to kill her child? What if the reason was that she felt like killing herself, then her child? What if she was ready to finally admit to someone that she had been abused as a little girl and that having another little girl around the house (Caylee) was, for reasons she wouldn't have been able to explain yet, making her feel like she was at death's door.

From all the available data, Cindy wouldn't have wanted to know. And not wanting to know—and, therefore, convincing Casey to stay at home instead of going to the hospital—had the potential to put Caylee in harm's way.

Forget "potential." Caylee *is* dead. It didn't happen right after Casey worrying about having a nervous breakdown, but it didn't happen that much later, either. So if a reader were to believe the proponents of Theory #1, then the nightmare scenario described in the paragraphs above is worth considering.

In an ideal world, Cindy would have brought Casey to an older female psychiatrist.

A woman old enough to be Casey's mother would have been the toughest for her to trust, the one likely to bring out her symptoms most dramatically and, therefore, the one with the best chance of engaging the demons that inhabited her soul.

Imagine how differently events might have unfolded if Casey had been introduced to a warm, engaging, and intelligent woman of say, fifty-five, who *listened* to her and *confirmed* some of her private thoughts and let her *express* some of her sadness and *challenged* her when she seemed to be evasive and maybe even, if God was on their side and Casey took a real chance to be vulnerable again, even sat with her while she cried—about everything, but mostly about never having been loved unconditionally, not once, not ever, and therefore, never having learned to love herself. I am speaking of a woman, of a healer, who would empathize with her and not inhale her, one who would demand to know not only what Casey had stolen, but *what had been stolen from her*. Just sitting with a compassionate much older female who had *boundaries* could have been the beginning of Casey venting the rage and self-hatred building up explosive pressure inside her.

I have written before about my own experience starting to see a psychiatrist. Mine was named James Mann. He was about eighty when I first visited with him. I was chief resident in psychiatry at New England Medical Center, in Boston. My mentors had really gotten on my case about the fact that I hadn't yet been in psychotherapy myself. They knew it was an important part of becoming a therapist.

Mann, seated in an upholstered armchair with deep pillows, listened to me patiently as I tried to fabricate a few innocuous problems we could bat around together, but then he held up a hand.

I stopped talking.

Mann's penetrating but remarkably kind gaze settled on me. He smiled warmly. "Do you ever get the feeling, as you're speaking," he said, "that you're completely full of shit?"

I laughed. How could I not? I'd been doing whatever I could not to speak of the really painful things I could have spoken about—like the fact that a good friend of mine had been killed just months before. "Yes," I told him. "Sometimes, I do."

Mann smiled. He leaned forward in his armchair. "Here's the thing, Keith," he said. "It's your time, and it's your money. But, more importantly, it's your life. And if you want to waste all three, I'll still sit here with you."

That was enough to start me on a path of truth-telling with Dr. Mann that was the most healing experience of my life.

Casey should have had such a doctor in her life. She needed one and she had as much as asked for one.

At a minimum, Cindy could have listened to Casey's plea—maybe her final plea while Caylee was still alive—that she be allowed to connect for one week—*just one week*—as a mother with her *own* daughter, to stop playacting for seven days, to stop lying about going to work and having a nanny, to let a little light past the fortified stone walls of her mind and heart and soul. But even that was refused. One hundred sixty-eight hours, out of a lifetime. Even that was a threat to Cindy's ownership of Caylee—and Casey.

A mother–daughter bond between Casey and Caylee might have brought Cindy too close to memories of having been the only girl amongst brothers, the one they marginalized and taunted as a spoiled "princess." It could have left Cindy too perilously close to hearing echoes of whatever emotional trauma she had suffered herself.

No, Cindy seems to have traded away every moment of potential healing to reinforce her stranglehold on her daughter, whom she apparently believed shared all her thoughts, to write just the way she wrote, to want the very same things she did. She acted as though she believed Casey was her best friend, her confidante, her source of unconditional love. She believed, one could theorize, that Casey was the mother *of Cindy's child*. That's right. I believe the obliteration of boundaries and toxic enabling had gone that far. I believe Casey had been treated as her own mother's womb and breast—an accessory reproductive system that had delivered her mother's baby and nursed it. That's why George was in that delivery suite—as the metaphorical father of Caylee (if not, as some have argued, the actual, biological father). That's why Caylee was handed to her grandmother.

That's why—many psychiatrists might argue—Caylee was dead now, whether murdered or accidentally drugged into oblivion or ignored as she drowned. That's why the closest Cindy could get to Casey now was a string of evasive phone calls that she was at her nanny's house, then at the Hard Rock Hotel, then in Busch Gardens, then back at Universal Studios in Orlando, then quickly off to Jacksonville.

She was nowhere to be found. She was finally, horribly, explosively, inextricably free.

Casey next told her mother that Jeff and she were getting closer. Caylee was spending time with Jeff's mother in Jacksonville.

That didn't seem to make all that much sense to Cindy, since she had been told that Jeff's mother was recovering from cancer, but no matter.

Casey told her mother she wouldn't come home until Saturday, July 5, or Sunday, the sixth. That didn't happen, because Casey's car supposedly needed service. But the two of them talked each day from the seventh through the eleventh. She finally said she was coming home on Saturday, the twelfth.

But again, the plans were scuttled. Casey told Cindy that Jeff and she were talking about moving in together. They were even considering marriage.

None of the above actually happened. As already noted, Casey had no job. She had no nanny. She was not at Busch Gardens or in Jacksonville. She had not spent time with Jeffrey Hopkins, who, in fact, hadn't seen her in about a year.

Hopkins would later testify that he met Casey in middle school and that they saw each other only in passing, later in life. They were acquaintances, not good friends. Both of them apparently worked at Universal Studios during 2002, but he didn't recall ever seeing her there. He bumped into her on July 2 at a place called the Waterford Lakes Ale House, and they exchanged numbers. But he never called her, and she never called him. He testified that he'd lived in Orlando his whole life and had never lived in Jacksonville.

Lying was one of the ways Casey had learned to keep a little, tiny bit of herself under wraps, to keep the candle of her soul just barely flickering, perhaps just one more personal invasion away from being permanently extinguished. She was an expert at it. World class.

The real events of those days are not fully known. But what seems clear is that Casey had released herself, in some terrible way, from Cindy's control. With all opportunities to heal her having been ignored, her internal self—that broken, gnarled creature behind walls of denial and pain—was no longer contained. Something dramatic had freed Casey from Hopespring Drive.

One of the things we know for sure is that Casey did borrow a shovel from her neighbor on the seventeenth or eighteenth of June.

We also know that on the evening of June 18, she made calls on her cell phone from Tony Lazzaro's apartment, including a two-and-a-half-minute call home. Then her cell phone went dead for thirteen and a half hours until she texted Tony the next morning.

Whatever happened in those thirteen and a half hours, and whatever had happened in the days preceding them, no one should wonder any longer at how detached from it all Casey appeared to be—and actually was. She had already severed her connections with pain, rage, and suffering long ago, severed her connection to herself, and developed an incredible capacity to suppress her real emotional and psychological identity.

The best final defense against complete immersion in one's tortuous past is complete flight from it. Free of Caylee, Casey was no longer anchored to any reality at all. She was Jay Gatsby on steroids, reinventing herself, inventing others, inventing the past and the future. She was on a dead run from reality, from the loss of her daughter, into the defense mechanisms she had already honed so well.

If Casey's own report of her childhood, after all, in any way reflects the facts—even if she accused the wrong individuals of abuse perpetrated by others—then no one should be shocked that losing her daughter to an accident, or an abduction, or a moment of vindictiveness, or a pathologically misguided desire to bring her peace would leave her seemingly untouched. If an eight-year-old can perform fellatio on her father and then go to school and play dodgeball and learn subtraction and memorize vocabulary words and play in the school band, and then go home and hug her mother, who is trying to suffocate her, then she can perform any role, without ever stepping out of it—even the without-a-care-in-the-world party girl whose two-year-old is dead, inside a trash bag.

She had many well-honed, time-honored tools, after all, to bolster her emotional on/off switch, what was essentially an "ability" to dissociate. She began deploying them right away.

She started with flirting, romance, and sex, adding that to

the ever-present, ubiquitous text messaging, Internet surfing, and MySpace posting.

On June 19, Casey invited a friend named Troy Brown, as well as her friend Iassen Donovan, to meet her at Fusion Ultra Lounge, a club where Tony would be performing. She also called a man named Matthew Crisp about renting an apartment at Cranes Landing Apartments, then met him, along with Tony, and filled out an application form.

On Friday, June 20, Casey was at or around Tony's apartment much of the day. She used Tony's Internet Protocol (IP) address to upload a flyer related to Fusion. She also backed into her parents' garage for the third time in a week, then disappeared again.

Casey went out with a big group of friends the night of the twentieth. She entered a "Hot Body Contest" at Fusion—and won. She partied there until the morning.

She must have felt especially free competing in that contest. People were focused on her breasts and abdomen and buttocks, not on her thoughts or feelings—or her past. They were voting on a winner based on appearance. Based on sex appeal. Everything that mattered was skin deep—or, at most, groin deep. And Casey had had lots of experience with men focusing on her groin. Even her father, George, had stood at the foot of her bed as she lay with her legs spread and was prepped to deliver Caylee.

Maybe Casey threw back a few shots to chase any demons even further from consciousness. Maybe she tried Ecstasy, the feel-good drug so popular in clubs, to fortify the walls around this singular truth: that she had died spiritually, that what was dead inside her had become virulent and that her daughter was gone.

But dancing that night of the Hot Body Contest, with her hair flowing and her body writhing, and booze carrying her away from her self, and music carrying her away from her self, and the hungry eyes of men and women at Fusion carrying her away from her self, she must have felt entirely free, when in reality, she was entirely lost, entirely absent. Gone.

She may have started using more alcohol, routinely, to keep her underlying emotions at bay and may, indeed, have added illicit drugs to the mix. She mentioned as much to a friend.

Casey stayed the weekend with Tony. Caylee was nowhere to be found.

On June 23, Casey and Tony Lazzaro reportedly ran out of gas near the Anthonys' house. She walked to Hopespring Drive, reportedly convinced Tony to break the lock on her parents' shed, and took two gas cans with her.

George Anthony discovered and reported the theft of his gas cans on June 24. He has claimed that Casey returned to the house that day in the afternoon. She told him she was there to get more clothes for work and went to her room. He inquired about the well-being of Caylee and was assured she was doing fine. He also mentioned the theft of the gas cans. "Casey," he said, ". . . if you took them, that's fine. If you're using them, that's fine." He wanted to play detective a little bit, so he told her that he would be rotating Cindy's tires during the coming weekend and needed one of the little metal triangle platforms he used to keep Cindy's car from rolling while he worked on it. He told her he remembered putting it in her car and that he'd like to grab it. What he really wanted was to see if his gas cans were in her trunk.

He told the Assistant Florida State Attorney what happened next:

> So we had a little bit of a back and forth, I guess a little banter about me wanting to get it. And I said: Casey, I know exactly where it's at because I'm the one that put it in your car. And I said: Where it's at, I said, it's down by the spare tire. It might be hard for you to get out. And since I put it down there, I'm a lot stronger than you, I'll just get it out.

But just as George was getting ready to go out through the garage, Casey burst past him, saying she would get what he was looking for. She opened the trunk, handed him the empty cans, and sputtered, "Here are your fucking gas cans."

"I was stunned," he reported. "I said [to Casey]: Why did you make me look like—I don't know if I called myself an ass or an idiot in front of the sheriff's department, I said, and make a report [that they were stolen]?"

According to George, Casey told him, "Dad, I don't [have] time. . . ."

He wasn't going to press the point. He never did. "I said: Fine. We'll discuss it later."

Casey got in her car and left.

It is important to note that during his interview with law enforcement officials, George Anthony was shown photographs of the gas cans in question. And in a stunning demonstration of what really seemed to matter to him in the setting of his granddaughter's death, he insisted again and again they must have been mishandled by the folks in charge of keeping evidence down at the police station. They looked dirty, for one thing. And there was a piece of duct tape stuck haphazardly over the vent in the can. He couldn't let go of that issue. "Because," he said, "I like that gas can. It's sort of part of me. It's twenty years old."

Caylee Anthony, after all, was only two.

The next day, Wednesday, June 25, Casey called Amy Huizenga and complained about a terrible smell in her car and wondered whether her father might have run over something when he borrowed it. Specifically, she said it smelled "like something died in my car."

Former Los Angeles Police Detective Mark Fuhrman believes he knows why Casey was complaining about a noxious odor. His words aren't for the faint of heart, but Fuhrman isn't one to pull punches or shrink away from tough realities. "If you keep a dead child in a trunk for days, where temperatures are reaching 172 degrees, you're talking about rigor mortis having set in. You're talking about the breaking down of cell walls, a bloating process, insects starting to infiltrate tissues."

Those who believe, as Fuhrman does, that Theory #1 explains why Caylee Anthony was missing on June 25, should be aware of how completely the tragedy of Caylee's body liquefying inside a car's trunk, in which temperatures have soared to 172 degrees, fits the psychological moment, as well. Because the driver of the car, visible through glass windows, is a woman who has turned her back on the past, denied all her suffering, suppressed her true identity, and has just won a hot-body contest, on a night when she probably smelled like Chanel perfume, like a dream. She has jettisoned all ugliness and trauma and relegated it to an unseen, locked, pitch-black place where it has boiled over.

In this way, Theory #1 makes Caylee the physical representation of everything dead inside her mother, just as experts like Dr. Arno Gruen would have predicted.

On June 26, Casey probably spent the day at Tony Lazzaro's apartment. She downloaded tattoo art of the words *Bella Vita*. Translated from Italian, it reads, "Beautiful Life." She also downloaded tattoo art of a partly rotten apple carved to look like a skull. The apple would have been the more honest image to be tattooed with. *Bella Vita* was the predictable one—the one that said the opposite of everything that had really happened, the one that was another skin-deep defense against reality.

On June 27, Casey texted her friend Amy Huizenga, stating that she had run out of gas again and added that "there was definitely part of an animal plastered to the frame of my car." She told her that Caylee was at the beach with her nanny and her grandmother, Cindy. She also made calls to Tony Lazzaro, Jesse Grund, and her lifelong friend Ryan Pasley.

Since Casey was supposedly stranded, Tony Lazzaro went to pick her up from the parking lot of Amscot, a check-cashing and Western Union store. When he pulled up to her Pontiac, she was already standing outside the car, with bags of groceries taken from the Anthonys' house and clothes in hand. She told Tony her father would take care of picking up the car and, for reasons that are not known, she left her purse inside it.

Casey was still juggling men. She asked her former fiancé Jesse Grund to come by Fusion that night, but he declined. She texted her former boyfriend Ricardo Morales and asked what he might be up to the next night.

For Casey, sex would have been another anesthetic escape, as freeing as a hot-body contest. If she could just be told what to do and do it well enough, while keeping her own needs far from consciousness, then she could, for all intents and purposes, disappear. No one would be looking for her if they were looking at her naked. And since she was (according to my sources) so good in bed, she could make her lovers disappear, too—into their pleasure. She didn't need to worry about "connecting" with them if she was "hooking up" with them.

She did, indeed, go to the Fusion Ultra Lounge with Tony. She seemed to be happy working that night, passing out shots to the customers. It was a perfect job for Casey. She was the dispenser of anesthetic to the crowd, the prophet of painlessness, the ambassador of oblivion.

The next day, Casey's car was still abandoned in the parking lot. She purchased a few tickets to the movie *Wanted,* about a mild-mannered accountant on anxiety medication who discovers he is the son of a professional assassin and decides to join the secret society of killers to which his father belonged. It's almost too obvious to say that a movie about someone who has repressed all hostility, has experienced psychiatric symptoms because of it, and who then becomes a killer, might speak to her.

She and Tony also rented another movie at Blockbuster.

Caylee hadn't been seen by Tony or his roommates for a long time. Clint House, one of the roommates, told me, "From the middle of June to the end of June, we didn't see Caylee anymore. She'd been over a lot before that. And she was great. But then, she was gone. And I was asking, 'Where is she? We miss her.' And Casey would be, like, 'Oh, she's with her grandparents,' 'Oh she's with her nanny.' We didn't know Casey was a pathological liar. She came off as an awesome person. Bubbly. Sweet. Caring. She seemed like the perfect human being."

Too good to be true.

On June 29, 2008, Casey and Tony spent the day together.

Casey used her mother's credit card, forging her name to make a few purchases at JCPenney and Target.

On the thirtieth, Casey's car was towed by the manager of the Amscot store to an impound lot. She used Tony Lazzaro's Jeep to drive him to the airport for his trip to New York City.

Casey kept driving Tony's car while he was away (despite not having permission to do so) and immediately started hanging around with other men. On July 1, she asked Jesse Grund if it would be all right if she showered at his apartment before work. He agreed to let her. Then, she apparently spent the night at Tony Morales's apartment.

On July 2, Casey stole about four hundred dollars from her friend Amy Huizenga. When Amy couldn't find her money and asked Casey about it, Casey described a scene for Amy that eerily evoked what she later claimed was her mother, Cindy's, way of writing off the idea that Lee might be sexually abusing her. According to Amy's interview with Detective Jerold White of the Orlando County Sheriff's Office, Casey claimed that Amy had lost the money while sleepwalking.

"I didn't know she stole it, I knew it was missing," Amy said. "[Casey] told me that I woke up in my sleep and, um, set aside money for the Puerto Rico trip [which Amy was planning to go on]. . . . I had no reason not to trust Casey. . . ."

The interview proceeded:

Detective Jerold White: Okay, so let me get this right. . . . . A week before your trip, four hundred dollars comes up missing, Casey was in the house, she tells you . . . that you were sleepwalking. . . .

Amy Huizenga: She told me before I knew the money was missing, like, I was counting money and she told me the story.

Amy just couldn't bring herself to think Casey might steal from her, so she decided she must have hidden the money too well. "Yeah, so I was, like, well, you know eventually it will turn up," she told Detective White. ". . . You know, like, my, they're two of my best friends that I live with, [so] if four hundred dollars and twenty shows up, they're gonna know whose it is."

The same day that Casey stole Amy's money, she went to Cast Iron Tattoos and got the tattoo on her right shoulder that read, *Bella Vita*.

The next day—the day Cindy wasted ten dollars at Universal Studios looking for Casey and Caylee—Casey reached out to Jesse Grund to alert him not to give her mother any information if he were to receive a call from her. She explained that something complicated was going on in her family and that she would handle it.

She went to a party at the home of William Waters and, according to what Waters later told Corporal William "Eric" Edwards of the Orlando Police Department, immediately recruited him as another man—another anesthetic—in her life. She told him she had a daughter, but that she was with her nanny:

William Waters: . . . She took care of my house. . . . . I got a cut on my face. She was right there to grab a cold towel and put it on me. And she swept my house, cleaned it, and she just took care of everything. I, I had no problems with her in my house while we were all playing football and kickball. I walked in, she had everybody in order and [was] taking care of things.

Corporal Eric Edwards: First time you ever met her?

WW: Yeah. That's why like all my friends were like, "Dude, you," they just seen how, I was totally like a love bug. I'd like, like, love being, being around her. She was, her energy was awesome and she was fun to be around. I . . .

EE: You dug her right off the bat?

WW: Yeah, kind of. Because I knew she had a, Amy

told me she had a boyfriend and don't even, you know, don't pursue, blah-blah-blah. So you just, you know, became friends. Hang out and you know, and just go out and play kickball, push each other around, and, and . . .

EE: No kiss?

WW: No. Not at all. She, never. Like she would never.

EE: The fifth. You say at nine thirty in the morning she shows up on your doorsteps?

WW: Yes, sir.

EE: Tell me about that.

WW: Uhm, she came down, because I texted her that morning. I was like, "Are we going to hang out again?" And, or, "When are we going to hang out?" And she said whenever I wanted. So then I went and took a shower. Uh, I went upstairs, talking to my roommate about how, how awesome she was. And, uh, and I went down. Went and took a shower, came out of my room, and she was walking on the steps. So I had this big grin on my face. I was like, "So what, so what are we going to do?"

So I needed to go to, uh, IKEA and she needed to go to IKEA because supposedly she was getting a place soon. So, uhm, I got ready and we left my house around eleven thirty. . . . . And we were just pretty much picking out things we wanted to put in our, in our houses. Her future house and I'm re-decorating my house.

Keep in mind that Casey Anthony had no home and no income with which to secure a home. At the time she was with William Waters in Orlando, her mother believed she was in Jacksonville with Jeffrey Hopkins. And Casey was able to happily pick out furniture for her nonexistent apartment, despite her daughter having gone missing or being dead, and despite the fact that she would be picking her boyfriend up from the airport in just hours.

The pathological ability to cleave oneself from reality

and move fluidly through the day, as Casey did, is absolute evidence that she had almost completely suppressed her real identity and feelings.

Later on July 5, she did, in fact, pick up her boyfriend, Tony Lazzaro, from the airport. They went over to Buffalo Wild Wings for some food and to meet some friends.

On July 6, Casey went shopping at Kmart and texted her friend Troy Brown that she might stop by his place. She never did.

On July 7, Casey allegedly posted a message to her MySpace account titled, "Diary of Days." It read: "On the worst of days, remember the words spoken, Trust no one, only yourself. With great power, comes great consequence. What is given can be taken away. Everyone Lies. Everyone Dies."

Some people have theorized that "Diary of Days" was Casey's response to Cindy Anthony's MySpace post, "My Caylee Is Missing."

Were that true, then Casey would essentially have been telling her mother that their bond had been severed, that she should consider herself alone in the world now, that exercising so much power over others had backfired.

Another possibility is that the events of the preceding weeks had sent Casey spiraling beyond the pathological orbit she had been confined to on Hopespring Drive. She may literally have been euphoric and disinhibited, speaking about herself as an extremely powerful, even godlike individual being hunted—as though she had leaped off the screen of the movie *Untraceable* or *Jumper,* the two films she had rented on June 16.

Later on July 7, Casey sent a text message to William Waters that read, "You're really the sweetest guy I ever met."

On July 8, Amy Huizenga left for Puerto Rico and let Casey borrow her 1997 red Toyota Corolla while she was away. Casey used the checkbook Amy had left in the glove compartment to make a purchase for $111.01 at Target. Then she went grocery shopping with another stolen check of Amy's.

On July 9, Casey posted a picture of herself on her MySpace account while she was out partying.

On July 10, she went shopping again at Target and for groceries, using Amy's checks. She's seen by a friend's mother at Target and looks "happy."

Casey had plans with William Waters to go on a helicopter ride that day. He was already quite taken with her. But she canceled, explaining that she needed to spend time with her grandmother.

At 11:47 P.M., she posted a comment about a rock group named Fuzzy Red Balloons: "oh my sexy boys," she wrote, "i love [them] . . . !"

One of the group's most popular songs is titled "Evil Eyes," and includes the lyrics, *I've got the time, if you don't care, / you can take me anywhere.*

Indeed. Casey was floating free of everything and everyone. She was like a drug herself. If you had the time, and you didn't care, you could do a few lines of CMA, anywhere.

Yet, the truth had been making itself known to Casey herself in the night. With her defenses partly neutralized by sleep, demons were visiting. Anthony Lazzaro had noticed it from the first night he arrived back in Orlando, from New York City. He later shared his recollections in an interview with Corporal William "Eric" Edwards of the Orlando Police Department:

Corporal Eric Edwards: . . . You say that, uh, Casey . . . was waking up in cold sweats during the middle of the night. Can you tell me about that?

Anthony Lazzaro: Yes, uh . . . she, uh, would wake up and, or wake me either in the middle of the night, or I would just wake up in the middle of the night and see that she was sweaty in bed. And I would ask her, uh, why and she said that she would have [a] nightmare . . . she was having a nightmare or something. . . .

Once Casey had had a few moments to shake the terror from her mind, she would try to explain away her night terrors by telling Lazzaro they were all about her fear that he was going to end up leaving her.

That probably made Lazzaro feel especially close to Casey. Indispensable. Of course, he didn't know that she was still spending time with Jesse Grund and Ricardo Morales and had found a new love interest in William Waters.

In fact, on July 11, Casey texted Waters to ask him if he could meet her and Tony at a sake bar. He declined. He had real feelings for her and didn't want to see her with another man. "Why would I put myself through that?" he texted back.

Not very much is known about the next few days, other than that Casey kept forging checks to go shopping and bought one ticket to *Hellboy II,* a movie about a mythical world that declares war on humanity and attempts to take over the earth.

It was an apt choice. Events were unfolding very rapidly, and Casey would be back at 4937 Hopespring Drive, where humanity had been defeated, very soon.

On July 14, 2008, she posted a very telling update to her MySpace account. She wrote that she was listening to a song she loved from the rock group Nine Inch Nails:

The lyrics include these words:

> *I am still inside here*
> *A little bit comes bleeding through*

The song goes on to describe someone who wishes that events could have unfolded in some other way than they did, but felt powerless to change things because she is lost inside herself.

It is hard to imagine a more fitting ballad describing Casey's life. No real voice. No real love. Hiding from pain. Anesthetized. Still locked behind thick walls. Just a little bit of her bleeding through, now and then.

A rare moment of tears for Casey Anthony, who listened to most of the testimony in her capital murder trial with a stoic countenance. (Courtesy: Red Huber/*Orlando Sentinel*/MCT via Getty Images)

The author, Keith Ablow, MD, was often called upon by the media for insight into Casey Anthony's psychological makeup and her family's behavior during her trial. Here, he comments on Casey's father's testimony to anchor Martha MacCallum on the Fox News Channel. (Courtesy: The Fox News Channel)

George Anthony seemed to be feigning tears as he testified at his daughter's murder trial. Sources described Mr. Anthony as a "non-person," without real emotions. (Courtesy: Red Huber/*Orlando Sentinel*/MCT via Getty Images)

On February 10, 2009, the Anthony family held a public memorial for Caylee Anthony. Her grandparents, George and Cindy (pictured here with their son Lee), would later seek a trademark for the name Caylee Anthony and sold photos of her to a television network for tens of thousands of dollars. (Courtesy: Red Huber/*Orlando Sentinel*/MCT via Getty Images)

Casey Anthony speaks to her parents after her arrest for the murder of her daughter Caylee. Her defense counsel would later accuse her father of forcing her, beginning at age 8 and continuing for years, to perform oral sex on him—and possibly of having sexual intercourse with her. (Courtesy: Red Huber/*Orlando Sentinel*/MCT via Getty Images)

Cindy Anthony, Casey's mother, here in court. Cindy and her husband George were both in the delivery room when Casey deliverer her daughter Caylee. Cindy held the baby first. (Courtesy: Red Huber/*Orlando Sentinel*/MCT via Getty Images)

George Anthony, here in court, had a history of lying, stealing, and gambling. According to the author's sources, he dreamed of being a character, like Pluto, at Disney World. (Courtesy: Red Huber/ *Orlando Sentinel*/ MCT via Getty Images)

With her daughter dead nearly a month, and her remains not yet found, Casey Anthony got a tattoo reading "Bella Vita," Italian for "Beautiful Life." (Courtesy: AP Photo/ Red Huber, Pool)

Casey Anthony, holding hands with her attorneys, awaits the jury's verdict in her capital murder trial. (Courtesy: Red Huber/*Orlando Sentinel*/MCT via Getty Images)

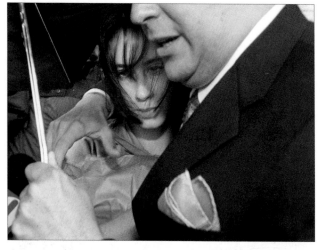

Casey Anthony was described by her ex-fiancé's father as having a special way of turning toward any man who put his arm around her, as though she adored him and were seeking protection from the whole world. Here, her attorney, Jose Baez, shelters her. (Courtesy: Red Huber/*Orlando Sentinel*/ MCT via Getty Images)

Casey Anthony with her boyfriend Anthony Lazzaro. While she was sleeping with him, she was texting other men telling them how special they were to her. (Courtesy: Teddy Pieper and John Azzilonna)

George Anthony, Caylee's grandfather, helped organize the search for Caylee. According to a woman named Krystal Holloway (aka River Cruz), he was having sex with her at the same time as volunteers were searching. (Courtesy: Red Huber/*Orlando Sentinel*/MCT via Getty Images)

Casey Anthony attracted the sexual interest of men and women, wherever she went. She is pictured here at the Fusion Ultra Lounge, where she entered and won a "hot body contest," while her daughter Caylee was missing. (Courtesy: Teddy Pieper and John Azzilonna)

The roots of her predicament reached back at least five generations and a hundred years.

She had been imprisoned inside herself a long, long time, every day crouched in a space as dark as the inside of a garbage bag, as airless as the trunk of a car at 172 degrees.

THREE HUNDRED BUCKS

The truth about Casey's fake odyssey to the Hard Rock Hotel and Busch Gardens and Jacksonville, including a fake romance with Jeffrey Hopkins and plans to become engaged to him, began to leak out on July 11. A notice posted on the Anthonys' front door alerted them to a certified letter being held at the post office. According to Cindy and George, they didn't see the notice until Sunday, July 13. Neither one of them had the time to go down to the post office to pick the letter up the following day. So, on Tuesday, July 15, George went and grabbed it.

The letter was from Johnson's Tow and Recovery. It said that they had towed Casey's Pontiac Sunfire from the Amscot parking lot back on the thirtieth of June. It was being held at an impound lot on Narcoossee Road in Orlando.

When George Anthony was interviewed by authorities on August 5, 2009, he described what happened next, as follows:

> I drive down to Johnson's Towing and I met the attendant who was at the front glass area, a lady, told her what I was there for and she told me how much it was going to be to get it out.
> And I said: Whoa. Whoa. Whoa. I says: Question for you. I said: If you towed it on the thirtieth, why did you wait two weeks before we got a notice on it? This makes no sense to me. When we're two miles away

from you, why couldn't you have called me or something like that?

And she said: Sir, that's not up for us to do. State
requirements for towing—and she went into thing with
with me.

I said: Well, I don't agree with what you're doing,
but how much is it going to cost? She told me five hundred and some dollars. I said: But the letter said two
hundred and some.

She says: Well, that's because that was only for the
first three or four days.

I was, like: You've got to be kidding me.

I called Cindy, told her what was going on.

She says: Well, George, I'll have to go and get the
money.

And I says: Well, while you're getting the money
out of our account, I said, I'm going to go ahead—we
need a title for it. And I said: I'll go ahead and meet
you down at the towing service. I told her where it was
at. Both of us—as a matter of fact, both of us met at
our house.

I got some gas in the gas can, as a matter of fact this
can of ours, or one of—some other can that we have,
put some gas in it and Cindy and I went down to Johnson's Towing and tried to discuss the fee, why it took
them so long to contact us—

Again, the extent to which George and Cindy Anthony
were demonstrating their inability to focus on Casey as a
human being (not to mention Caylee) is breathtaking (word
choice, intentional). After all, they had been under the impression that Casey had driven her car to Jacksonville—with
Caylee. They knew that Casey had a habit of lying. They had
never met her supposed nanny named Zanny. And they hadn't
spoken with Caylee in thirty-one days. Yet their focus—much
like that of Cindy on her wasted ten dollars at Universal and
George's on his prized gas can—was on whether they should
be charged two hundred or five hundred dollars to retrieve

Casey's vehicle. They were obsessed with the fact that they believed they were being overcharged by three hundred bucks. Not only did George bring it up repeatedly the day he went to Johnson's Towing, but also he kept bringing it up in his interview with the Florida Assistant State Attorney. The attorney actually had to interrupt him to try to refocus him on his daughter:

Q: Let me stop you for one second and ask, before we get to that: Did you try to call Casey after learning that the car she uses has been towed?

A: I didn't talk to Casey about that. I don't know if Cindy did that specific day or that night. Don't really know. I really don't know.

Q: All right. So you're at the tow yard to talk to them about—

George simply couldn't contain himself. He was lucky he wasn't facing competition from Cindy for the attorney's time. She might have wanted to bend his ear about the ten bucks she was out from searching for Casey on July 3, 2008.

A: . . . about the bill, why they couldn't contact us, why couldn't at least he went by our house . . . why they didn't get Orange County to contact me. You know, there were so many questions I asked. You know, why just tow something and all of a sudden, after two-plus weeks, we find out—

Q: Right.

A: —you know, our car has been towed and now we owe you guys five hundred and some dollars? That makes no sense to me. You know, why not a little bit of—cutting somebody a little bit of a break.

We were there for probably at least a good part of an hour, and got negotiated, and Cindy finally got the price down a little bit, but it just didn't come down as far as I was concerned, but—

The attorney had to interrupt him, lest he go on and on and on about the unfair price the impound lot was charging for him to retrieve Casey's car.

Q: Okay. So at some point do you go out to the vehicle with one of the people that works there?

At no time did George Anthony demand to know why Johnson's Towing had waited so long to alert him about having Casey's car in their possession, based on the fact that he had been worried about Casey and Caylee. At no time did he yell, "Why would you guys keep my daughter's car for two weeks without telling us? What if something had happened to her? What if she'd been kidnapped? What if she were dead? How could you know? We've been out of our minds worried about her."

Nope. George and Cindy spent the better part of an hour negotiating something a little less than five hundred dollars to pick up the Sunfire. And, contrary to George's report, it was Cindy who did the lion's share of the negotiating.

If what you've read about the Anthonys before in this book hasn't been enough to give you some insight into what being raised in their household might be like, just think about how the mundane details of daily life might trump all your psychological pain. Think about how keeping things neat and clean might overshadow your need to talk about a messy emotional issue you might be confronting. Think about how you could feel left for dead in a home where everything had its place, except for your feelings, where every dollar was counted, except what could be stolen from your mother's clutches or your father's gambling stash. Imagine being left, essentially, for dead by the parents to whom you had been born. Would you want to internalize that reality? Or would you want to deny it with every mental gymnastics routine you could?

No wonder Casey had tossed her father's "fucking" gas cans at him. They were so very important to him. They were "part" of him, in his own words. He had not a hair out of place, but his kids' lives were a wreck. He spent weekends detailing every family member's car, until they were perfectly clean and shiny, but he'd gambled away enough dough to throw his family into financial chaos. He liked to say that he'd moved on from the family car business when his father had an opportunity to sell it, but he'd really moved on after he threw his dad through a plate glass window. He played it straight, but he was staring at his daughter's crotch when she gave birth. He was all about denying his underlying messiness, loose ends, hostility, and depravity, and keeping up a front. If only Casey had been able to tell him to go fuck himself many years before, she might not have turned into what she had become. If only. But she was out of touch with her grief and rage. She had too completely suppressed her identity to assert it.

When the all-important financial negotiations with Johnson's Towing had finally concluded, George walked over to Casey's Sunfire with Simon Burch, the operations manager for the tow yard.

From George's interview with law enforcement personnel: "And I walked around and just prior to me getting to the car, I see there's no damage on the car, which I was thankful for."

Huh? He made it clear elsewhere to law enforcement authorities that at that time he was worried about whether the body of his daughter or granddaughter might be rotting in the trunk. But he was "thankful" that there didn't seem to be a scratch or a dent on the Sunfire.

This was George Anthony unmasked. This was George Anthony for real. This is apparently what *mattered* to him.

His comment was eerily echoed by Cindy Anthony, when she was interviewed by Scott Bolin, of the FBI, after her granddaughter had been missing for approximately five months:

Cindy Anthony: You wouldn't leave a car especially that was in good condition. That car runs.

Scott Bolin: Yeah

CA: Great shape, I mean.

SB: I've seen it.

CA: Yeah it's a nice-looking car.

SB: Yeah.

CA: And um, has a lot of life in it. And we had just, you know, put some money into tires and stuff, and there's no way that we were gonna, you know, get rid of the car.

SB: Right.

CA: And it doesn't make sense to me that she would . . . not want to go back and pick up the car. And eventually at some point.

SB: Keep in mind, there's a lot of things that could happen.

CA: I understand.

SB: That doesn't make sense.

Agent Bolin seemed to be struggling to comprehend why Cindy would be focused on how pretty the Sunfire was and how she and George had just invested in new tires for it. But that's because he didn't know that she could push aside a person in favor of a thing. He wasn't working off the theory that she was a psychological assassin. And if she was, that wasn't her fault, of course. She had lived through her own trouble, and I believe it had left her psychologically sterile. Emotions didn't seem to register with her as real. That may be why Casey had buried her genuine thoughts and feelings, along with anything else close to her heart, and had deployed one psychological defense after another to keep them buried, until she was completely estranged from them. That's why I think she became, in real life, the Stranger about whom Camus wrote so eloquently in fiction.

George's interview with the Florida Assistant State Attorney continued:

Q: Now, as you approach the car, you've talked a number of occasions about the odor?

A: Yeah. There was a strong odor coming from the car. There was. I'm not going to deny it. I can't deny it because—

Q: And you formed an opinion about the nature of that odor as you approached; is that correct?

A: Well, it was an overpowering odor. It was something that anyone within a few feet of this vehicle could have smelled something. And—

Q: And did you believe the smell—did you recognize the smell as being a smell of human decomposition?

A: Not human decomposition. I knew it was decomposition there. I knew there was decomposition there. I knew there was something that just didn't smell right to me. As I went around to the driver's side, opened up the driver's door, and it took my breath away for a second. It really did. I mean, it's ninety-some degrees outside. The car had been sitting there for over two weeks.

I remember opening the driver's window, trying to vent the car a little bit. And I remember I stuck the key in the ignition and as I did, I knew the—the car wouldn't start. And I told the guy, I said: Well, it's probably out of gas.

And the attendant that was there, he's the one that says: Oh, my gosh, this really stinks. . . .

Q: Let me stop you for a second before you go on to that; okay? As you approached the car, did it come into your mind that the odor might be from the decomposition of either your daughter or your granddaughter?

A: Not at that point. No, sir. . . . . I looked around the inside of the car. I couldn't see anything except my granddaughter's car seat and some shoes and some other stuff. The car was, you know, messy inside. [Far be it from George to miss *that*.]

And I remember getting out of the driver's seat and walking towards the back of the car. And I didn't say it directly to this gentleman. I did say it to my—under my breath. I said: Please don't let this be my daughter or granddaughter.

And as I opened up the trunk, the only thing that was there was a bag full of garbage, a white bag with the tie on it, twist tie. There was an Arm and Hammer liquid detergent. I don't remember what size. I guess about that size [indicating]. There was a pizza box and there was maggots inside of that box—I mean, in that bag. I remember specifically because they were making a cracking sound, like hamburger on a skillet. I remember that specifically.

I did not touch it. The attendant reached inside and he says: This is your smell.

He grabbed it, the trunk got shut, and he walked over and disposed of it inside the—

Q: All right. At some point up to this point in time, did you recognize the smell as something you had smelled before?

A: It reminded me of something that I had smelled probably years ago when I was in law enforcement. Yeah. It did.

Q: What was that?

A: A—could be some decomposition of possibly human remains, a possibility.

Q: You would agree that—with the statement that once you've smelled human decomposition, you never forget it?

A: Yeah. There's some certain things in life you just don't forget.

George drove the Sunfire home. Cindy followed him in her car. He wanted to open the windows to air it out, but it was raining, so he had to sit in the stench for miles.

The drive could have been the best therapy he'd ever gotten, if only he'd been driving with Sigmund Freud or Arno Gruen or my own psychiatrist James Mann in the passenger seat. Because one of those fellows may have pointed out the

magnificent poetry of George driving home in a car he feared
might reek of the decomposing flesh of his granddaughter, a
car he had detailed to perfection so many weekends while he
wore perfectly creased pants, a car he had given his daughter, who would later through her attorney at trial accuse him
of forcing his penis into her mouth under cover of darkness.
One of these therapists might have suggested that all the
scrubbing and ironing and pristinely pressed uniforms in
the world wouldn't keep George's demons at bay. The only
answer would have been to stop running from them, turn
around and face them. You can't conquer anything ugly by
covering it up. It's like trying to treat an infected wound by
sewing shut the skin with more and more sutures—every
one of them perfectly, pristinely tied. Underneath, the infec-
tion is only growing more angry, more unwieldy, more certain to track inward and kill the host's heart or shred the skin
and explode outward.

When Cindy met him at home and smelled the car for
the first time, she shouted, "Jesus Christ! What died?"

Of course, they put the car in the garage, opened all the
windows, and tried to get the smell to go away. Imagine the
wry grin on Freud's face had he been there to see that.

Now, imagine this: The next thing that Cindy Anthony
did was to go back to work at Gentiva Health Services, the
home care nursing company where she was employed. She
told coworkers that the car smelled like a dead body and that
Caylee's car seat, favorite doll, and some clothes were in it.
Her supervisor, perhaps wondering why in the world Cindy
Anthony would be at work when her granddaughter might
be dead, sent her home early.

Cindy had also directly ordered George to go to his job
as a security guard over at the Fashion Square Mall. He had
obeyed, even though he was inclined to search the car for
clues, instead. After all, he had just found the vehicle abandoned, in the setting of not having spoken to, nor seen, his
granddaughter for thirty-one days, and having possibly
smelled the odor of decaying human flesh in the vehicle.

According to George's report, he and Cindy hadn't discussed the idea of calling the police.

The Florida Assistant State Attorney wanted to know why. George's answer really said it all, "Because Cindy said she was going to handle it. I was upset with Casey. I said: I want to know where she is. She says: George, I'll handle it. So that was the extent of our conversation."

"I made him go to work," Cindy later told authorities. "He wanted to stay home."

That's the extent of fathering that Cindy Anthony was going to allow her husband—either because she apparently wanted complete and utter control over him and everyone else or because, given the man she had chosen to marry, she apparently couldn't count on him to do anything other than get in the way or both. So she sent him off to make a few bucks at the mall. After all, she was out the hundreds she had had to pay the tow yard, not to mention the ten bucks she had wasted at Universal.

BRINGING CASEY HOME

While George and Cindy were reclaiming Casey's car from Johnson's Towing, she was over at Cast Iron Tattoos scheduling an appointment for July 19, to get another tattoo. She told the tattoo artist that she would bring Caylee by the shop to visit, too.

Why tattoos? Maybe because she felt liberated—whether by violence or tragedy—from what I believe was a psychological death chamber at 4937 Hopespring Drive. Even through the filter of her obvious psychopathology, maybe she felt a faint glimmer of the identity she had suppressed her whole life. Whether the words "Beautiful Life" inscribed on her shoulder were meant to signify hers or Caylee's matters very little. In Casey's mind, it may have seemed that she and her daughter had broken free, even if one of them had died escaping and had gone to God.

Next, Casey went over to the Orlando Bank of America branch and withdrew $250 from her friend Amy Huizenga's account. Amy was flying home from her trip to Puerto Rico, and Casey seemed to want to use as much of Amy's money as she could before she got back. She also tried to pay a $574 AT&T bill using a check from the account, but was informed the balance had dropped too low.

Casey then picked Amy up at the airport.

Amy dropped Casey off at Tony Lazzaro's place, and eventually headed over to the Florida Mall to go shopping.

Late that afternoon, Cindy returned home from Gentiva

Health. She searched Casey's car and found a piece of paper inside it with Amy's number on it. She called the number and explained that Casey's car had been found, that Casey had been telling her all manner of tall tales about being in Jacksonville and that she was worried about Caylee. She wasn't sure, anymore, that anything Casey had told her over the past month was true. She asked if she could come pick Amy up at the mall. Amy hesitated, but finally agreed.

Cindy also took clothing out of the car, including a pair of Casey's slacks, and washed them. They smelled, after all. Why would anyone leave messy clothes around at a time when her granddaughter could be missing or dead?

Cindy told Amy that Casey was probably in so much trouble that she could easily end up arrested. She was able to convince her to bring her to Casey. On the drive over to Tony's apartment, she explained that Casey had been stealing from her and from others for years.

Amy told her about having lost four hundred dollars of her own and how Casey claimed to have seen Amy sleepwalking while talking about putting it in a safe place. Cindy told her she wouldn't be seeing that money again. She also told her that whatever she'd heard about the Anthonys splitting up was not true and that Casey certainly wasn't taking ownership of their home. Amy wouldn't be living at 4937 Hopespring Drive, after all.

Amy led Cindy upstairs to Tony's apartment and knocked on his door. Cindy stayed out of sight, in a corner, until the door opened. Then Amy asked Casey to come into the hallway.

Cindy walked into plain view.

Finally, mother and daughter stood face-to-face.

"You're taking me to see Caylee," Cindy demanded of Casey, according to Amy's recollection.

"She's fine," Casey insisted angrily. "She's with the nanny. You don't need to see her. We need our space."

The fact that Casey uttered those words was meaningful. She and Caylee *had* needed space. They had needed to breathe. Even a little. But it was far too late for that. Casey was breathing easy, having destroyed the emotional circuit connecting her to her mother, and Caylee was with God.

In Casey's mind, perhaps she felt more alive, more together with her daughter, while living away from her parents, although having only memories of Caylee. That's the degree to which Cindy had inserted herself in the mother–daughter relationship between Casey and Caylee. *We need our space.*

If Theory #1 were correct, and Casey had killed her own child, at least (her irrational mind might actually argue) *she* was the one who had decided to liberate the little girl from hell. She had finally taken possession of *her* child. She had taken what was hers back from those who would abscond with her soul. *She* had sent her to a better place.

Now, Casey stood in the hallway with a woman essentially looking for *her* daughter. She stood with the would-be mother of Caylee. A trickster. A kidnapper. But now, she couldn't have her. Now, the trick was on her.

The two women kept arguing about whether or not Casey would take her mother to see Caylee. Casey insisted the little girl would be too tired for a visit, that she was in good hands with her nanny.

Anthony Lazzaro was inside his apartment playing a video game with his roommate Nathan. He told law enforcement authorities what happened next:

> About a half hour later . . . Casey and her mother, Cynthia Anthony, came to the door, Casey stormed in and looked like she was in tears. Uhm, and her mom said, "Get your things. . . . . You're coming with me." And Casey said, "No, I'm coming back." She said, "Okay, but I'm coming back." And she [Cindy] goes, "No, get all your things." And then . . . [Cindy] made a comment to me while I was sitting on the couch, because she was waiting at the door and I said . . . hello, you know, because I never, I've seen pictures of the woman, but I never met her. So I was saying, you know, being friendly. Like, you know, "Hello. You can come in."

Like, because she was waiting at the door. And, uhm, she came in and she goes, "I hope you're rich because Casey's going to take all your money and leave you high and dry." And me and my roommate were just looking at her like, like, what? "What? I have no, what are, what are you talking about?" Like because I had no idea about, uh, her with I guess the money. I guess the whole situation with the mother, Amy, and Casey were about the money situation. Uhm, I guess that's what they talked about because that's why I guess Amy was there with the grandmother. Uhm, but, uh, so that happened. She said that and then Casey said, "Shut up," and they, she stormed outside and the grandmother [Cindy] followed her.

It is interesting that Cindy didn't ask Lazzaro a thing about whether he had seen Caylee. She didn't ask him whether Casey had said anything that might lead Cindy to be able to find Caylee. She wanted him to know that he would be out money if he stayed with Casey. That—it would seem—was the biggest possible loss she imagined a person could suffer.

Remember, Cindy had argued for nearly an hour over how much the bill should be at Johnson's Tow and Recovery.

Of course, Cindy may have only wanted to pause long enough with Lazzaro to make him back off any thought of a relationship with her daughter. Because that would mean Casey and Caylee would end up living somewhere else. And Cindy had already had to go head-to-head with Jesse to crush the same possible outcome from occuring with him.

Amy, Casey, and Cindy got in the car. Cindy kept insisting that Casey needed to take her to see her granddaughter. She also brought up the lies Casey had been telling Amy.

Casey refused to take Cindy to see her granddaughter.

Finally, they dropped Amy off at her apartment.

Cindy tried convincing Casey once more to bring her to Caylee, to no avail.

Maybe Casey felt panic, or maybe she felt power. She might not be driving the car, but she was the one in control.

Her mother had been the first to hold Caylee, probably the one who had come up with her name, the one who had originally chosen the theme for her nursery, the one who had insisted Caylee not be adopted by Casey's friend Kiomarie (which probably would have saved her life), the one who awakened each time Caylee needed to nurse or be bottle-fed and brought her to her mother (maybe even staying by the bedside to observe, then snatching the child back), the one who had indicated it didn't matter who Caylee's father might be, the one who had argued Jesse Grund out of the house when he was playing dad to Caylee and watching TV with her, the one who had declared triumphantly that there was no father on Caylee's birth certificate, the one who had threatened more than once to take custody of Caylee and send Casey away.

Well, things had really changed. Cindy had no control, other than to decide whether to turn the steering wheel right or left, hit the brakes or accelerate. She could rant all she wanted about being taken to see Caylee. She could scream, cry, threaten. The game of control had been played, and it was over, and she had lost, in a shutout. The daughter seated beside her, the one who had suffocated psychologically for want of emotional oxygen, had all the control now. She wasn't going to be the one who surrendered custody of her child, after all. She wasn't going to be the one calling home, trying to arrange to visit her child. She wasn't going to be the one wondering how her child was faring with a grandmother who couldn't forget that she squandered ten dollars searching for her granddaughter or a grandfather who was relieved that the car in which he thought she might have died had no scratches on it. She wasn't going to wake up in the middle of the night in a cold sweat, feeling sick to her stomach and sore between her legs, wondering whether she had touched her own trauma or was channeling that of Caylee.

No, Casey was going to be free. It was going to be a Beautiful Life, after all.

One of my mentors, the late and great Theodore Nadelson, MD, a champion of personal freedom, once told me, "You can count on one thing about slaves: They always revolt.

The mind figures out a way to get free—in one way or another. It can take a long time, and it isn't always pretty, but it always happens."

"After they dropped me off," Amy later told law enforcement authorities, "probably about an hour after they dropped me off, I was, like . . . I don't know how, but I feel like I should check my bank account. I was, like, I don't know how anything would have happen[ed], but this seems like a good idea just to make sure, if anything, I just checked it, no big deal. I just went online. Um, [I] checked my account [and it] was at zero."

Casey had withdrawn everything from more than one account in her life—literally and figuratively.

A DIZZYING ROMANTIC TIME LINE

To get a sense of just how much time and energy Casey Anthony was expending on romantic entanglements, I offer this time line. Some of the names of men noted below are not included elsewhere in the book, simply because detailing all Casey's love interests in a single volume would not be practical. Where exact dates are not known, a month is indicated:

2004

DECEMBER: Caylee Anthony is conceived.

2005

JANUARY: Casey Anthony meets Jesse Grund at Universal Studios, and they begin dating.

AUGUST 9: Caylee is born.

AUGUST 18: Jesse Grund has a DNA test performed on Caylee. It is negative.

NOVEMBER 15: Casey fills out an application to cash checks at Amscot and lists Jesse Grund as her spouse. They are, of course, not married.

2006

JANUARY 1: Casey and Jesse get engaged.

MARCH: Cindy Anthony is furious when she finds Casey and Jesse Grund in bed together (although they are fully clothed) with Caylee.

MAY: Casey and Jesse Grund end their engagement.

JULY 10: A man named Joshua O'Barr, whom Casey tells friends she had a one-night stand with, resulting in Caylee's conception, kills himself. He was never proved to be, nor ruled out as, Caylee's father at trial.

2007

JANUARY: Casey begins dating Brandon Snow.

FEBRUARY: Casey claims to friends that she is pregnant by Brandon Snow and that her mother, Cindy, is furious.

FEBRUARY 14: Casey claims she has suffered a miscarriage. She and Brandon Snow are no longer dating.

MARCH: Casey begins casually dating Chris Stutz.

MAY 4: Erik Baker, who Casey also claimed was Caylee's father, dies in a car accident. He, too, was never proved to be, nor ruled out as, Caylee's father.

MAY 8: Jesus Ortiz, a third man rumored to be Caylee's father, dies in a car accident. He was never determined to be, nor ruled out, as Caylee's father.

JUNE 1: Casey meets and begins dating Steve Jones. She also meets Ricardo Morales.

JULY 22: Casey tells Mark Hawkins, whom she casually dated for a short time, "You are seriously one of the sweetest guys I have ever met."

AUGUST: Jesse Grund gives Casey a ride home from a friend's graduation party.

OCTOBER: Casey and Steve Jones break up.

NOVEMBER 18: Casey spends time at Jesse Grund's apartment.

2008

JANUARY (FIRST WEEK): Casey and Anthony Rusciano have sex.

JANUARY 23: Casey and Ricardo Morales start dating.

MARCH 13: Google search for *bustdown* performed at the Anthony home. *Bustdown* is urban slang for a woman who will have sex with anyone.

APRIL 1: Casey and Caylee spend the night at Ricardo Morales's apartment.

APRIL 14: Casey and Ricardo Morales break up, but continue an on-again, off-again relationship.

MAY 3: Casey has a flirtatious Facebook chat with Anthony Rusciano.

MAY 5: Casey goes on a date with Chris Stutz.

MAY 6: Casey exchanges erotic instant messages (IMs) with Anthony Rusciano.

MAY 11: Casey and Caylee spend Mother's Day at Chris Stutz's parents' house.

MAY 13: Casey has a flirtatious IM chat with a man with the screen name RPHawks300, rumored to be Ryan Pasley.

MAY 14: Casey has a flirtatious IM chat with Anthony Rusciano.

MAY 14: Casey goes to Voyage Nightclub with Ricardo Morales.

MAY 17: Casey and Caylee spend the night at Chris Stutz's parents' house.

MAY 19: Casey has a flirtatious IM chat with Anthony Rusciano.

MAY 20: Casey creates a Cupid.com profile.

MAY 21: Tony Lazzaro requests Casey's friendship on Facebook, though they have not met before.

MAY 22: Casey and Ricardo Morales get into an argument, but they also have sex.

MAY 23: Casey has a flirtatious IM chat with Anthony Rusciano.

MAY 24: Casey meets Tony Lazzaro in person, for the first time, at a party where he is the disc jockey.

MAY 25: Casey attends an Anything but Clothes party with friends. Casey sees Brandon Snow and becomes very emotional. She is overheard saying, "I still love you. I want to be with you."

MAY 26: Casey has a second flirtatious IM chat with a man with the screen name RPHawks300, presumed to be Ryan Pasley.

MAY 27: Casey logs on to her Cupid.com profile for the last time.

MAY 29: Casey and Caylee spend the night at Ricardo Morales's apartment.

MAY 30: Casey visits Jesse Grund.

MAY 30: Casey and Caylee spend the night at Ricardo Morales's apartment.

MAY 31: Casey attends a pool party at Jesse Grund's apartment complex, where Tony Lazzaro is the DJ. She introduces Jesse to Tony. This is Tony and Casey's first date.

MAY 31: Casey spends the night at Ricardo Morales's apartment.

MAY (END OF): Casey has sex with Anthony Rusciano.

JUNE 1: Casey has sex with Tony Lazzaro for the first time.

JUNE 2: Casey tells Ricardo Morales that she "kissed" Tony.

JUNE 4: Casey goes to Voyage Nightclub with Tony Lazzaro and some friends.

JUNE 6: Casey tells Ricardo Morales that she'll have dinner at his house, but cancels and goes to Fusion Ultra Lounge with Tony Lazzaro.

JUNE 7: Casey and Caylee sleep at Ricardo Morales's apartment.

JUNE 9: Casey and Caylee pick Tony Lazzaro up from school and have lunch together.

JUNE 9: Casey and Caylee spend the night at Ricardo Morales's apartment.

JUNE 10: Casey and Ricardo Morales have sex, for the last time. She tells a friend that Ricardo told her he loved her, but that he's no longer the only man for her.

JUNE 11: Casey changes her Facebook profile to say she is "in a relationship" with Tony Lazzaro.

JUNE 12: Casey has a flirtatious IM chat with Ryan Alex Green. She tells him, "You're an amazing guy—one of my favorites."

JUNE 13: Casey asks Ricardo Morales to go to Fusion Ultra Lounge.

JUNE 13: Casey spends the night at Tony Lazzaro's for the first time.

JUNE 14: Casey and Jesse Grund speak on the phone.

JUNE 14: Casey sends a MySpace message to Tony Lazzaro that says, "You're absolutely my favorite."

JUNE 16: Casey has a flirtatious IM chat with Ryan Alex Green.

JUNE 16: Jesse Grund calls Casey.

JUNE 16: Casey spends the night at Tony Lazzaro's apartment.

JUNE 17: Tony Lazzaro skips school to spend the day with Casey.

JUNE 18: Casey visits Chris Stutz (while driving Tony Lazzaro's Jeep).

JUNE 21: Jesse Grund calls Casey.

JUNE 21: Casey spends the night at Tony Lazzaro's apartment.

JUNE 22: Casey and Mark Hawkins speak on the phone.

JUNE 22: Casey spends the night at Tony Lazzaro's apartment.

JUNE 23: When Casey runs out of gas, Tony Lazzaro picks her up, and they take gas cans from the Anthony shed.

JUNE 24: Jesse Grund calls Casey.

JUNE 24: Casey calls Mark Hawkins.

JUNE 25: Casey calls Mark Hawkins.

JUNE 27: Casey and Jesse Grund go to the beach together.

JUNE 27: Casey and Tony Lazzaro go to Fusion Ultra Lounge together.

JUNE 27: Casey sends a Facebook message to Ricardo Morales, inquiring about his plans.

JUNE 28: Casey runs out of gas and calls Jesse Grund for assistance, but he is unable to help. Tony Lazzaro picks Casey up instead. Casey watches a movie at Tony Lazzaro's apartment.

JUNE 29: Casey spends the night at Tony Lazzaro's apartment.

JUNE 30: Casey drives Tony Lazzaro to the airport, for his flight to New York.

JULY 1: Casey goes to Jesse Grund's apartment to shower before "work" and she spends the morning there.

JULY 1: Casey spends the night at Ricardo Morales's apartment.

JULY 2: Casey spends the night at Ricardo Morales's apartment.

JULY 3: Casey sends a text message, regarding "problems with her family," to Jesse Grund.

JULY 4: Casey calls Jesse Grund.

JULY 4: Casey attends a party at William Waters's house.

JULY 5: Casey spends the day with William Waters.

JULY 5: Casey picks Tony Lazzaro up from the airport and begins living with him full-time.

JULY 7: Casey sends a text message to William Waters that says, "You're really the sweetest guy I ever met."

JULY 10: Casey cancels her date with William Waters.

JULY 10: Casey tells Mark Hawkins she is planning to go to California, where he lives.

JULY 11: Casey asks William Waters to join her and Tony Lazzaro at a sake bar, but he declines.

JULY 15: Cindy Anthony picks Casey up from Tony Lazzaro's apartment.

Casey would have, no doubt, literally preferred to be taken to any one of her men's apartments, rather than returning to Hopespring Drive. That had always been the idea. She'd been using her winning personality and her sexy body to stay as far from her inner memories, thoughts, and feelings—especially the ones rooted on Hopespring Drive—as possible. Now, there appeared to be no escape.

911

Cindy and Casey returned to 4937 Hopespring Drive together.

Cindy tried to call George on his cell phone around eight o'clock that evening, but he didn't answer. He dialed her back a bit later. And bizarrely, this is how he described what happened next to authorities:

George Anthony: I remember stepping out after I had seen that she called me. I tried calling her back. All I got was her voice mail. Left a message for her: Hey, sweetie, what's going on?

Idle little chitchat. Fifteen, twenty minutes go by. I didn't hear from her. I call our home phone, our landline at the time. The same thing. All I got was, you know, this-is-the-Anthony-residence-type deal.

Florida Assistant State Attorney: Okay.

GA: I got to be a little bit concerned because it's really weird for me not to get a hold of Cindy through one of two ways, either through her cell phone or our home phone.

I ended up calling my son, and I said: Hey, Lee, I'm really concerned. Can you go down and see Mom?

Lee was living at another location. And I said: Hey, I said, it's been a bad day. Casey is sort of in trouble. We got the car.

Okay, Dad [Lee said]. I'll go down and check on Mom.

At about, I don't know, probably just before nine o'clock, eight forty-five, something like that, I finally got a hold of my son again.

Yeah, Dad. I'm home. Mom is okay. Whenever you can make it home, you know, we need to talk.

I said: Okay, fine.

Finally talked to Cindy again. She said: How soon are you going to come home?

. . . And I said: Well, I said, if you need me to come home now, I will.

She says: Well, just whenever you can make it.

And I told her, I said: It will probably be about ten, ten thirty that night; by the time I . . . [get] home.

If a tendency to dissociate from one's reality runs in families, then George and Casey shared the trait. Not only had George gone to work at a movie cinema after finding his daughter's car smelling of death (by his estimation), not only had he failed to take a call from his wife while he was at work, but he had also left "idle little chitchat" on her mobile phone's voice mail when he finally did call her. He had actually, from what he could remember, said, "Hey, sweetie, what's going on?"

Now, wouldn't any normal individual retrieving such a message be yelling into the night, "What's wrong? We just found the car that our daughter said she was driving all over Florida, and it was towed weeks ago, and it smells like death, and we don't know where our granddaughter is! Are you completely and utterly insane?"

Cindy was the one who ultimately got that message, though, or the one George left on the phone at home, or got word from Lee that George wanted to speak with her. So when she spoke with George, she told him not to hurry home, that he should finish his shift and make the extra, say, fifty bucks. According to what George told authorities, Cindy didn't even tell him that she had found Casey.

Now, does that sound a little controlling to you?

Cindy had already driven with Casey down to the Orlando Police Department on Pershing Avenue and sat outside, hoping that she could bring Casey in, threaten her with charges of stealing the Sunfire (which Cindy and George owned, not Casey), and let the officers pressure her to find out where Caylee might be. When she saw that the station was closed, she started heading home and dialed 911.

Orlando Police Department: Hello.

Cindy Anthony: Hi, I drove to the police department here on Pershing, but you guys are closed. I need to bring someone in to the police department, but you guys are closed. . . . Can you tell me where I can— the closest one I can come to?

OPD: What are you trying to accomplish, bringing them to the station?

CA: I have a twenty-two-year-old person that has, um, grand theft, sitting in my auto with me.

OPD: So the twenty-two-year-old person stole something?

CA: Yes.

OPD: Where did they steal it from?

CA: Um, my car, and also money. . . . My car was stolen. We've retrieved it today. We found out where it was at, and retrieved it. I've got that, and I've got affidavits for my banking account. I want to bring her in. I want to press charges.

OPD: Where—where did all of this happen?

Cindy was transferred over to the proper jurisdiction for her complaint—the Orange County Sheriff's Department.

As her call was being transferred, Cindy told Casey, "My next thing will be down to child [and family court] . . . and we'll have a court order to get her. If that's what you want to play, then we'll do it and you'll never . . ."

That was an interesting threat—that Casey would never

see Caylee again. One has to wonder whether Casey had heard that threat before—and believed it.

Casey asked her mother for one more day to produce Caylee, but Cindy turned her down.

911 Dispatch was back on the line.

911 Dispatch: 911, what's happening?

Cindy Anthony: Umm . . . I have someone here that I need to, umm, be arrested, in my home.

911: They're there right now?

CA: And I have a possible missing child. I have a three-year-old that's been missing a month.

911: A three-year-old?

CA: Yes.

911: Have you reported that?

CA: I'm trying to do that now, ma'am.

911: Okay, what did the person do that you need arrested?

CA: My daughter.

911: For what?

CA: For stealing an auto and stealing money. I already spoke with someone they said they would patch me through the Orlando, umm, Sheriff's Department, have a deputy here. I was in the car, I was going to drive her to the police station and no one . . . They said they would bring a deputy to my home. When I got home to call them . . .

911: She's there right now?

CA: Yes. I got her. I finally found her after a month. She's been missing for a month. I found her, but we can't find my granddaughter.

Cindy gave a description of Caylee and made it clear that Casey was unwilling to say where Caylee could be found.

Dispatch agreed to have a deputy drive to the Anthony residence.

In the meantime, Casey's brother, Lee, arrived at home. It

was just before Cindy and Casey pulled back onto Hopespring Drive themselves. He noticed Casey's car in the garage with the windows open and the trunk open. He later told authorities the smell was "horrible" and "hit you like a wave."

Cindy Anthony pulled in just moments later. As they got out of the car, it was obvious they had been arguing.

"Your sister knows where Caylee is, and she won't take me to her," Cindy told him, according to documents released by the State of Florida. "I'm going to call the police and you need to talk to your sister."

They all walked inside.

Casey went to her room and sat on her bed.

Lee stood in her doorway, while Cindy came and went from Casey's room, and the two women argued back and forth. Casey kept insisting Caylee was with her nanny, doing well, and Cindy kept refusing to accept anything short of seeing her.

Lee pleaded with his sister. "I will go. Tell me where I go to, to see Caylee myself. I'll go for five minutes. I'll do it your way. I'll go and just make sure that she's okay."

"That's unacceptable," Cindy said. "I want her here. I want her home. I, I don't, I don't want just to see her. I want to hold her. I want her to be here."

Lee was between a rock and hard place. He kept asking his sister, "What's going on? What's the deal?"

Casey kept maintaining that everything was all right, but then, according to Lee, she opened up. "Mom has thrown it in my face many times before that I'm an unfit mother. Maybe she's right. Maybe I am." And she went further, telling Lee that Cindy had referred to Caylee before as a mistake—a good mistake, but a mistake nonetheless.

Casey certainly sounded as though she had finally yielded to Cindy's arguments that she should not be Caylee's mother.

Lee kept pushing Casey to let his mother see Caylee, even given Casey's complaints. "Why won't you allow us to see Caylee?" he finally asked, exasperated.

According to Lee, Casey answered, "Well, maybe I'm a spiteful bitch."

One month outside the Anthony house had brought Casey more closely in touch with her underlying rage than the twenty-two years that had preceded it. Now, she knew she was angry, she just couldn't see the whole picture yet. She wasn't yet able to fully feel the grotesquery of lying with her legs spread with her father present in that obstetrical suite, of having her baby handed over to Cindy, of having everything else happen to her on Hopespring Drive to suffocate her nearly into oblivion.

Nearly. But, the lyrics she loved so much attested to something still alive inside her, and that remnant of self was very, very angry and volatile:

> *I am still inside here*
> *A little bit comes bleeding through*

"Well, I don't get it," Lee went on. "What's in it for you? Why are you letting the police get involved with this? This doesn't make any sense to me."

"Well, maybe this should have been done a long time ago," Casey said, according to Lee. "I've stolen money from Mom. I've been a bad daughter. I've stolen money from you. I've been untrustworthy. Maybe I have been a bad mother, daughter, and sister."

Casey was right. More should have been done sooner. What she didn't have was insight into why more *hadn't* been done: Because fixing her would have made her better able to resist her mother. A pathogen does not want immunity in its host.

Lee looked over at his mother and gave her the go-ahead to call the police. He didn't know what else to do.

Cindy Anthony headed outside, but it isn't clear she made another call.

Lee went to sit in the living room. He just didn't understand why Casey wouldn't open up to him. Of course if you believe Casey's later contention that he had sexually abused her, that would explain it.

It is interesting that during Lee Anthony's formal law

enforcement interview just two weeks later, conducted by Corporal William "Eric" Edwards, Lee couldn't seem to maintain a demeanor consistent with the seriousness of the fact that his niece was missing and might be dead. He kept laughing and chuckling—no fewer than twenty-five times. It would seem that every member of the Anthony family had multiple defenses against reality and real emotion.

Cindy walked back inside. "The cops are on their way," she said, loudly enough for Casey to overhear. She walked out the door again.

Lee decided to try one more time with his sister. He walked back into her bedroom. She was sitting on her bed, looking down. "Casey, here's what I don't get," he said. "Really, what's in this for you? You know as much as Mom doesn't like the fact that you're running up her credit card bills and all, she's never called the police. So why would you let this be the reason why you'd get in trouble? I don't get it. What's your motivation right now? I just don't understand."

Casey looked up at him.

"So you got to understand this is what's going to happen when the officer arrives," he went on. "Because I don't understand what you're going to do here. The officer is going to say, 'You know, good evening, Mrs. Anthony. Uhm, where's your daughter?' That's exactly what he's going to say."

Exactly? Well, maybe Lee had just made his own Freudian slip: There was only one Mrs. Anthony on Hopespring Drive, and while she might have acted like Caylee's mother, she wasn't. She was her grandmother.

"And what are you going to say?" Lee went on.

"She's with the nanny. She's sleeping," Casey said.

Sleeping. Sleepwalking. Dead. Casey was speaking, after all, to the brother whom she would later write about sexually assaulting her while she was asleep—unhooking her bra, gawking at her with a flashlight, and fondling her.

"Great, Mrs. Anthony," Lee continued playacting, "I'm so happy to hear that. That's going to be a relief for everybody. So hop in the car. Your mom's going to follow. Let's go get her."

Casey looked like she had finally awakened to the moment at hand—a moment of reckoning.

Lee waited ten, fifteen seconds, then shrugged his shoulders, as if to say, *What's it going to be? What are you going to say?*

Casey took a deep breath; then she buried her face in her hands and began to cry. "Lee, do you want to know the truth?" she said. "I haven't seen Caylee in thirty-one days. I haven't seen my daughter in thirty-one days."

Lee didn't want to shut his sister down from telling him more by attracting his mother's attention. "Where have you been?" he whispered to Casey. "When's the last time you saw her?"

"She was kidnapped," Casey said, tears in her eyes.

Having overheard Casey crying and Lee whispering, Cindy burst into the room. "What have you done?" she blurted out. "Why are you crying? What's going on?"

Casey seemed to morph from sadness to anger as soon as she heard her mother's voice. She looked defiantly at her. "I don't know where Caylee is," she said.

"Who took her? Who took her?" Cindy asked.

"The nanny did," Casey said. "She was kidnapped, Mom."

Cindy slammed her fist down on the mattress. "We could have found her a month ago! Why did you wait?"

Casey seemed steadier with her mother in the room—rageful, rather than distraught. It was one of those moments the neighbors talked about—when Casey was liable to tell her mother to "fuck off."

Lee ran out to the kitchen for a pen and pad of paper so he could start writing down information to give to the police, or begin making some calls on his own.

Before he could get back to the room, Cindy was on the phone to the police again:

911 Dispatch: What's your emergency?
Cindy Anthony: I called a little bit ago. The deputy sheriff's . . . My granddaughter has been taken. She has been missing for a month. Her mother finally

admitted that she's been missing. I want someone here now.

911: Okay, what is the address that you're calling from?

CA: We're talking about a three-year-old little girl. My daughter finally admitted that the babysitter stole her. I need to find her.

911: Your daughter admitted that the baby is where?

CA: That the babysitter took her a month ago. That my daughter's been looking for [her]. I told you my daughter was missing for a month. I just found her today, but I can't find my granddaughter. She just admitted to me that she's been trying to find her herself. There's something wrong. I found my daughter's car today, and it smells like there's been a dead body in the damn car.

911: Okay, what is the three-year-old's name?

CA: Caylee. *C-a-y-l-e-e* Anthony . . . I have not seen her since the seventh of June.

911: What is her date of birth?

CA: Um, eight, nine—um, oh, god, she's three. 2005. . . . Caylee's missing! Casey said Zanny took her a month ago. She said that she found, um. . . . We're so worried, we can barely keep still. [sobbing]

911: Is your daughter there?

CA: Yes.

911: Can I speak with her? Do you mind if I speak with her? Thank you.

CA: [in the background] I called them two hours ago, and they haven't gotten here. Casey finally admitted that Zanny took her a month ago. I have to try and find her.

911: Ma'am, ma'am.

CA: [in the background] Casey. Here, it's the sheriff's department. They want to talk with you. Answer their questions.

Casey: Hello?

911: Hello.

Casey: Yes.

911: Hi. What can you, can you tell me what's going on a little bit?

Casey: I'm sorry?

911: Can you tell me a little bit of what's going on?

Casey: My daughter's been missing for the last thirty-one days.

911: And you know who has her?

Casey: I know who has her. I've tried to contact her. I actually received a phone call today. Now from a number that is no longer in service. I did get to speak to my daughter for about a moment, about a minute.

911: Okay, did you guys call and report a vehicle stolen?

Casey: Um, yes, my mom did.

911: Okay, so there's been a vehicle stolen, too?

Casey: No, this was my vehicle.

911: What vehicle was stolen?

Casey: Um, it's a '98 Pontiac Sunfire.

911: Okay, I have deputies on the way to you right now for that. But now your, now your three-year-old daughter is missing? Caylee Anthony?

Casey: Yes. Caylee Marie Anthony.

911: White female.

Casey: Yes, white female.

911: Who has her? Do you have a name?

Casey: Her name is Zenaida Fernandez-Gonzalez.

911: Who is that? The babysitter?

Casey: She's been my nanny for about a year and a half, almost two years.

911: Why are you calling now? Why didn't you call thirty-one days ago?

Casey: I've been trying to look for her and have gone through other resources to try to find her, which is stupid.

At some point, Cindy apparently called her area director at Gentiva Health. "Oh my God, Debbie," she reportedly told her. "If something happened to the baby or if the baby's dead, I don't know what I'm going to do."

George Anthony returned home just minutes later. It was just before 10 P.M. He pulled into the driveway behind Cindy's car.

Cindy was pacing back and forth outside the garage. She told George what she knew: that Caylee had been missing for thirty-one days and that Casey had said that her nanny, named Zanny, had taken her.

According to what George told authorities, he didn't think immediately about the odor of death he had smelled inside Casey's car. He just held Cindy while she wept.

He didn't go inside the house at all to see Casey. Maybe Cindy told him to stay put.

Five minutes later, several sheriff's deputy cars were in front on 4937 Hopespring Drive.

Orange County Sheriff's Deputy Ryan Eberlin interviewed Lee Anthony outside the Anthony residence, then spoke to Cindy and George. Then he spoke privately with Casey.

Casey claimed the last time she had seen Caylee was actually at about 1 P.M. on June 9, 2008, when she dropped her off with her nanny, Zaneida Fernandez-Gonzalez, at 2863 South Conway Road, apartment 210, on her way to work at Universal Studios.

Michelle Murphy, Casey's friend, shared a theory with me about why Casey would have told such bold lies to the police—lies that could be easily investigated and proven untrue. "I think Casey wasn't used to being confronted or held accountable. I think she literally thought the police would simply take her word that she worked at Universal and had a nanny and move on, because everyone else had."

Casey had learned to trade on anything but the truth, so likely felt little or no anxiety while lying. Her fears were of reality, of what she had truly suffered, of whom she had actually lived with for the past twenty-two years, of what it meant to have delivered her baby in full view of her father and have had that child whisked into the arms of her mother, of what it meant that she had never been taken for any significant help of any kind, despite telltale signs that she was psychologically disordered, of what it meant to be the offspring of a woman who seemingly counted a ten-dollar loss in the same calculus as the loss of a granddaughter, and a man who could walk around a car he feared had been the death chamber of his granddaughter and inspect it for scratches.

Casey wrote out a statement for Officer Eberlin:

On Monday, June 9, 2008 between 9am and 1 pm, I, Casey Anthony, took my daughter, Caylee Marie Anthony, to her nanny's apartment. Caylee will be 3-years-old on August 9, 2008. She was born on August 2005. Caylee is about 3 feet tall, white female with shoulder-length, light brown hair. She has dark hazel eyes (brown/green), and a small birth mark on her left shoulder. On the day of her disappearance, Caylee was wearing a pink shirt, with jean shorts, white sneakers, and her hair was pulled back in a ponytail. On Monday, June 9, 2008, between 9am and 1pm, I took Caylee to the Sawgrass apartments, located on Conway Rd. Caylee's nanny, Zenaida Fernandez-Gonzalez, has watched her for the past year and a half, to two years. Zenaida is twenty-five years old, and is from New York. She is roughly 5 foot 7 inches tall, 140 pounds. She has dark brown, curly hair, and brown eyes. Zenaida's birthday is in September. I met Zenaida, through a mutual friend, Jeffrey Michael Hopkins. She had watched his son, Zachary Hopkins, for about 6 months, to a year. I met Zenaida in 2004, around Christmas. On the date listed above, June 9, 2008, after dropping Caylee off at Zenaida's apartment, I proceeded to head to my place of employment, Universal Studios Orlando. I have worked at Universal for over 4 years, since June of 2004. I left work around 5pm, and went back to the apartment to pick-up my daughter. However, after reaching the apartment I realized that neither Zenaida, Caylee, or either of her two roommates were home.

I have briefly met Raquel Farrell, and Jennifer Rosa, on various occasions. After calling Zenaida to see where she and Caylee were, and when they were coming home I waited outside of the apartment. I had called her that afternoon, her phone was no longer in service. Two hours passed, and around 7pm, I left the apartment, and headed to familiar places that Zenaida would go with Caylee. One of Caylee's favorite places is Jay Blanchard Park. I spent the rest of that evening, pacing and worrying at one of the few places I felt "at home" my boyfriend Anthony Lazzaro's apartment. For the past four weeks, since Caylee's disappearance, I have stayed at Anthony's apartment in Sutton Place. I have spent everyday, since Monday, June 9, 2008, looking for my daughter. I have lied and stolen from friends and family, to do whatever I could by any means, to find my daughter. I avoided calling the police, or even notifying my own family out of fear. I have been, and still am afraid of what has, or may happen to Caylee. I have not had contact with Zenaida since Thursday, June 12, 2008. I received a quick call from Zenaida. Not once have I been able to ask her for my daughter, or gain any information on where I can find her. Everyday I have gone to malls, parks, any place I could remember Zenaida taking Caylee. I have gone out and tried to find any information about Caylee, or Zenaida, whether by going to a popular bar, or restaurant. I have contacted Jeff Hopkins on several occasions to see if he had heard from, or seen Zenaida. Jeff currently lives in Jacksonville, Florida. On Tuesday, July 15, 2008, around 12pm, I received a phone call from my daughter, Caylee. Today was the first day I have heard her voice in over 4 weeks. I'm afraid of what Caylee is going through. After 31 days, I know that the only thing that matters is getting my daughter back. With many and all attempts to contact Zenaida, and within the one short conversation, on June 12,

2008 . . . I was never able to check on the status or well-being of my daughter. Zenaida never made an attempt to explain why Caylee is no longer in Orlando, or if she is ever going to bring her home.

An officer was dispatched to the Sawgrass Apartments, but learned that Apartment 210 was vacant—and had been for 142 days.

Another officer was dispatched to Amy Huizenga's apartment to collect more data.

And a third officer headed to Tony Lazzaro's apartment to interview him and his roommate. He retrieved Casey's cell phone.

Lee Anthony went by Tony's later that evening and picked up the rest of Casey's belongings, including Cindy's laptop (which Casey had been using), a leopard print duffel bag, a white backpack, her purse, and a black bag with some papers in it.

When he got back to 4937 Hopespring Drive, Casey was standing in the driveway in a circle of police officers.

Ponder for a moment the image of Casey standing in that circle, surrounded by officers charged with finding the truth, whose investigative skills relied on pursuing logical lines of inquiry. They may as well have been standing there alone, given how deeply Casey Anthony had suppressed her identity and how completely she could "flip a switch" (according to her friend Michelle Murphy) and shut down all the current running to what was left of her genuine thoughts, emotions, and connection to reality. It would have been, in fact, more productive to exclude her from the investigation entirely as a source (although this, of course, could never actually happen). Because Casey Anthony's aversion to the truth could actually trump their love of it. Skilled as she was in spinning tall tales to deny the abuse she would later claim to have suffered, to deny the horror of lying with her legs spread in front of her father, to deny what seems to have been a constant campaign by her mother to extinguish her as a human being and take her baby, she had the potential to spin the officers around at dizzying speed, until they knew not where lines of inquiry had evaporated into a dream state.

Casey Anthony was no Adolf Hitler, but her thought patterns and behavior patterns seemed honed from his advice on how to manipulate and confuse others. "The size of the lie," Hitler once said, "is a definite factor in causing it to be believed, for the vast masses . . . are in the depths of their hearts more easily deceived than they are consciously and intentionally bad. The primitive simplicity of their minds renders them a more easy prey to a big lie than a small one, for they themselves often tell little lies but would be ashamed to tell a big one."

Casey had an audience of police officers around her who may have been used to suspects who could try to come up with an alibi, or lie about a date or a time, or hide a weapon, but they probably had never tried to get the truth out of a ghost or a shadow.

Lee walked into the house with Casey's belongings. An officer was there with his parents.

George Anthony, true to form, was reportedly upset that Casey's things smelled like cigarette smoke. There he was, just several hours from having driven home in utter stench, possibly from rotting flesh, in the middle of a nightmare that would end with his granddaughter's bones being found in the woods, and he was worried that Casey's purse and clothes might leave the odor of tobacco on his precious carpet or furniture. This was the man Casey Anthony had grown up around. This was the person she would have looked to for comfort when she fell down and skinned a knee, when she had an accident before getting fully toilet trained, when she needed a shoulder to cry on. And he was obviously someone who would have made it clear that anything messy—like, say, *living*—would rankle him.

"Disappear, and I will love you," he may as well have told her.

Even with the officer present, Cindy insisted she be able to go through Casey's belongings herself.

The officer instructed Lee to dump the contents in a pile on the ground. Then, almost inexplicably, after Lee did so, the officer left.

The pile had Casey's IDs in it, receipts, her car key, Amy Huizenga's car key, a few diapers and some baby wipes, but no snacks or juice or anything of the sort for Caylee. The pile also contained Casey's wallet, and what happened next almost boggles the mind.

Lee Anthony later described the scene for Corporal Eric Edwards:

Lee Anthony: My mother at that point had opened up my sister's wallet. . . . [She] had actually already opened up my sister's wallet because she was looking through the contents of this large wallet, [and she] saw unfolded, it had to be a minimum of a hundred and forty, maybe as much as two hundred dollars just from seeing the number of bills, straight twenty-dollar bills that were taken out. And the reason why I know the officer wasn't in there is because my mom grabbed the money and goes, and, and put it in her pocket. And no one else was in there.

Eric Edwards: She's just stealing her money back from the girl who stole it.

LA: Exactly [laughs]. Exactly. And I think they even, uh, made a comment to that extent.

Oh, Cindy. She really was something else. To think that she had the presence of mind to grab some fresh twenties from a pile of evidence that might link her daughter to the death of her little granddaughter. Mind not that her granddaughter was presumed missing and might be dead, this was a good day for her, financially. She'd talked the folks at Johnson's Towing down from their usual pricing and she'd retrieved as much as a few hundred in cash from Casey's bag.

Do you really believe, for an instant, that Casey Anthony was born without empathy? Do you really believe, for an instant, that she was born a thief? If we focus only on two pages from her life story—one in the obstetrical suite with her father looking at her nakedness and one in the "living" room of 4937 Hopespring Drive, with her mother reportedly pocketing cash from her wallet (as police were beginning the investigation in her granddaughter's disappearance)— don't we already have reasonable doubt that hers were problems from the womb?

Was there really anyone allowed to live a real life at all in the Anthonys' home? Was there anyone allowed to breathe?

Again, I am reminded of Camus's character named Meursault, in his novel *The Stranger*. Meursault has been arrested for the murder of his mother. He describes speaking for the first time with his lawyer:

> The investigators had learned that I had "shown insensitivity" the day of Maman's [his mother's] funeral. "You understand," my lawyer said, "it's a little embarrassing for me to have to ask you this. But it's very important. And it will be a strong argument for the prosecution if I can't come up with some answers." He wanted me to help him. He asked if I had felt any sadness that day. The question caught me by surprise and it seemed to me that I would have been very embarrassed if I'd had to ask it. Nevertheless, I answered that I had pretty much lost the habit of analyzing myself and that it was hard for me to tell him what he wanted to know. I probably did love Maman, but that didn't change anything. At one time or another all normal people have wished their loved ones dead. Here the lawyer interrupted me and seemed very upset.

I wonder if Eric Edwards was upset hearing Lee Anthony say that his mother had the presence of mind to focus on a few hundred dollars and take it out of Casey's wallet on July 15, 2008. I wonder if he was upset noticing that Lee couldn't stop chuckling during his formal interview. I wonder if the police officer at the Anthony home was upset hearing George complain that Casey's belongings smelled of smoke. I wonder if the investigators in this case sensed the vacuum of emotional oxygen at 4937 Hopespring Drive. I wonder if they were struck by the absence of love in this family that had finally run out of the energy to sustain life.

APARTMENT 210

Casey Anthony and Deputy Adriana Acevedo drove over to the Sawgrass Apartments together a little after midnight. Casey led Acevedo and Corporal Brendan Fletcher to Apartment 210. There was, of course, no one there. The unit had been vacant several months and was used only as a leasing model.

Casey returned with Acevedo in her patrol car to Hopespring Drive.

Just before 4 A.M., Detective Yuri Melich arrived at the Anthony residence. He reviewed Casey's statement, asked her if she intended to stick to it, then interviewed her:

Detective Yuri Melich: Okay. Going back to your statement. You dropped off your ah, you dropped off Caylee on June 9, and walk me through . . . You dropped her off to go to work?

Casey Anthony: Uh-huh.

YM: Okay. Get off work and go from there.

CA: I got off of work, left Universal driving back to pick up Caylee like a normal day. And I show up at the apartment, knock on the door. Nobody answers. So, I called Zenaida's cell phone and it's out of service. Says that the phone is no longer in service. Excuse me. So, I sit down on the steps and wait for a little bit to see if maybe it was just a fluke if something happened. And time passed I didn't hear from anyone. No one showed up at the house so I went over to Jay Blanchard Park and checked a couple other places where maybe possibly they would've gone. A couple stores, just regular places that I know Zenaida shops at and she's taken Caylee before. And after about seven o'clock when I still hadn't heard anything I was getting pretty upset, pretty frantic. And I went to a neutral place. I didn't really want to come home, I wasn't sure what I'd say about not knowing where Caylee was. Still hoping that I would get a call or you know find out that Caylee was coming back so that I could go get her. And I ended up going to my boyfriend, Anthony's, house, who lives in Sutton Place.

YM: Did you talk to Anthony about, um, what happened with Caylee?

CA: No, I did not.

YM: Had Anthony ever seen Caylee before?

CA: Yes, he has.

YM: Have you talked to anyone about Caylee, about your incident with Caylee? Or the fact that—

CA: Outside of—

YM: —she's missing?

CA: —a couple of people, a couple of mutual friends.

YM: Who did you talk to about it?

CA: Um, I talked to Jeff, Jeffrey Hopkins.

YM: Uh-huh.

CA: I also attempted to contact Zenaida's mother and never received a call back from her.

YM: Do you know Zenaida's mother's name?

CA: Um, wow . . . and, um, I think it's Gloria.

Wow. She really didn't sound as though she'd expected such a tough question as, "*Do you know [your nanny's] mother's name?*" You know—the one you called when you were looking for Zenaida?

Gloria. Why not? Gloria Gonzalez had a nice ring to it. It was no more created from whole cloth than having a nanny to begin with, or talking to Jeffrey Hopkins.

Casey went on to invent another coworker named Juliette Lewis.

YM: You talked to Jeffrey, who else did you talk to?

CA: I talked to Juliette Lewis. She's one of my co-workers at Universal.

YM: She works . . . You still work at Universal?

CA: Yes.

YM: What ah, what do you do at Universal?

CA: Event coordinator.

YM: Okay. What is Juliette, what position is she? Where does she work?

CA: She's also an event coordinator. We work in the same department.

YM: You have a number for Juliette?

CA: Ooh, offhand . . . I can't think of one.

YM: She in your SIM card?

CA: No, she's not. Some of them are recent numbers. Her number just changed because she just moved back up north. She . . . within the last two months has finished moving up to New York. She's subleasing her apartment.

YM: So, Juliette . . . doesn't work at Universal anymore?

CA: No, she does not?

YM: When did she leave Universal?

CA: About two months ago.

Reviewing Casey Anthony's statements, even with the benefit of now knowing that they are wholly fabricated, readers could easily begin to doubt themselves and think that maybe she and the rest of the world had simply had some gigantic misunderstanding. Maybe Jeffrey Hopkins *had* spoken to Casey. Maybe someone named Juliette Lewis actually *did* exist. Maybe Gloria Gonzalez and Zenaida Gonzales had lived in Florida and perpetrated an evil scheme to steal a little girl. Maybe Casey really *did* have a job at Universal. Her capacity to invent stories almost outstrips the human ability to generate doubt. That's how unfettered she was by facts.

Detective Melich took her on another drive. Casey pointed out a second-floor apartment on Glenwood Avenue where she said Zenaida had lived during part of 2006. It was a seniors-only facility, however. Melich didn't know at the time (although he would learn this later) that the building stood right across the street from Casey's lover Ricardo Morales's apartment.

Casey was seemingly using bits and pieces of her real life story, slightly altered, to create a new, fictional biography. As a woman with so little anchoring her to a true self, she was "free" to do this. She'd done it for many years, after all. Her friends, including Michelle Murphy, knew it, but said nothing, because they enjoyed her company and didn't want to argue with her or humiliate her. Her brother, Lee, knew it and actually kept others from challenging her. Her father, George, knew it (especially after he'd learned that Casey didn't even work at the Sports Authority store where she had claimed to), but he'd dropped the issue when Cindy ordered him to. Some of her boyfriends probably knew it, but they loved having sex with her and laughing with her too much to focus on it. Her grandmother Shirley knew it, but hadn't pressed charges against Casey for theft when she stole funds from her and her husband—twice. Her uncle Rick—a good and decent man—knew it, but had learned that trying to make his sister, Cindy, stop enabling (i.e., destroying) her family members was impossible. And Cindy, of course, knew it, but wasn't going to get Casey any help, no matter what. Because if Casey ever got well, Casey would have gotten the hell away from Hopespring Drive, taken her daughter with her, and never looked back.

Casey's uncle Rick Plesea seemed to know his niece's habits a lot better than her parents did. "I would say this about Casey," he told police later. "If she sees something, she will spin it into her own little world to make it work for her, whatever kind of lie it is."

Even the name Zenaida Gonzales seemed like Casey had grabbed on to it because it fit the fictional nanny named Zanny whom she had invented. Gonzales was a real woman, but she was no nanny. She'd stopped by the Sawgrass Apartments on South Conway Road on June 17 and filled out a guest card. At the time, she was looking for an apartment for her and her children. Perhaps Casey had run into her there at some point.

Casey's ability to rewrite her story on the fly had, no doubt, been honed during all those hours spent on MySpace and Facebook and Cupid.com, fashioning "profiles" that were no more than shiny, seductive suits of armor. And since everyone "bought" what she posted and replied with little smiley faces and lots of exclamation points and pithy one-liners and invitations to parties, she must have figured that the whole world could be lulled into a state of suspended disbelief.

Maybe that's why, in the days before being located by her mother and dragged back "home," Casey took refuge in movie cinemas, losing herself in films like *Untraceable* and *Jumper*. She would have been at home not only with the content of fantasy films about unlimited freedom, but also with the whole notion of entering a darkened room and hiding from any stubborn reminder of what she had done and what others had done to her.

Detective Melich and Casey next drove onto 2863 South Conway Road, where Casey confirmed that Zenaida Gonzales had most recently lived in apartment 210. Casey told him that the apartment was nicely furnished and had children's toys inside. She also described her nanny's car as a silver Ford Focus.

She really could spin a tale.

Third on the fantasy tour was a town house development called Crossings at Conway, where Casey claimed that Zenaida's mother lived and Zenaida herself had resided for parts of the past few years. She couldn't recall which town house in the community was the exact one, however.

No sense going too far out on a limb for nothing.

Detective Melich knocked on a few doors and asked the people who answered if they had ever heard of Zenaida Gonzalez or her mother, but no one had.

Casey was unfazed.

Finally, Melich drove her home and dropped her off.

Casey texted Amy Huizenga and many of her friends:

Caylee is missing. She has been for 32 days now. Please if you have information call me on cell or at home.

Amy texted back asking for information about who might have Caylee, to which Casey replied,

Her nanny. Someone I trusted took her. No calls until yesterday.

She also texted Tony Lazzaro,

. . . if they never find her [Caylee], guess who spends eternity in jail?

The boldness with which Casey had taken officers to the Sawgrass Apartments, and Glenwood Avenue, and Crossings at Conway wasn't typical of witnesses or suspects with something to hide. She hadn't stayed silent and called an attorney. She hadn't come up with a more plausible scenario, like leaving Caylee to be watched by someone at a park, in order to go flirt with a man she'd spotted down the street, only to return and find her daughter had vanished. She hadn't maintained that she'd been so angry about her mother wanting custody of Caylee that she'd left her parents' house by herself on June 15, leaving Caylee alone with George.

Casey apparently didn't feel that a more credible cover story was necessary. Any fact that an investigator might unearth that contradicted her fictional version of events had no better claim on the truth, anyhow. Once you've cut ties with your self and with reality, you aren't bothered by blatant inconsistencies or even obvious lies. You can't necessarily fashion a compelling alibi, because you can't remember what it felt like to doubt anyone, or be doubted by anyone.

To perpetrate a fraud that is difficult to unravel, you need to have some hold on truth—at least enough to know the taste and tone of it and smell of it.

Nothing about Casey's story made sense, nothing about her participation in the investigation made sense, nothing about Casey made sense at all, which is why it was going to end up being very difficult to use reason or logic to find out the truth about her or what had happened to her daughter.

Try pinning anything on a ghost and see how far you get. Casey was a *Jumper,* just like in the movie. Here. No, there. No, no—over *there.* Sports Authority, Jeffrey Hopkins, Universal, Orlando, Jacksonville, Busch Gardens, Anthony Rusciano, Ricardo Morales, William Waters, Facebook, the Hard Rock Hotel, Tony Lazzaro, high school graduation, Jesse Grund, Valencia Community College, Zaneida "Zanny" Gonzales, MySpace, Hopespring Drive, the Sawgrass Apartments, Cupid.com, Crossings at Conway, Amy Huizenga moving into Hopespring Drive, Casey moving in with Jeffrey Hopkins, marrying Hopkins, living with Tony, sleeping with Ricardo, still in love with Brandon Snow, showing up at William Waters's door.

Before Detective Melich left the Anthonys house, he spoke with George. He asked him who Caylee's father was. George told him that Casey had once confided that Caylee's father's name was Eric, but that Eric had died in a car crash during 2007. Casey had kept the obituary for a long time, but then lost it.

About the only thing that Detective Melich should have noted about that story—presumably originally authored by Casey—was that it involved two takeaways, each designed to sprinkle bread crumbs for his mind to follow, then blow them all into thin air.

Broken into steps, the George Anthony "Double Takeaway" looked like this:

[Storyteller says . . .] Caylee's father's name was Eric.
[Listener thinks . . .] Eric . . . Okay, we're getting somewhere. I'll go look for him.
[Storyteller says . . .] But he's dead.
[Listener starts to lose interest]
[Storyteller kindles hope . . .] But Casey had his obituary.
[Listener thinks . . .] If you can get me that, I can use it to contact the father's family members.
[Storyteller says . . .] But she lost the obituary.

In my opinion, the only sort of person who would have listened to such a tale and accepted it as reflecting any kind of reality at all would be someone like George, who was too busy picking lint off his clothes and spraying air freshener to cover up smells to notice or care whether another human being was making sense. If he was able to be analytical at all, he would never have shared such a story with Detective Melich and suggested it was relevant. He would have prefaced the whole verbal wild-goose chase, by saying, "Listen, I know this makes zero sense, but here's what Casey once told me. . . ."

But how can a man who hasn't even confronted his daughter about her fake job also think of her as enough of a person to merit rational analysis? How can a man who walks around looking for scratches in the paint of the car he fears may have been a temporary tomb for his granddaughter's body also empathize with another human being enough to gauge what that person will and won't believe?

George even went into work the next day. "I had to go back to work," he would explain to investigators. "As a matter of fact, I remember waking up, I went back to my employer because I had to drop off the information from the night before of this event that I had worked."

"Hey, George," any balanced human being may have wanted to reply, "you didn't have one friend in the world who could take some paperwork into headquarters for you? I mean, your granddaughter was missing, and you thought the car she'd left your house in thirty-one days earlier smelled like human decomposition. You didn't think your boss would understand you not showing up with your report from working security at the movies?"

George remembered something else, too. When explaining to investigators that he really hadn't talked with Casey much the night she finally returned home, he mentioned that she had, however, told him about Zenaida Gonazales being the last person to see Caylee. "She was supposed to have been a very attractive lady," George remarked.

"She just described her to me," he told investigators, "you know, about being twenty-five, five foot seven inches tall, 130, 140 pounds, on a scale of one to ten, you know, on and on, and straight white teeth. . . ."

Very attractive, huh? On a scale of one to ten? Really, George?

Now, why would the fictional Zanny having a nice body be important to a man whose granddaughter might be dead and whose daughter could be tried for murder and executed? Or was feminine anatomy the *only* thing he could truly focus on, the only thing truly important to him?

No, I believe Casey had never been seen as a person by her parents, and now she was a ghost taking police officers trick-or-treating out in their squad cars. She was borrowing streets and buildings from the recesses of her memory and treating them like her own personal movie set. She was acting and didn't know any better and assumed everyone else would read the scripts she was handing them and let well enough alone.

Not Yuri Melich. Melich was a child-abuse investigator. He'd seen things that most people would never want to see and can barely imagine. He'd seen what Freud once called "those half-tamed demons that inhabit the human beast."

Melich was the lead detective on more than twenty-one criminal investigations when he'd worked homicide at the Orange County Sheriff's Office. Back during 2007, he and his partner had been assigned three homicide cases within a twelve-hour period and solved all three within two weeks.

One of those cases was an execution-style killing with no witnesses.

After Melich had dropped Casey back at her house, he hit the streets again. He interviewed staff members at the Sawgrass Apartments complex. None of them had seen Caylee. Their only interaction with Zenaida Gonzalez had been when she filled out a guest card to view a model apartment (which is probably when Casey overheard her name).

Melich continued on to Universal Studios. He learned that Casey hadn't worked there since being fired on April 24, 2006. Even though she had told him that her friend Jeffrey Hopkins still worked there with her, he'd been fired during May of 2002.

Maybe Melich had a flair for the dramatic or a lively sense of the grotesque because, rather than confronting Casey with what he knew back at her house or down at the police station, he arranged to have her meet him right at Universal Studios.

REALITY AT UNIVERSAL STUDIOS

When Casey arrived with officers at Universal Studios, she told the security guard at the employee entrance that she worked there and had lost her ID. When she was asked for her supervisor's name, she gave it as Tom Manley. But no Tom Manley worked at Universal.

Detective Melich had met the group at the entrance. He and the other officers arranged to escort Casey to her office, despite the fact that she wasn't listed as a current employee. She walked through the Universal lot, entered a building with them, strode halfway down a hallway, then stopped, all of a sudden. Then she looked at Melich and calmly admitted that she didn't work at Universal Studios anymore, at all.

The officers—Detective Melich, Sergeant John Allen, and Detective Appie Wells—arranged to use a small conference room for a second interview with Casey. She agreed it could be recorded. It was 1:20 P.M. on July 16, 2008.

What follows is a portion of that interview. It is included at some length because it demonstrates just how detached Casey had become, how suppressed her real identity truly was. That explains why she seemed neither anxious nor sad nor angry during the interview. It was as if any of the officers could have reached across the table and passed a hand right through her. She offered no palpable resistance yet yielded no ground. In terms of her emotional stance, it was as if she were not there at all.

Detective Yuri Melich: Casey, we talked earlier this morning and we're working a case looking for your daughter, Caylee, is that correct?

Casey Anthony: Yes.

YM: Okay. We came here to Universal Studios, we're sitting in [a] little conference room. Obviously the door's unlocked. We just closed it so we could have a little privacy and talk to you.

CA: Uh-huh.

YM: And ah, couple more questions came up I need to ask you about. Remember our, how I opened this whole thing in the morning?

CA: Yeah.

YM: About saying that you know we need to get complete truth and the snowball effect and, and—

CA: Absolutely.

YM: —how it goes? Okay. Um, we're about halfway down that hill, three quarters down that hill and it's a pretty big snowball. Which means that there's a lot of stuff going on right now.

CA: Uh-huh.

YM: And I can tell you just for certainty, everything you've told me so far has been a lie. I can tell you with certainty and let me explain why. Since I left you this morning—

CA: Uh-huh.

YM: —I've gone to every address that you've told me. I've looked up every name. I've talked [to] every person that you . . . you wanted me to talk or try to.

CA: Uh-huh.

YM: I've reached out. . . . I've talked to your ex-boyfriend, I've talked to Amy. Ah, I talked to Tony. Um, I came over here, I've already talked to all the employees.

CA: Uh-huh.

YM: And found out all these names you're giving me are people that either never worked here or been fired a long time ago . . . okay. So, where we are right now is in a position that doesn't look very good for you.

Now, here it should be noted that Yuri Melich was under-estimating his interviewee. While Casey may not have tried to whitewash her actions for the police before, she had a very long history of having done so for others. She wasn't someone who was going to be scared straight. She probably could have passed a lie detector test, because lying was natural to her, not an effort of will. Her pulse probably wouldn't have risen. She wouldn't have perspired. Reality had no claim on her, whether its defender was her grandmother, her mother, her lover, her friends, or Yuri Melich.

CA: Uh-huh.
YM: And this is gonna be your . . . your escape hatch, so to speak. This is gonna be the point where you stop all the lies and you stop all the fibs and you tell us exactly what's going on.
CA: Uh-huh.
YM: I'm just being, you know, being straight with you.
CA: Yeah.
YM: 'Cause obviously I know and you know that everything you've told me is a lie, correct?
CA: Not everything that I told you.
YM: Okay. Ah, pretty much everything that you've told me. Including where Caylee is right now.
CA: That I still, I don't know where she is.
YM: Sure you do. And here's—
CA: I absolutely do not—
YM: Listen to me, let—
CA: —know where she is.
YM: —let me . . . let me explain something. Together with combined experience in this room, we all have about thirty years of doing this.
CA: Uh-huh.
YM: Okay, both myself and Sergeant John Allen

worked for homicide division for several years. We've dealt with several people, we've conducted thousands of interviews between the three of us. And Appie's twenty years, so just between three of us we've got several years. And I can tell you for certainty that right now, looking at you, I know that everything that you've told me is a lie. Including the fact that you know your child was last seen about a month ago. And that you don't know where she is. Yeah, I . . . I'm very confident just by having talked to you the short period of time that you know where she is.

CA: I don't.

The ratio of spoken words between Yuri Melich and Casey Anthony was about five hundred for Melich and thirty-five for Casey, give or take.

It wasn't really clear, by that arithmetic, who was interviewing whom.

That ratio didn't shift in Melich's favor. Casey took even more control:

YM: You . . . you do. And here's the thing, we need to get past that because we could sit here and go back and forth all day long about I don't, I do, I don't, I do. It's pretty obvious that with everything you told us, nothing has been true. You know where she is. Now my question to you is, is this. We need to find Caylee. I understand that right now Caylee may not be in very good shape. You understand what I'm saying?

CA: [No verbal response]

YM: She may not be the way we or the way your family last remembers her. We need to find out from you where Caylee is. This . . . this . . . this right now is just . . . this has gone so far downhill and this has become such a mess.

CA: Uh-huh.

YM: We need to end it. It's very simple, we just need to end it.

CA: I agree with you. I have no clue where she is.

YM: Sure you do.

CA: If I knew in any sense where she was, this wouldn't have happened at all.

YM: You know . . . listen.

CA: It wouldn't have happened whatsoever.

YM: This stuff about Zenaida the caretaker or the nanny taking care of—

CA: It's the truth—

YM: Everything you've told us is a lie. Well, now there's a couple of ways that this goes. Right now, we can, you know, we . . . I've never met you before. So I can look at you in a couple ways.

CA: Hm.

Okay, well, right about now is when, had I been in that room with Detective Melich and Casey Anthony, I would have tapped him on the shoulder and—had I the benefit of what I know now—asked to help him out for just a minute.

"Detective," I would have said, "do you know that Ms. Anthony was thirty weeks pregnant and continued to deny it to relatives?"

"Uh, no, I didn't know that," I imagine him saying.

"And do you know that, for all those thirty weeks, she had been telling her mother she was a virgin?"

"Uh, no."

"And do you know that she maintains that, at twelve years old, she had the ability to wake up in the dark with her breasts exposed and her brother beside her bed illuminating her with a flashlight, and then have breakfast with him and her parents in the morning?"

"No, no, I wasn't aware."

"And do you know that she asserts that she would routinely perform oral sex on her father at eight years old, then head to grammar school and play kickball with her friends?"

"No."

"And do you know that she is very well aware that she could call a lawyer right now and say nothing to you, but doesn't feel any need for that whatsoever, because she thinks you are a very curious fellow whose mind seems to proceed in linear fashion, tied to this time and place, rather than *jumping* off the grid, entirely, and believing things that never occurred, in places that never existed, at any time she fancies?"

"I'm not certain I follow."

"Exactly."

"So what are you suggesting?"

"Well, see, if you have a lot of work to do on this case, I'd pretty much pack it in as regards this interview. Because I just don't see the woman I've described giving two shits what you think. Got it? You're in the ring with the Muhammad Ali of the big lie, on the grid with the Joe Namath of denial. Go, do something else. You're just gonna get yourself hurt."

Of course, I wasn't in that room, nor would I be so flippant with a true professional like Melich. But the point still stands: Casey Anthony was not tied to the truth. An investigator is tied to the truth. It is his lifeblood. Therefore, he is at a distinct disadvantage in any discussion that requires two people to agree on one reality.

The interview—or scheduled fifteen-round bout—went on, with Casey winning using the "Rope-a-Dope" strategy made famous by Ali, lying back on the ropes, absorbing blows, offering no resistance, wearing out her opponent:

YM: I can look at you as a person, who's scared, who's concerned, and who's kind of afraid of what's gonna happen because of something bad that happened before. Or we can look at you as cold, callous, and a monster, who doesn't care. Who's just trying to get away with something . . . that something bad had happened and trying to cover it up.

CA: Uh-huh.

YM: It's gonna be one of those two options. Now . . .

you seem like a very bright young lady. You don't seem like someone who had no education.

CA: Uh-huh.

YM: All right. Now, what we would have to do is we have to determine which way is this gonna go. Are you . . . are you a person who's scared about the consequences of what happened? Or are you scared about something that happened? Or are you, are you really this cold, callous person, who doesn't care about what happened. It's one of those two options.

"Um, I'll take door number three, please, Monty," Casey may as well have said, invoking the show *Let's Make a Deal* hosted by Monty Hall. She was too young to have seen that program, and this was an investigation, not a TV show, but that was the game she was playing, anyhow.

CA: I'm scared that . . . I don't know where my daughter is.

YM: So . . .

CA: I would not have put my entire family . . .

Here, Sergeant John Allen, one of the other officers in the room, started trying to help his colleague out. Anyone would get tired trying to reason with the Riddler.

Sergeant John Allen: Hold . . . hold on, I want to ask you something.

CA: Yes, sir.

JA: Like he said, you, you seem like a pretty bright person, okay. You're here willingly, right?

CA: Uh-huh . . .

JA: Nobody's forced you to talk to us, right?

CA: No.

"Are you kidding," Casey could have said, "I'm having *fun*. I'm getting lots of attention, and I'm here at Universal Studios, and I'm going to message my friends about this later and probably post it on MySpace and Facebook. I'm a *suspect*! I'm going to be *famous*. Wow. This is some ride. It's like I'm back at the movies!"

JA: You, you want us to . . . You're here because you called, you want us to help find your daughter, right?

CA: Uh-huh.

JA: Now, let me, let me ask you something. I want you to put yourself in, put yourself in some . . . put yourself in my shoes for a minute, okay. Since you've talked to him [Melich] this morning. In an attempt to try and help find your daughter, you've give him bad addresses. . . . Okay?

CA: Uh-huh.

JA: You drove me all the way out here. We walked from the gate back here all the way to your office, right?

CA: Uh-huh.

JA: Okay. To the, to an office that you don't have. We got all the way to the building into the hallway out here before you finally says, Well, I really don't have an office here. But . . . we were walking to your office, right?"

CA: Uh-huh.

JA: Okay, so I mean does any of this make sense to you?

CA: I understand how all that sounds. I—

JA: No, no, no, no, no, here's the problem with that, though. Here's the problem with that, okay. Um, you can carry the weight of this room for a long time, it's not gonna get any easier, okay. What he's trying to tell you right now. I'm gonna tell you, you know, and in the amount of time that I've done this, almost thirty years, okay . . .

"No, no, no, no, no, let *me* tell *you*," Casey could have said (in my own imaginary scenario). "I have carried the weight of a family that denied my existence entirely for over two decades. I have carried the weight of suppressing my humiliation at lying spread-legged and shaved in front of my father. I have carried the weight of my mother enabling me right out of my mind and soul. You are nothing. Your thirty years mean nothing. You have never met anyone like me, because I am not like anyone at all, not even like my*self*. I do not exist. Hence, you cannot make me feel afraid or guilty or worried or even tired. I will outdistance you and your partner and any investigator you would like to bring into this room, because I am a *Jumper*. And if what you seem to think happened to my daughter actually were to have happened, it would be no different for me than watching a sad movie—maybe less. So, take your thirty years and shove it up your ass. I have been in the making, in the airless psychological tunnels of my toxic family, for a hundred years—probably much longer. Now, what were you saying, again?"

JA: I've learned this, people make mistakes. Everybody makes mistakes. We, every . . . all three of us have all made some mistake . . . mistakes in our lives. . . . We've done some things we're not proud of—okay. But then there comes a point in time you either own up to it, you say you're sorry, you try to get past it. Or you lie about it, you bury it, you lie about it, and you bury it, and you bury it and it just never, ever, ever, ever, ever goes away.

CA: Uh-huh.

JA: At this point, we can explain that you're afraid. You know that you were ashamed, or maybe something bad that happened. You were afraid that maybe what happened. But now we're giving you this opportunity and you continue to lie and you continue to lie. . . . By burying this, okay, you are not going to get yourself to a better place, okay? What you're going to do is you're going to cause everybody around you to suffer, okay? And at some point, this is going to come out, it always does. . . .

CA: Uh-huh.

"You know, you are a very interesting man," Casey might have said, in my completely imaginary scenario. "But this theory of yours that burying things leads to catastrophe has just never had any reality in my existence. For instance, I was able to convince my own parents that I was a virgin when I was thirty weeks pregnant. I had them convinced I was working two jobs and had a nanny taking care of Caylee. I hid what my dad did to me from everyone, even from my*self*—most important, in fact, from my *self*. I'm just not like you people."

Again, in my entirely made-up world (taking my cues from Casey Anthony's writing here), she stops suddenly, smiles shyly yet seductively, looks deep into Detective John Allen's eyes, and says in an utterly convincing tone, "You are honestly the nicest, sweetest, cutest guy I have ever met. I mean, when this is over, would you want to go ballooning or something together?"

JA: It always comes out—okay? Now your best bet is to try to put this behind you as quickly as you can. Go to your parents and tell 'em you know some horrible accident, whatever happened, happened. Get it out in the open now—okay? Instead of letting them worry, and worry, and worry, and worry, okay? How old are you?

CA: Twenty-two.

JA: At some point, okay, you're gonna want to . . . to mend things with your family.

I can't resist writing this imaginary response for Casey: "You mean, the people who destroyed me? I would rather they all be dead, you moron."

CA: Uh-huh.

JA: Okay. You let this drag out for another three days, another week, another two weeks, okay. You make us solve this some other way. We'll solve it, we always do—okay? Okay, I mean it . . . it . . . there's

no point in coming forward to say, oh my God, this is
what really happened, once we figured it out, okay?

CA: Uh-huh.

JA: You ever had anybody do anything wrong to you?
Did anybody hurt—

CA: Of course.

JA: —you in any way, okay. Let me ask you a question. When somebody's hurt you in the past. And
they've come to you and said, I'm sorry, okay? I
really am, from the bottom of my heart sorry for
what happened. Do you forgive 'em?

CA: Yes.

JA: What about somebody that does something to you
and lies, lies, lies, lies, lies. You forgive them?

CA: It's a lot harder to sometimes.

Again, I can't resist adding these fictional words, "But I
had done that, until recently, with my mother, who psychologically murdered me; and my father, despite what he did to
me and also watched me give birth; and my brother, regard-
less of the pain he caused me; and my grandmother, who
ruined my mother."

In truth, what's really remarkable is that Detective Allen
didn't pause to ask Casey just what it was that had been done
to her. That may actually have opened up a door. It would've
been a one-in-a-million shot, but that was better than his
odds were with his current line of inquiry.

JA: A lot hard[er] to. Tell me the last time somebody
hurt you over and over and then let you suffer for a
period of time. And then lied about it, then you
caught 'em—okay? Well, what . . . When you caught
'em, that apology didn't mean a hell of a lot, did it?

CA: No.

JA: Okay.

CA: No.

JA: All right. Right now, your best bet is to get it out
in the open whatever happened, and tell us now,

okay? So, we can, we can kind of start getting past this. Try to help you explain, okay? 'Cause keep in mind you're talking to people . . . There's nothing you're gonna tell . . . us that's gonna surprise us, okay?

CA: Uh-huh.

JA: I've had to sit down with . . . with mothers who rolled over their babies accidentally. I've had to sit down with mothers whose kids have drowned in swimming pools. I've had to sit down with mothers who had boyfriends who beat their kids to death. Ah, you know who . . . who felt horrible about what happened. And then try, and I had to go to them and help them try to explain to their families, okay? And then I've also had to deal with people who have done horrible, unspeakable things to children. And then lied about it and lied about it and lied about it, okay? And I'll bet you somewhere near I probably dealt with somebody who maybe made a mistake, but continued to lie about it. Maybe they weren't such a bad person. But maybe the whole world didn't see it that way. Maybe their family didn't see it that way 'cause they kept lying, lying, lying, and lying about it. And then when it finally . . . and then months down the road or days down the road when they finally decided to come forward, okay? People were past it. . . . [If] you told me that you lied to me for the last time . . . I would . . . listen to what you had to say. . . .

CA: Yeah.

JA: Yeah, we . . . we've had to, you know, we've had to go into court and try to help people explain situations. We've had to go in court at times and say, you know the person just never said . . . they kept lying to us and lying to us and lying to us, okay? We're all human beings.

It must be said, at this point, that Detectives Melich and Allen were coming perilously close to the point at which a "normal" but psychologically vulnerable individual could issue a false confession. It is well known that a lengthy interview, without access to breaks, with repeated suggestions of plausible scenarios that could explain a person's violence, coupled with empathy and offers of assistance, can prompt a person to simply fabricate a confession. Emotionally needy suspects who are completely innocent can be "seduced" into confessing to crimes they never committed by the promise of having someone "on their side"—especially a powerful man. And, in any case, agreeing to guilt can seem, unconsciously, like the easiest route out of a painful interrogation.

Also, Casey's behavior to that moment, including her willingness to take investigators to her nonexistent workplace, should have alerted Melich that in my opinion further questioning of her should not be conducted without a psychiatric evaluation. She was not behaving in a normal manner, and no one at that moment could have credibly asserted that she was competent to continue answering an investigator's questions.

But Casey Anthony probably wasn't at risk to give a false confession, because she probably didn't much mind being interrogated, anyhow. And she was unlikely to resonate with offers of empathy, because she didn't have access to unwieldy emotions. You have to feel afraid in order to hunger for comfort. Casey automatically shut down at painful moments, flipping the circuit breaker on her real feelings and moving on.

The only thing about which the detectives were correct was the fact that Casey Anthony (and her mother) had, indeed, summoned law enforcement to Hopespring Drive. They had triggered this investigation. But that should not have given Detectives Melich and Allen any solace or confidence. It should have made them wonder whether they were being "played" by a card shark who, in the end, wouldn't even agree that a full house beats a pair of deuces—as long as she were the one holding the deuces.

Really, truly, they were wasting their time. Even Meursault's inquisitors had left him alone pretty quickly, once they realized they were with the Stranger.

> **JA:** You brought us here, okay? All right, I want you to look at this from an outsider's perspective— somebody somewhere down the road—and we have to decide, you know, how this all plays out.
>
> **CA:** Uh-huh.
>
> **JA:** What would you do? How would you see that person? How would you see that person different[ly]? You might see somebody, maybe a young mother who made a mistake and you know maybe initially was afraid to tell the truth. But at some point came forward and said, a horrible thing happened. I'm sorry. I feel terrible about it. But I have to tell you.
>
> **CA:** The horrible thing that happened is, this is the honest-to-God's truth. Of everything that I've said I do not know where she is. The last person that I saw her with is Zenaida. She's the last person that I seen my daughter with.

That was the equivalent of a body slam in professional wrestling that sends one's opponent running to the corner to slap his tag team partner's hand. And that's exactly where Detective Allen was headed. Yuri Melich was rested and ready to jump in the ring. But he wouldn't be pinning Casey or getting her to "tap out," ever.

> **Detective Yuri Melich:** Um, see here's the problem and I—
>
> **CA:** Yes.
>
> **YM:** —think Sergeant Allen, Sergeant Allen is trying to get to this . . . Is we . . . we know that's not the truth. We know . . .
>
> **CA:** It is.
>
> **YM:** Listen, listen . . .
>
> **CA:** Absolutely is.
>
> **YM:** Listen, we know that that's not true. . . . Because

if that were the truth, everything you would've told us would've been on the money. The addresses you would've taken us [to] would've been on the money. Everything else would've matched. If you had told us the truth, we wouldn't be here at Universal Studios at a place that you've been fired [from] since 2006 . . . with you trying to explain to us, you know, you got an office and all that stuff.

CA: Uh-huh . . .

YM: But here's . . . here's . . . here's what we're trying to get by is that there's . . . you're . . . you're . . . you fall under one of two categories.

Wow. Yuri Melich was about to launch into his lecture again, about how Casey could be perceived either as an evil woman with no conscience or as an unfortunate, overwhelmed mother who had done something very bad but, ultimately, something very understandable.

In the movie *The Incredibles*, Mr. Incredible attempts to distract his would-be nemesis, an animated bad guy named Syndrome, by letting him go on and on about his philosophy:

Mr. Incredible: I was wrong to treat you that way. I'm sorry . . .

Syndrome: See? Now you respect me, because I'm a threat. That's the way it works. Turns out there are lots of people, whole countries, that want respect, and will pay through the nose to get it. How do you think I got rich? I invented weapons, and now I have a weapon that only I can defeat, and when I unleash it . . .

[Mr. Incredible throws a log at Syndrome, who dodges it and traps Mr. Incredible with his zero-point energy ray.]

Syndrome: Oh, ho ho! You sly dog! You got me monologuing! I can't believe it. . . .

Mr. Incredible's strategy to distract Syndrome by making him fall in love with his own words was just another version of Ali's Rope-a-Dope. And Detective Melich kept monologuing—wearing himself out. He went on for several minutes about Casey's responsibility to the truth and to others, noting how much pain people were feeling, and how Casey could put a stop to all of it. And when he was finally done, she replied, simply, "I've been trying."

ROUND TWO

Sergeant Allen seemed to be needed again. "Wait a minute, wait a minute, okay. Let's go through this again," he interrupted.

He did go through it all again. He went through Casey's entire story of what she did and what she did not know about what had led to Caylee supposedly disappearing:

Sergeant John Allen: Okay. Stop me at the part that I say, it's not true okay.

Casey Anthony: Uh-huh.

JA: I want to go through this, and I want you to stop me at the part that isn't the truth, okay?

CA: Uh-huh.

JA: You take your daughter and you drop her off on June the ninth. [Again, this fictional event was later established to have supposedly occurred on June 16.]

CA: Uh-huh.

JA: Okay. At somebody, at a babysitter's house, okay. Now, this is a babysitter that lives at this apartment, okay. That's been vacant . . .

CA: I dropped her off at that apartment.

JA: Okay.

CA: At those stairs . . .

JA: Okay. You first called the police about this, when your mother and father, okay . . . Ah, actually, you don't call the police to report your daughter missing. What happens is, your parents find their car has been towed—

CA: Uh-huh.

JA: —from Amscot, and your parents ask you where your daughter is. And you tell them your daughter . . . or your parents, that you haven't seen you daughter for over a month, right?

CA: [No verbal response]

JA: That's true, okay? So, I haven't told anything . . . so, so far, I haven't said anything that's not true, okay?

CA: That's all true. . . .

JA: Okay. When the police do get involved . . . when you're, when your parents involve the police in an attempt to locate your child because they're worried.

CA: Uh-huh.

JA: The first thing you do, okay, is you lie to the detective whose job it is to try to find your daughter and get her back into safe hands, okay? You give him all kinds of bad addresses to look at, right, okay?

CA: [No verbal response]

JA: So far I'm on track right?

CA: Uh-huh.

JA: Okay. Then, you bring us out to Universal, where you say you work, in an office.

CA: Uh-huh.

JA: To try to help find stuff that will help us find your daughter. I'm on track so far, okay?

CA: Uh-huh.

JA: And we get here, we walk all the way down the hall to where you tell us, you don't really work here. You don't have an office here, okay.

CA: Uh-huh.

JA: So far, everything I've said is true, correct?

CA: Uh-huh.

JA: Okay. Now, that sounds reasonable to you, okay. I'm telling you this story, I'm saying to you, listen, I dropped my child off five weeks ago, at the baby-sitter's house. And she just disappeared.

CA: Hm.

JA: Now, I didn't call the police and tell them. Matter of fact, I made some attempts to locate her on my own. But I didn't really get the police involved or, you know, do anything like that, okay? And, oh, by the way, um, I got my mom and dad's car towed, and then when my parents asked me what happened to my daughter, I told 'em I hadn't seen her in five weeks. So, they call the police, okay? Now, what I did is, I lied to the police when they got there, okay? I told 'em a whole bunch of crap that isn't true. Gave 'em a bunch of bad addresses to go look at, where I know my daughter's not there. And I did all this to try to help find my daughter. Make sense to you, right?

CA: That's what I said, yes.

JA: No, no, I'm asking you, that makes sense to you. My—

CA: That part of it, no, not at all. . . .

JA: 'Cause everything we're doing here is about finding your daughter, okay? So, I want you . . . to explain to me, how coming here, to come to an office that you don't have, I want you to tell me, how that's helping us find your daughter. Because . . . you got three people here to try to help you, that's why we're here, to try to help you find your daughter, okay?

CA: Uh-huh . . .

JA: Now, I want you to tell me how that's helping us find your daughter. . . .

CA: Caylee's been up here, maybe we could talk to security, see if she's come through the front. I know she's come to the park. She's gone to Disney. She's been at Sea World.

JA: Whoa, ho-hold on—
CA: She's been to other places.

Maybe Sergeant Allen had a sense, at that point, what he was up against. Casey wasn't even getting tired. She wasn't tempted to throw in the towel. She hadn't even hit her stride. She wanted to go to the front desk at Universal and ask the staff some questions. She wanted to take the investigators to some other places, too. Another field trip . . .

Allen seemed to have been thrown a little off balance. And Casey wanted to spin him around a little more. Play a little Pin the Tail on the Donkey.

JA: Let's go back to, let's . . . let's . . .
CA: I've been reaching to try to figure out a place where she actually is.
JA: So, once again, okay, 'cause you never did answer my question. You're reaching and helping find her by bringing us here, to this office, that you don't have. It's helping us find her, how?
CA: It's . . .
JA: Because what you're doing right now, is you're doing everything you can to find your daughter. You have three experienced detectives right now, whose sole focus is here to help you find your daughter, okay. And we're here, 'cause you brought us here, correct?
CA: Absolutely.
JA: You directed us here, because we're going to your office to find evidence.
CA: Hm . . .

Detective Melich was rested and ready to do battle again. Trouble is, ghosts don't scare easily. They don't scare at all.

Detective Yuri Melich: So, why'd you do it?
CA: Honestly, I wanted to come up and try to talk to

security. Maybe pass around a picture of Caylee.
I legitimately have not seen my daughter in five
weeks. I don't want anything to happen to her.
Except, I trusted her with somebody. Somebody
that had been taking care of her. That had been
taking good care of her. Someone that she was
comfortable with, that I was comfortable with.

YM: What about, what about Jeff [Hopkins], you said
Jeff worked here about, ah, about two months ago?

CA: No, he hasn't worked here for quite a while.

YM: Ten months? How long?

CA: It's been at least ten months.

YM: . . . 2002. He hasn't been employed here since
2002. What about, ah, the girl?

CA: Juliette?

YM: Yeah, what about her?

CA: She left two months ago, that's exactly what she
had told me.

YM: Juliette Lewis never worked at Universal Studios.

In fact, Juliette Lewis is the name of an American actress
and musician who became famous for her roles in the thriller
Cape Fear and *Natural Born Killers* and the serial killer
film *Kalifornia*.
Yuri Melich sounded like he was almost ready to sur-
render.

YM: All right, well, you've told us so many untruths
right now, I'm confused.

Sergeant Allen took over.

Sergeant John Allen: And we're here to, to go to what,
to do what? We're here because, why?

CA: Try and put things together.

JA: No, we're here in this building because . . . We've
put a lot more together, than I think you realize
we've put together. My question to you is, we're in

this office because . . . we got here because . . . we got here how, to do what?

CA: [No verbal response]

JA: Our purpose in coming here was to do what? Go where?

CA: I guess there wasn't a purpose. There wasn't a purpose whatsoever to come up here. . . .

ROUND THREE

The third officer in the room, Detective Appie Wells, decided to take her best shot at Casey next.

Wells asked Casey about a telephone call she claimed to have received the day before from Caylee.

Detective Appie Wells: Did you actually talk with . . . What day was it you talked to her?

Casey Anthony: Yesterday.

AW: You remember what time of day?

CA: Around noon. It was from a private number. [There was no caller ID.]

AW: Okay, what'd she tell you? What'd your daughter say to you?

CA: She said, "Hi, Mommy."

AW: And that's it?

CA: And she started to tell me a story, talking to me about her shoes and books and . . .

AW: It's important that you tell me. I mean, maybe there's something in what she said that can help us figure out where she is. What did she say?

CA: I tried to ask her where she was—

AW: Okay.

CA: —and she just kept talking about the book that she's—

Sergeant Allen jumped back in the ring.

Sergeant John Allen: Right.

CA: —reading. We have videos of her reading the story, and she's telling me the story—

JA: She was telling . . . you about a book, that would seem not . . . no sign of any type of stress at all?

CA: Not at all.

JA: Great, that's wonderful. Let me ask you a question. Your daughter hasn't seen you in over a month, and she's not, she—

CA: She was excited, she was excited, sorry, to talk to me. But at the same time, it's crazy that she didn't get upset when she talked to me. Which . . . had it been my mom, I know it would have been . . . totally different.

JA: Is that another thing . . . that makes sense to you?

CA: She never gets upset when she talks to me. Whether I haven't seen her for an entire day, or if I had to work late at night, I didn't see her almost an entire day, until the next one. . . .

JA: The last time, the last time somebody took her, and you didn't see her for five weeks was when?

CA: Never.

JA: Okay. Now, you haven't seen her in five weeks. She has not seen you in five weeks.

CA: No.

JA: Okay. She's been with this woman for . . . or somebody for five weeks. Hasn't been in her own home, hasn't seen her mother in five weeks.

CA: Uh-huh.

JA: That didn't upset her.

CA: She was fine.

JA: She was fine, she talked about the, y'all talked about the book. I mean, is all that stuff you're saying true, right?

CA: She's always like that. You can even ask my mom, she's the same way.

Here, Casey may have been telling something close to the truth. She had no insight into the story of what I view as her psychological destruction as a human being, couldn't describe for the officers the experience of slowly suffocating while choked off from emotional oxygen on Hopespring Drive, but she knew something about her mother, Cindy: At least in Casey's estimation, she didn't miss anybody when they were gone. She seemed oddly disconnected. And according to what Casey has written, Cindy believed her granddaughter was turning out the same way. Cindy seemed to believe all CMAs were pretty much the same as she was. She didn't necessarily see other people as unique individuals. In fact, from all data available to me, she may well have felt very threatened by anyone's individuality—hence, the psychological suffocation of Casey.

As I have said, psychological realities can transmute themselves—tragically—into physical ones, as generations pass, and no healing takes place. Psychological death can become physical death.

JA: Okay, let me go back to the, when was the last time you didn't see her for five weeks? When was the last time something like this happened, where she was gone and you didn't see her for five weeks? The last time this happened, when?

CA: Never.

JA: Okay, so this is the first time. Okay.

CA: This is the first time I've been away from her for more than a day.

JA: Okay. The first time you ever been away from her for more than a day, and she wasn't the least bit upset?

CA: No.

Detective Appie Wells: Now, if this is the first time she's ever been gone for . . . away from you for more than a day. I'm a parent, too.

CA: Uh-huh.

AW: I would've been, I would've been just beside myself.

CA: I have been.

AW: I would've called the police immediately, and that's the part that I just don't understand. . . .

CA: I didn't know . . . what to do.

Sergeant John Allen: You didn't know what to do?

CA: I didn't know what to do. At that point, I'm thinking, Okay, they haven't been gone that long. Maybe I can find them. Maybe I can track them down. . . .

JA: Right, I understand all that, okay. I want you to focus on what we're doing here, okay.

CA: Uh-huh.

JA: All right. Because I want to make sure we get this right. After, after having, after having not seen your daughter for five . . . or heard from or not knowing where your daughter was at, for five weeks . . . she calls you on the phone. You have a conversation with her, where she talks about the books and this other stuff.

CA: Uh-huh.

JA: But then you ask her to speak to an adult, and then she hangs up. Or the phone hangs up, okay. Correct?

CA: Uh-huh.

JA: The very next thing you do after that is what? Call the police because now something really strange has happened, so you must've called the police right, after that. Did you call the city police or do you remember who you called? Which police agency did you call yesterday?

CA: I didn't call anybody at noon after I got that phone call. I sat down—

JA: You . . . Whoa . . . You didn't think that was odd? This con . . . you didn't this, this . . .

CA: I thought it was extremely odd.

JA: But not odd enough to call the police and try to get help.

CA: [No verbal response]

Detective Melich wanted to try a little something different with Casey. He'd gotten a call from Casey's lover Ricardo Morales and thought that confronting her with an inconsistency between her story and Ricardo's might give him a foothold to climb toward some sort of truth or shared reality. He was wrong.

Detective Yuri Melich: Rick [Ricardo Morales] is in the office, and Rick's finishing up the interview and that was actually Rick calling me. You know Ricardo right obviously, your ex-boyfriend?

CA: Uh-huh.

YM: We brought him down to the office, and he's been talking to a couple of our detectives down there. And he was able to help us because he's telling us something obviously, completely different, than what you're telling us. And I was just able to . . . pull the surveillance camera from the video across the street, at the old folks home, that you drove me by.

CA: Uh-huh.

YM: And ah, we're gonna get it enhanced, to see if we can actually get some good detail on pictures and faces. But Ricardo was saying that you spent the night with him on the ninth and left on the tenth. And this is being, this is being corroborated right now, which again shows that you're continuously lying about the ninth being the day that—

CA: I stayed over at . . . at his house . . . on the ninth of this month [July]. . . . Not of last month. I was not at his place the ninth of that month [June].

YM: So, you stayed at your ex-boyfriend's the ninth of this month, when you're staying at your other boyfriend's house, Tony, the rest of the month?

CA: He'd been out of town, so I was staying over at another friend's place while he was gone. I wasn't staying in his apartment. I was staying with Amy and Ricardo and JP. . . .

YM: So, why didn't, why didn't you tell us you were staying there. We drove right by the house this morning, didn't we, when we went to . . .

CA: [No verbal response]

YM: Okay, and you're at this old folks home, which is another lie, right?

CA: Uh-huh.

YM: 'Cause Zanny never lived there. Am I correct?

CA: Uh-huh.

This exchange shows why Casey had so many friends. She could bounce off a challenging comment or an argument or a criticism like a pinball off a rubber bumper. Challenge her with a few facts, and her story could change to encompass the new information. No hard feelings. Nothing to get nervous about. Nothing to argue about.

YM: Yet across the street from this old folks home, right there on Glenwood, is where Ricardo lives.

CA: Uh-huh.

YM: With Amy and JP.

CA: Uh-huh.

YM: All of whom are at our station talking to our detectives right now. So, obviously, you know, we're . . . we're not stupid, okay. And, what you're doing right now, is you're treating us like we're stupid, in which I take that, you know, to be a personal insult. I can't speak for them [apparently indicating the other two officers]. Here . . . here's where it comes down to. None of us are sitting here believing what you're saying, because everything that's coming out of your mouth is a lie. Everything. And unless we start getting the truth, unless we start getting the truth, we're going to announce two possibilities with Caylee. Either you gave Caylee to someone that you don't want anyone to find out about, because you think you're a bad mom. Or something happened to Caylee, and Caylee's buried somewhere, or in a trash can somewhere . . . and you had something to do with it . . . either way, right now, it's not a very pretty picture to be painting. Either way, either way right now, with everything that you're telling us, you're painting yourself as a very bad person. Your family's gonna suffer for this. Your friends are gonna suffer for this. And remember what I told you about all these people coming? They're gonna crucify you for this. Because of all the lies that you've been telling us. We need to stop this right now. Everything you've told us is a lie. You're looking me in the eyes, you're looking at . . . everything you've told us is a lie. Every single thing.

CA: No, it isn't. . . . [Caylee] is with someone else.

YM: . . . No, she's either in a Dumpster right now, or she's buried somewhere, she's . . . she's out there somewhere, and her rotting body is starting to decompose because what you're telling us . . . And here's the problem, the longer this goes, the worse it's gonna be for everyone, everyone. The worse it's gonna be for everyone. Right now, everything you've told us, we've locked you into a lie. Every single thing that you've told us has been a lie. We're proving all that. Now, right now, it's gonna be one of two things. Either we find Caylee alive, which is gonna help you out extremely by telling us the truth. Or we find Caylee not alive, which, if you start telling us the truth, might still paint you in a better picture. But here's where it needs to end. Here's where the truth needs to come out, okay. No more lies. No more bull coming out of your mouth. We've been very respectful, we're taking our time and talking to you. But we're tired of all the lies. No more lies. What happened to Caylee?

CA: I don't know.

YM: You do know.

CA: I don't know—

YM: What happened to Caylee?

CA: —where she is. That is the God's honest truth. . . .

Okay, the bout was almost over, anyhow, but I'd have to have called it a TKO in the third round for Casey Marie Anthony. She'd used the Rope-a-Dope (and, mind you, neither Melich nor Allen nor Wells was anything close to a dope) and the "Mr. Incredible Monologuing Trick" and the circuit-breaker technique to exhaust her inquisitors and leave them wandering the ring, confused and dispirited. I bet she didn't have a bead of sweat on her. I bet her pulse had never risen over eighty. She was probably already thinking whom to text first when she could get to her cell phone and how long it would be before she could sleep with Tony Lazzaro again, or Ricardo Morales, or Anthony Rusciano, or . . . who knows?

The amazing thing is that none of Casey Anthony's intellectual tug-of-war with three detectives who had talked vicious gang members into confessions probably required any conscious thought on her part at all. Her hyperbolic "ability" to deny reality had been honed over decades and was triggered automatically by anyone who sought to pierce her armor or cause her any strife. Being evasive wasn't an effort; it was like water running downhill, like a helium balloon floating away. It felt natural to her now, after all the years she had spent trying *not* to feel.

She had admitted to nothing other than lying about lying about the truth about lying about the truth about lying. Or something like that. It really didn't matter. That was the point. And even if Melich and company had not had enough, I'd have saved them from themselves. They may have suffered lasting "head" trauma from staying in that room with Casey Anthony too long.

YM: Let me, let me just go ahead, because this is still running, I noticed it. Raise your right hand for me. Just like this morning.

CA: Yeah.

YM: You swear everything you've told me is the truth now about the lies and—

CA: Yes.

YM: —everything else? Okay.

"The truth . . . about the lies and . . . everything else." Melich sounded like he had nothing left. He sounded punch-drunk. He'd once solved three homicide cases within two weeks. He'd just been knocked out cold by a hundred-pound, twenty-two-year-old former Kodak kiosk employee with a fresh tattoo that read, *Bella Vita*. "Beautiful Life." And chances are, she still had enough steam to go fifteen with anyone else who cared to step into the ring, go out for a tour of random addresses, or take her to bed.

Does that sound cavalier to you? As I invoked Mr. Incredible, professional wrestling, Muhammad Ali, and the rest, did you find yourself losing track—even for a nanosecond—of the reality that Caylee Marie Anthony's bones were found in a black garbage bag in the woods? Did you find yourself, just for a fraction of an instant, thinking more about Casey's jousting with three investigators, taking them down one by one? If so, you were inside the mind of Casey Anthony for that brief vacation from reality. The difference is that you—and I—come back to reality. Reality has its own gravity that pulls us back to solid ground—Caylee's bones, that black garbage bag, the woods. Not so for Casey. Her sense of reality—which should have been anchored from the first days of her life in her sense of *self*—seems to have been completely eroded by parents who I believe would have found any manifestation of her true self to be unacceptable and terrifying, something to resist at all costs, lest it remind them of what was dead inside *them*. It was still alive, somewhere deep, deep inside Casey, struggling for a breath of real emotional oxygen, through filters like Facebook and

MySpace and Cupid.com and hot-body contests and shots down at Fusion Ultra Lounge, and tall tales of every variety. It was still alive inside her even when she had anonymous sex with men she knew—anonymous because she was absent from it, accommodating their needs and hiding hers, perhaps even making the denial of her *self* the warp and weft of the erotic experience itself. To be restrained or choked or both during sex could have been, for her, the most stimulating drama of all, since it at least would have brought her in touch more closely with the fact that she had been deprived of oxygen, in one form or another, all her life, especially, chances are, during adolescence, when she may have been fighting at least a little for an identity.

That fight—that life-and-death struggle to be a real person—can get very ugly, indeed. People sometimes are driven to kill themselves in final and singular acts of autonomy, claiming at least their right to live or die from those who would give them no claim at all on them*selves*. And sometimes, they kill others.

ARRESTED DEVELOPMENT

Casey Anthony was placed under arrest on charges of child neglect, making false official statements and obstructing a criminal investigation at 8:09 P.M., on Wednesday, July 16, 2008.

The arrest affidavit, written by Detective Yuri Melich, read, in part:

> On July 15th, 2008 at 0045 hrs. I was notified by Sgt. Reggie Hose about a report of a missing child, later identified as Caylee Anthony (2 yoa).
>
> The initial report indicated the child was last seen at 2863 S. Conway Road around apartment #210 on June 9th, 2008 [this date is later corrected to June 16, 2008] between 0900 and 1300 hrs. According to the child's mother, the child was last left with the babysitter (Zenaida Gonzalez at the above S. Conway Road address). Since June 9th, the defendant has not been able to locate Zenaida or her child and she never reported the incident to law enforcement until tonight. . . .
>
> I briefed my supervisor (Sgt. John Allen) and responded to 4937 Hopespring Drive to begin my investigation. I first met with the defendant inside the residence and spoke with her alone and away from other family members. . . .
>
> The defendant lived at this address on Hopespring Drive until June 9th, 2008. On June 9th [again, the

accurate date is actually June 16], she left with her daughter Caylee to go to work at Universal Studios. This was between 0900 and 1300 hrs. En route, she says she stopped by 2863 S Conway Road and met with Zenaida Gonzalez who babysits Caylee. She left Caylee with Zenaida at that building at the stairwell that leads to apartment 210. She says she's known Zenaida for four years and Zenaida has babysat Caylee for the past one and a half years. When the defendant left work around 1700 hrs. and came back to pick up Caylee, she says she got no answer at the door. She tried calling Zenaida's cell phone (number unknown) and got no answer. She started going to places that Zenaida was known to frequent but didn't locate her child.

The defendant said she was "pacing and worrying" and went to her boyfriend's house where she felt "safe." Her boyfriend is Anthony Lazzaro. Since June 9th, the defendant says she's done her "own investigation" in trying to find her daughter. . . .

The defendant agreed to show me the three last known locations for Zenaida in hopes of identifying her. The defendant rode with me in my unmarked car to meet with a market unit and other Deputy Sheriff to attempt contact at one of these locations. We first went to the corner of Glenwood and Robinson where she pointed out a building on the northwest corner. She pointed at the second floor window and said Zenaida had lived in that apartment in early 2006 to mid 2006 when she moved into another house owned by Zenaida's mother (Gloria). The building she pointed out was later identified as 301 N Hillside Drive, a seniors only facility. The defendant said the apartments were three stories and the window above Zenaida's belonged to Zenaida's roommate. As a note, the initial responding deputies had found a handwritten note with the address of 232 Glenwood in the defendant's car prior to my arrival. This address was directly across from the building she just pointed out to me.

We then went to 2863 S Conway Road #210 to confirm this was the same apartment she showed deputies earlier that night and where she had left the child on June 9th. She confirmed that was the apartment.

We then went to the Crossings at Conway town home community near Michigan Avenue and S. Conway Road. This is where Zenaida's mother allegedly owned a condo and where she claims she'd dropped her child off several times between mid 2006 to early 2007. We rode through the complex, down every street and the defendant said she couldn't remember what the address was. We knocked at three different addresses (4729, 4283, and 4273) making contact with three different tenants, all of which did not know Zenaida or her mother Gloria. The defendant said she didn't remember the house because she stopped paying attention to it since she came so many times.

I dropped the defendant back off at her residence on Hopespring, telling her I would call her if I needed anything. Prior to leaving, I was approached by her father George who stressed his concern that his daughter is holding back information. He and his wife (the defendant's mother) fear something may have happened to Caylee. . . .

I then went to Universal Studios and met with Investigator Leonard Turtora. After briefing him on what I was there for, he checked several names in their database and came up with the following results. The defendant was fired from Universal on 4/24/06 and she was NOT currently employed there. Jeffrey Hopkins (an alleged outcry witness) did not work for Universal Studios but he was fired in 5/13/02. Juliette Lewis (another alleged outcry witness) was not found as a current or former employee of Universal Studios. Zenaida Gonzalez (who the defendant claimed was the seasonal employee) was also not found as a current or former employee of Universal Studios.

While with Leonard, I called the defendant on my

cell phone and put my phone's speaker on so all could hear. The defendant confirmed that she did currently work for Universal as an event coordinator. She said her office extension was 407-224-1000 x104. Leonard said this was not a valid extension and even tried calling it. She said her direct supervisor was Tom (Manley). They have no Tom Manley employed there. The head of the events department is Tom Mattson. Leonard called him and confirmed they did not have the defendant listed as an employee, either past or present. I asked the defendant where her office was (she claimed to have her own office) and she couldn't give me the building number or location. When asked if she had her current work ID she said she didn't know where it was.

I asked Sgt. Allen to see if he could arrange to have someone go back to the Hopespring address and meet with the defendant to see if she'd agree to come to Universal Studios. At 1230 hrs. Sgt. Allen and Detective Appie Wells went to the Hopespring address and met with defendant who agreed to accompany them to Universal Studios. Investigator Turtora agreed to assist us with this.

Once at Universal Studios, I met with the three at the employee's entrance. Investigator Turtora was present. The defendant, who didn't have her ID, explained to the security officer at the entrance she was a current employee and lost her ID. When the security guard (Steve) asked who her supervisor was, she told him it was Tom Manley. When told no Tom Manley worked there, she had no answer. Investigator Turtora agreed to escort the defendant to where she said she worked. We followed her into a building nearby and down the building's inner hall. She walked with purpose and acted like she knew where she was going. Halfway down this hall, she stopped, turned, and told us she hadn't told us the truth and she was not a current employee.

At this time, we found a small conference room in which to talk to the defendant. . . . In short, the defendant was confronted with all the inconsistencies in her story and the fact that I had proven she lied on almost every thing she had told me. . . .

It should be noted that at no time during any of the above interviews did the defendant show an obvious emotion as to the loss of her child. She did not cry or give any indication that she was legitimately worried about her child's safety. She remained stoic and mono-tone during a majority of our contacts. . . .

Here, I wish I myself could have added what I imagine Detective Melich had also likely observed during his contact with Casey. It would have read:

It should also be noted that Ms. Anthony was, at all times, affable toward us and, at times, even warm. She seemed to like us. She did not seem to appreciate, nor object to the fact, that our tone with her was extremely adversarial and that we obviously suspected her of wrongdoing, even of murdering her own child. She simply would not engage with us in any conflict, whatsoever. She never took steps to restrict our access to her by calling an attorney. She never fled. She never insisted on a break. It was almost as though she were not even with us in that conference room where we met. We left the room feeling as though she did not share our reality, or had no access to internal feelings—like fear, anger, guilt, perhaps even hunger or thirst. This raises the question of what happened in Ms. Anthony's life to completely—or very nearly completely—sever her from her internal self.

Okay, okay, I know Melich was doing his job as a detective. He wasn't about to do mine, as a detective of the mind. Back to Melich:

In the course of this investigation, I received calls from several persons who know the defendant. All claim she is a habitual liar and she has been known to steal from friends in the past . . .

Once at our central operation center, and after I started receiving the above phone calls reference the defendant and her child, the defendant was given one more opportunity to change her story. She did not. She was then placed under arrest for child neglect, and providing false information to us regarding this investigation.

INVESTIGATORS NOTE: As of this writing, we do not know the condition of the missing child Caylee Anthony. We do not know where the child is. Based on the repetitive lies that the defendant has told, we do not know with who the child is or even if the child is alive. As I received information, and relayed it to the defendant after her arrest, she continued to claim ignorance and at times, laughed about the situation. She still failed to show any outward signs of remorse or concern for her missing two year old daughter. I request that she be held on a NO BOND status until the child is located.

I can't help intruding one more time, embellishing Melich's report with my own vision of what he may well have observed:

When handcuffs were placed on the defendant, she showed no emotion. It was as though she were not under arrest at all. Nothing changed about her demeanor whether she was free of handcuffs or restrained by them. I felt, oddly, as though I had taken a phantom or a ghost into custody. She seemed in many ways to be physically but not psychologically alive.

The court agreed to hold Casey Anthony without bail. But, in truth, there could be no such thing as holding her, anymore.

NIGHT CALL

At 11:16 P.M., Casey called home from jail. She'd seen her mother interviewed on television. The transcript of her call follows.

Cindy Anthony: Casey?

Casey Anthony: Mom, I just saw your nice little cameo on TV.

Cindy: Which one?

Casey: What do you mean, which one?

Cindy: Which one? I did four different ones, and I haven't seen them all. I've only seen one or two so far.

Casey: You don't know what my involvement is in [inaudible]?

Cindy: Casey.

Casey: Mom.

Cindy: No, I don't know what you involvement is, sweetheart. You are not telling me where she's at.

Casey: Because I don't [expletive] know where she's at. You are kidding me?

Cindy: Casey, don't waste your call screaming and hollering at me.

Casey: Waste my call sitting in the jail?

Cindy: Whose fault is it you're sitting in jail? Are you blaming me you are sitting in the jail? Blame yourself for telling lies. What do you mean it is not your

fault? What do you mean it's not your fault, sweetheart? If you would have told them the truth and
not lied about everything.

Casey: Do me a favor and just tell me what Tony's
number is. I don't want to talk to you. Forget it.

Now, granted, Casey Anthony was under a great deal of
stress. She was, after all, in jail. But it is also consistent with
her cell phone–fueled, Facebook-powered personal life that
she didn't even have her own boyfriend's phone number committed to memory. Of course, it is also true he wasn't the only
one she may have had on speed-dial for those moments when
she needed to lose herself in a man's passion.

Cindy: I don't have his number.

Casey: Well, get it from Lee. I know Lee is at the
house. I saw Mallory's car was out front. It was just
on the news. They were just live outside the house.

Cindy: I know they were.

Casey: Well?

Casey: Can you get Tony's number for me so I can call
him?

Lee Anthony: Hello?

Casey: Hi. Can you get me Tony's number?

Lee: I can do that, but I don't know what good it's going to do you at this point.

Casey: Well, I'd like to talk to him anyway because I
called to talk to my mother and it is a [expletive]
waste. By the way, I don't want any of you coming
up here when I have my first hearing for bond and
everything. I mean don't even [expletive] waste your
time coming up here.

Many things Casey Marie Anthony had said (and would
say) during the course of the investigation were entirely
devoid of the truth. Here, however, she was expressing
some of the genuine, internal rage she harbored for her
family—a family, after all, that had orchestrated or allowed

the bleeding of nearly all humanity from her. Why, in God's name, would she want to talk to *them*? The fact that she reached out to them at all showed she still didn't understand that they had left her one of the living dead—like them.

Lee: You know, you are having a real tough year and making it real tough for anybody to want to try to, even if it is giving—

Casey: See, that is just it, every—

Lee: You are not even letting me finish.

Casey: Go ahead. . . .

Lee: First, you are asking me for Tony's phone number so you can call him and then you immediately want to start pressing toward me and don't even worry about coming up here for all this stuff and trying to cut us out.

Casey: I'm not trying to cut anybody out. . . .

Lee: I'm not going around and around with you. You know, that is pretty pointless. . . . Kristina [Kristina Chester, Casey's friend] would love to talk to you because she thinks you will tell her what's going on. Frankly, we are going to find out, whatever is going on is going to be found out. So, why not do it now?

Casey: There is nothing to find out. There is absolutely nothing to find out. Not even what I told the detectives. I have no clue where Caylee is. If I knew where Caylee was, do you think that any of this would be happening? No.

Lee: Anyway, you only have a couple of minutes with this so I'm not going to let you completely waste it. Here is Kristina.

Casey: No, no. I want Tony's number. I'm not talking to anybody else.

Kristina Chester: Hello.

Casey: Hi, I'm glad everybody is at my house but I'll have to call you later or I'll have to call to get somebody to get your number. Do me a favor and get my brother back because I need Tony's number.

Kristina: Okay. Is there anything I can do for you?

Casey: I'm sitting in jail. There is nothing anybody can do now.

Kristina: I'm just trying to be a . . .

Casey: I know you are, honey. I absolutely know you are and I appreciate it and everything you are trying to do but I'd like to call Tony. He's not at my house, is he?

Kristina: No. It's just me and your parents and Lee.

Casey: Well, can you do me a favor and get my brother back so I can get the number from him, please?

Kristina: Does Tony have anything to do with Caylee?

Casey: No. Nothing . . .

Kristina: Oh, then why do you want to talk with him?

Casey: Because he is my boyfriend and I want to actually try and sit and talk to him because I didn't get a chance to talk to him earlier. Because I got arrested on a [expletive] whim today and because they are blaming me for stuff that I would never do. That I didn't do.

Kristina: Well, I'm on your side, you know that?

Casey: I know that, I just want to talk with Tony and get a little bit of . . .

Kristina: If anything happened to Caylee, I'll die—you understand, I'll die.

Casey: Oh my God. Calling you guys [was] a waste—a huge waste. Honey, I love you. You know I'd never let anything happen to my daughter. If I knew where she was, this would not be going on.

Kristina: Then how come everyone is saying that you are lying?

Casey: Because nobody is [expletive] listening to anything that I'm saying. The media misconstrued everything that I said. The [expletive] detectives pulled [expletive] [expletive]. They got all of their information from me but at the same time they are twisting stuff. They already said they are going to pin this on me if they don't find Caylee. They've already said that. They arrested me because they said.

Kristina: They said that the person you left Caylee with doesn't exist.

Casey: Because, oh look, they can't find her in the Florida database. She is not just from Florida. If they would actually listen to anything that I would have said to them, they would have had their leads. They maybe could have tracked her down. They have not listened to a [expletive] thing that I've said.

Kristina: You know that whoever has Caylee, nobody is going to get away with it—

Casey: I know, nobody is going to get away with it but at the same time, the only way they are going to find Caylee is if they actually listen to what I'm saying and I'm trying to help them and they are not letting me help them. . . .

Kristina: How come everyone is saying that you are not upset and that you are not crying and you show no caring of where Caylee is at all?

Casey: Because I'm not here [expletive] crying every two seconds because I have to stay composed to talk to detectives, to make other phone calls and do other things. I can't sit here and be crying every two seconds like I want to—I can't.

Kristina: Okay, Casey, don't yell at me, I'm on your side . . .

Casey: I know you are on my side. . . . I'm not trying to.

Kristina: Nobody is saying anything bad about you. Your family is with you a hundred percent.

Casey: No, they're not. That is [expletive] because I just watched the [expletive] news and heard everything that my mom said. Nobody in my own family is on my side.

Kristina: Yes, they are.

Casey: They just want Caylee back. That is all they are worried about right now is getting Caylee back. And you know what, that is all I care about right now.

Kristina: Casey, your daughter, your flesh-and-blood and baby girl—

Casey: Kristina, please. Put my brother back on the phone, I don't want to get into this with you right now. . . .

Kristina: Lee said he doesn't have Tony's phone number.

Casey: Yes, he does. He has Tony's number in his phone. He needs to stop [expletive] lying. He just told me a second ago that he'd give me the number.

Kristina: So, if I go and get you Tony's number, are you going to finish talking to me?

Casey: I will call you tomorrow. I want to talk to him really quick. I wanted to actually try and call Mike. I haven't slept in four days. I have not slept in four days.

Kristina: Listen, if you are going to talk to anybody, you can talk to me.

Casey: I know I can talk to you but at the same time, I know that I can talk to Tony and that is who I want to talk to now. I have not gotten the chance to talk to him since this morning. Since all of this stuff happened with trying to set up the MySpace and I made the MySpace. [A MySpace entry had been created by Casey asking for help finding Caylee.]

Kristina: Do you know the password?

Casey: I made all of it.

Kristina: What's the password to MySpace so we can see if anybody has written any leads of where Caylee might be?

Casey: You can go online and see it. As far as messages, I don't know if anybody is going to be messaging.

Casey then exchanges MySpace log-in information with Kristina.

Kristina gives Casey Tony Lazzaro's phone number.

Kristina: Can Tony tell me anything?

Casey: Baby, Tony doesn't know anything. And, I have not even talked with him since this morning. . . .

Kristina: But you are telling the whole truth and nothing but the truth?

Casey: That I have no clue where my daughter is? Yes, that is the truth. That is the absolute truth.

Kristina: They'll find out and whoever—

Casey: Okay, Kristina, I'm hanging up, I've need to make this other call before I forget the number. So, I'll call you later.

Kristina: Okay, bye.

Casey was being held in jail, away from her family and away from her cell phone and away from her MySpace and Facebook accounts. If she sounded brittle, it may have been because she was detoxing from those drugs. That may be the reason why she so very much wanted to reach out for Tony Lazzaro—the most recent brand of man that she'd been smoking.

Her tone with Kristina, however, was not just that of an addict; it was that of an addict with no remorse. In order to have remorse, one must have empathy for others. And in order to have empathy for others, one must be able to first feel one's own pain, which Casey had, instead, run away from—all the way to a wilderness of fiction and fantasy and false freedoms that were nothing more than the petty, imperfect distractions of a woman hiding from her own internal feelings of humiliation, profound sadness and explosive rage.

The great psychologist Hervey Cleckley's research into those personality disorders in which a "mask of sanity" is worn to keep the world at bay, yields some insight here:

All the outward features of the mask are intact; it cannot be displaced or penetrated by questions. . . . The examiner never hits upon the chaos sometimes found on searching beneath the outer surface of a paranoid schizophrenic. . . . Only very slowly and by a complex estimation or judgment based on multitudinous and small impressions does the conviction come upon us that, despite these intact rational processes, these normal emotional affirmations, and their consistent application in all directions, we are dealing here not with a complete [person] at all but with something that suggests a subtly constructed reflex machine which can mimic the human personality perfectly. This smoothly operating psychic apparatus reproduces consistently not only specimens of good human reasoning but also appropriate simulations of normal human emotion. . . . So perfect is this reproduction of a whole and normal [person] that no one who examines [her] in a clinical setting can point out in scientific or ojective terms why, or how [she] is not real.

If this description fit Casey, in any measure, then maybe it also fit her father, George, who was able to focus sufficiently to inspect her abandoned car for scratches to its paint, though the interior smelled to him of rotted flesh, when his granddaughter had been missing thirty-one days. And maybe it also fit her mother, Cindy, who, during the ensuing weeks, would file with George to seek a trademark for the name Caylee Anthony and the slogan, "Justice for Caylee." She would also (with George's help) sell CBS photographs and footage of Caylee for twenty thousand dollars on one occasion, then cash in for hundreds of thousands from broadcast and entertainment companies later on. She was also the one who had never forgotten wasting ten dollars searching for her granddaughter and the one who had reportedly pocketed those irresistible fresh twenty-dollar bills from Casey's wallet while the police were at the house investigating Caylee's disappearance.

George's demeanor and behavior would, in particular, help make it impossible to convict Casey Anthony of murdering Caylee when she ultimately stood trial. According to the foreman of the jury, several jury members questioned whether George might have played a role in his granddaughter's death, whether he helped to cover it up or murdered Caylee himself.

One of the alternate jurors I spoke with concurred. That alternate juror stated that he would no more convict Casey of anything than he would George.

George and Cindy, of course, would famously appear for a three-part interview, beginning September 12, 2011, on the syndicated daytime show, *Dr. Phil*. The "foundation" they created was reportedly paid between $500,000 and $1 million. An entertainment executive who negotiated with them and their representatives told me in her opinion, confidentially, "Keith, they are about the money and nothing else. It's pretty sickening. It's revolting, actually. There is just nothing inside either one of them that seems human."

Oh, and don't forget that both of them had been there with their naked daughter—reduced to a state of existence, in that moment, no more human than a cold steel pipe—delivered unto them their granddaughter, Caylee, who was immediately cut from her umbilical cord and whisked away into Cindy's arms.

Whatever Casey Anthony had become, she hadn't had a snowball's chance in hell of becoming anything else at 4937 Hopespring Drive. Ultimately, jail was the most healing and holding place she had ever lived.

On July 22, 2008, attorney Jose Baez represented Casey at a bond hearing before the Honorable Judge Stan Strickland. He listened to testimony from Lee, Cindy, and George Anthony, as well as from Yuri Melich. In the end, he declared "the truth and Miss Anthony are strangers." He set bond at $500,000, well out of reach of the Anthony family.

On July 25, Cindy and George visited Casey in jail and spoke with her via telephone as she sat behind a glass panel.

"Are we going to be able to find her, do you think?" Cindy asked her daughter.

Casey said she hoped so.

"Do you think after this long, she'd still be local?" Cindy asked.

"She's not far," Casey said. "I know in my heart she's not far. I can feel it."

A REAL DEATH AMIDST
FAKE LIVES

On July 17, 2008, a K-9 unit with cadaver dogs was dispatched to the Anthony home. The dogs were trained to identify signs of human decomposition. They homed in on the rear passenger area of Casey's car and a patch of grass in front of Caylee's playhouse.

The obvious inference was that Caylee's decomposing body had been in Casey's car and that it had been near the playhouse she loved so much (which had an earthen floor that could have been an attractive place to hide her underground).

A search of the backyard also revealed an area of disturbed soil about a foot wide and five inches deep in back of the pool.

It seemed as though someone had shopped for a place to dispose of Caylee's remains.

George Anthony, meanwhile, was planning his own big-time investigation, which he said unfolded over the next weeks and months. Maybe he felt like getting back to the police work he'd done before those stints as a car salesman and pest exterminator and security guard at the movie cinema.

Cindy certainly didn't want him messing up anything. She'd seemingly picked him to share her life to begin with because he was too anemic of character to get in her way. And she'd commented to authorities that her husband was flailing around and pretty much worthless as the investigation unfolded.

But George decided, he told authorities much later, that he would "follow specific people around because [he] needed answers." He also told them he got a gun. He went out on the streets like Dirty Harry.

"I did," he said, "I went out and followed people around. I'll admit that to anybody. . . . . It's my duty not only as a father, as a grandfather, that I needed to get some answers from. And I did follow specific people around because I needed answers."

Some of the people George told authorities he felt might be hiding things and worth tailing were Jesse Grund, Tony Lazzaro, and Ricardo Morales. He said he wanted to follow Amy Huizenga around, too, but never did.

"There's a lot of inconsistencies of things that these people have said, that I've been told they've said," he stated. "I haven't actually read too much stuff. It's stuff that I've been told that they've said that just doesn't . . . register."

When George was pressed for the details of his detective work, however, it didn't seem he could come up with much:

Q: Who told you [this stuff]?

A: Hearsay. People out there, you know, talking. People that come up to you and say: Oh, I read Richard's [Ricardo's] stuff on this, or I read Tony's this. And it's just hearsay.

Q: Okay.

A: It's just hearsay stuff. And I'm just . . . Oh, interesting.

Q: All right.

A: Is there something I missed or something about this—

Q: Did you ask Casey directly if Jesse was involved in Caylee's disappearance?

A: The only thing she ever told me about him was: Be careful of him. That's the only thing she ever told me. . . . She really didn't talk too much about him or some of these other people, to be honest with you,

because we still think our house is bugged because
we still think people are listening in, and we're trying to do things as politely as we possibly can without people eavesdropping on our conversations.
But people do it every day.

There's stuff that you guys even brought up
today that I didn't even realize was being stated
out there. But, you know, it is what it is. You've
got to just deal with it, so—

Q: Okay. So what I take from this discussion is that
once Casey came home, you never asked her to
clarify what she meant about: Be careful of him?

A: No . . .

Well, this forensic psychiatrist would have wanted to ask,
What sort of investigator is that? If Jesse Grund were a man
worth following, who had inspired fear in one's daughter,
in the setting of one's granddaughter having gone missing,
wouldn't you have wanted to at least *ask* why your daughter
thought he was dangerous?

It looked like George was playing dress-up again. If only
they made a uniform for private detectives without a license,
Cindy, enabler of enablers, would probably have bought one
for him. Anything to keep him outwardly content and looking good, while in pieces psychologically.

George's interview with law enforcement moved painfully
forward:

Q: . . . But what did you ultimately find out about him?
Anything?

A: No. Because I—I come to find out is, you can't
take the law into your own hands. You can't do
something stupid. What if I would have caught him
doing something or found him with a particular—
then what would I have done? I had to know that
I'm not a law enforcement guy anymore.

Q: [Did] you think he could lead you to Caylee?

A: I don't know. I'd sure like to have an opportunity to talk to him. Do I think that there's more to him than meets the eye? Absolutely.

Q: But did you think he could lead you to Caylee at that point?

A: Uh-huh. I certainly do.

Q: Did you then?

A: I did then, I still think that he's involved in some way with this. I do.

Q: Okay.

A: But that's a gut feeling.

If George's evasiveness seems vaguely familiar, flip back to Casey's interview with Yuri Melich and his colleagues at Universal Studios. There was no real information forthcoming from George Anthony. He, like Casey, had seemingly disappeared over many years spent with Cindy. He'd started out as a cop and ended up as a gambler, hoping beyond hope to hold on to his job as a security guard at the movies. Granted, he may have been fractured when he met her, but he had been broken down to powder and dissolved in the powerful, toxic solvent of his wife's enabling. He was pretty much gone.

George also claimed to have followed Tony Lazzaro around. Of course, the Assistant State Attorney was interested in that, too:

Q: That's fine. What are the—what's the basis of your beliefs?

A: Oh, for I think—and this is just hearsay now . . . he's been involved with some very bad people, I guess. . . .

Q: All right. Is this something that you found out on your own through following him? I know you mentioned hearsay. . . .

A: Just—a lot of it on my own, little inquisitive things, just following—like I said, following him around. . . .

But when I found out about Club Fusion, I just
happened to go there one evening, and I just asked:
Anybody know Tony? . . .

Q: When did you go there?

A: I don't know. Towards the middle of—maybe
towards—probably about a week or ten days after
Caylee was missing. I'm just—I'm just giving a
rough idea.

George sounded like he would have hopped in a cruiser
just like his daughter Casey had done and taken law enforcement officials on a sightseeing tour to nowhere, in particular—
maybe even to his fake office at Universal.

The interview with the man of many uniforms continued:

Q: Right. But did you believe that Tony Lazzaro would
be able to lead you to Caylee?

A: Hope so. Between him and Jesse. I've come to find
out that he and Jesse knew each other prior to this,
too.

Q: Where and how?

A: Between some of the local clubs I guess they went
to. I guess they have some mutual acquaintances or
something like that. A lot more you guys don't know.

Q: Tell us.

Uh-oh, the attorney wanted specifics. . . .

A: I mean, that's—I'm just, like: Wow, that's interesting.

Q: Tell us.

A: That's the stuff that I've been—that's stuff that I
found in the beginning. . . . I sort of just backed
off. . . . Because I think law enforcement need to
do their job and anyone else who's connected with
this particular case needs to do research, do some
things, do some following. You just can't stop. You
can't stop when a child is missing, or a child is gone,

or someone's life is in jeopardy. You've got to do everything you can to get the right answers.

Q: That's what we're here for today. . . .

A: If I knew more about these people, I'd be more than glad to tell you. I wish I did. I can relate to you, though, this, and I've already relayed it to the sheriff's department. . . .

When [the] last search warrant was executed at our house in December, I had a three-ring binder that was probably as thick as those three—three—those pages that—those documents together, that stack [indicating].

Q: Sure.

A: I had written stuff down from the first day when Caylee came up missing up until the time we went to California. . . . [That trip was to make $20,000 or $200,000 or whatever selling stuff to the media.]

Q: Uh-huh.

A: It's gone. . . .

Oh, man. Where was Yuri Melich when you really needed him? Where was someone big and strong with a head of steam to get to the truth when someone started saying things that sounded just plain nutty?

George went on:

A: . . . The sheriff's department says they don't have it [George's *very* extensive record of his "investigation"]. Between the sheriff's department and one guy, Mr. Hoover, who was inside of my house, someone has it. I didn't misplace it.

Q: Okay.

A: It's gone. I had a lot of information in there. It was, like, a-hundred-seventy-some-odd pages, which I think that's probably the size of that [indicating]. There's a lot of stuff that I had written down, dates, times, people I talked to, things that I had done. It's gone.

Q: Okay.

A: I'm racking my brain, trying to remember everything. That would probably assist us a lot today if I had that. I don't have it.

Q: Okay. You started taking notes the second that you—or not the exact second, but shortly after you came home on the fifteenth? [June 15]

A: The night Caylee came up missing, besides this report that I made to the sheriff's department, I started writing stuff down on my own, people I specifically talked to, all the deputies that were at my house, the times, the dates, everything that happened. I did. I did that. Maybe that's the old investigator in me or something like that, but the best things you can do besides—the best thing you can do on something is documentation.

Q: Sure.

A: And if you have that, who can—

In my own fictional world, the Assistant State Attorney now leans over the desk and says, "All right, Mr. Investigator Schmestigator, enough with the 'my dog ate my homework' bullshit. We've got information that cadaver dogs smelled a dead body on your property—for real. We don't have time to be jerked around. Okay? Why don't you go buy a fistful of scratch tickets or something and knock yourself out? You're wasting our fucking time."

Okay, I feel better now. Let's get back to the real interview:

Q: Had you made any copies of that [your 170-page binder] up to a certain point and provided them to Mr. Baez?

A: I never did. I never did. Never gave it to him or anyone else. . . . That was just something I was doing on my own because I had felt compelled to do that. If there's something I felt was worthy, made a pass on, I would have done that. But like I say, everything was all speculation. Everything was just stuff that I was just working on my own, so—

Okay. Enough. If years spent with Cindy Anthony, RN, had left George Anthony as the person or nonperson giving the interview above, imagine what could happen to a little girl growing up in their home. That little girl, whose vagina was "all grown up," according to George, was Casey Marie Anthony. Maybe, when she'd left home June 15, 2008, she just couldn't stomach consigning her own daughter to the same hell. Maybe, in the end, she took some comfort from the fact that she herself was beyond Cindy's reach in jail, and that Caylee was beyond Cindy's reach in heaven. Talk about cheating the Reaper. The ultimate "double takeaway." Being dead offered the chance for rebirth. Being maintained in a state of suspended animation at 4937 Hopespring Drive was like living inside the novel *Coma*.

After she went missing, George and Cindy started searching for Caylee, of course. They had the whole she-bang—T-shirts, posters, you name it. They even had a "command center," although they kept moving it around. Five times. One parking lot to another. And people volunteered to help.

The cash from media sources paying for Caylee memorabilia was starting to flow in, and there was a lot more coming after that.

CRYING A RIVER

One of the volunteers helping the Anthonys search for Caylee was a woman who went by the name of River Cruz. Her real name was Krystal Holloway. She would spend hours and hours at the command center—which was, according to her, more like a makeshift "tent." She was tall and dark, and George took a liking to her. According to Ms. Cruz's testimony at trial, in fact, the two of them began sleeping together—while George was supposed to be devoting himself to the search for Caylee.

George has denied any sexual relationship with River Cruz, saying she was just another volunteer, despite his having sent her a text message that read,

Just thinking about you. I need you in my life.

Ms. Cruz told me she was volunteering for much more than the search for Caylee. "I initiated the sexual contact around August [2008], and we had sex about twelve times," she told me. "Cindy was always home sedated. Nonstop sleeping. I was giving him sex and money—about four thousand dollars—because he said he couldn't pay his bills."

According to Cruz, who was invited into the Anthony home, the interior was pristine—not a single item out of place. "It was very clean. Everything was in order," she said.

"George was like a kid acting out behind the back of his controlling mother," she went on. "Cindy was everything in that family. He's a wuss. She was always taking control of conversations. George always looked to her and deferred to her. She's a controlling bitch, and she's ice cold."

Cruz grew disenchanted with the search for Caylee because she intuited it was a for-profit ruse. "At some point, he knew the baby was gone," she said, "and they were still making money off the networks. . . . He was always turning his cell phone off when he was with me. Why would you do that if you were looking for your granddaughter?"

Cruz maintains that when she began pulling away from George because she considered the search a fraud, he tried to kill himself.

It is well known that George did, indeed, attempt suicide on January 22, 2009, but he has denied that Ms. Cruz had anything to do with it.

Before calling several people to let them know that he was doing himself in, he left a suicide note, reading, in part:

Cynthia Marie:

. . . I have decided to leave the earth, because I need to be with Caylee Marie . . .

I have never been the man any of you could count on. . . .

My loss of life is meaningless . . .

Cynthia Marie . . . 28+ years ago, you corrected me, a man who has now found his identity in life . . .

I blame myself for her being gone! You know for months, as a matter of fact for a year or so I brought stuff up, only to be told not to be negative . . .

I should have done more . . .

As I can tell by my writing and thinking, I am getting very stupid. Wow, what a word STUPID. Yes, I am. . . .

I will take care of Caylee—once I get to God "hopefully."

I want to hold her again, I miss her, I will always love us . . . at least I shaved today, wow . . .

I love you—Cynthia Marie.

Caylee Here I come.
Lee, I am sorry.
Casey—

"Yes? Yes?" I imagine Casey answering. Again, it's my fictional world beckoning. I should be allowed a little of my own fiction amidst *Keeping Up with the Anthonys,* no? "Dad?" Casey goes on. No answer. "Hey, Dad! Dad, why the hell were you looking at my vagina when I delivered Caylee? And why did you let Mom essentially steal her from me? And why didn't you lift a finger to get me psychiatric help when you should have known I so desperately need it? Do you really think Lee is going to end up being okay? He's already gone through one really bad depression. And who is this River Cruz woman who says she was blowing you while you were supposed to be out looking for my baby?"

Again, not to be mean, but I'm just not feelin' it. Number one, I don't know any grandparent who has attempted suicide over the loss of a grandchild. I've asked my colleagues, and none of them can remember any case of a grandparent trying to commit suicide over the loss of a grandchild. One's *child,* yes. It raises the question of George's exact relationship to Caylee. But that is a matter for the genetics experts, not me.

As I write this, by the way, I can feel the call to empathy. I *want* to feel connected to the words in George's suicide note and, thereby, to his suffering. I just can't. And since this is unusual for me, it is worth thinking about it for just a few moments. Because it can give us insight into the mind of Casey Anthony.

If a child grows up in an environment where no emotion seems genuine, where people have very limited—if any—bandwidth to truly connect with one another at a genuine human level (*empathetically*), then that child will herself shut down emotionally. After hundreds or thousands of attempts to be make her needs known and make herself understood and begin to understand those closest to her, she will retreat into psychological solitude and interact with others defensively, sometimes by not volunteering thoughts or feelings at all, but often by lying about her true feelings—and even asserting the opposite of what she thinks or feels. She will perform all manner of mental gymnastics to keep the incredibly sensitive vestige of her true self safe behind ever-thickening walls.

The patterns of behavior required to perpetuate the isolation of the true self are all manner of compulsions and addictions that promise to keep reality, profound disappointment, and pain at bay—compulsive lying, constant interpersonal drama, a plethora of sexual partners, and losing oneself in the Internet and social media are some of them.

Keep in mind that a person in this psychological predicament has to hide her true identity not only from others, but also from herself. Her wounds are not only are still raw, but they are also monsters that threaten to overwhelm her. They are remembered, after all, with the heart and mind of an exquisitely vulnerable child.

The trouble is that this remnant of the self does not lie idle, nor remain in its pristine state. No addiction will ultimately quell its suffering. It grieves its solitude and can spawn deep despondency. It nurses a grudge and can spark extreme rage.

Growing up with people who can't feel real empathy and don't elicit real empathy essentially leaves a person clinging for dear life to fiction.

Of course, it is a loser's game. You can't outdistance the past. The truth is always at your heels, and it always wins.

That would seem to have been Casey's predicament.

Cruz told me she reunited with George and tried to be supportive to him, until he gave her the sense that she wasn't welcome at Caylee's memorial service, held during February 2009. Apparently, he had stopped calling her and started sending her text messages. She didn't like that. "I blew him," she told me, simplifying her testimony at trial, sounding very credible, indeed, "and he blew me off." She chuckled. "So that was that."

MAKING BAIL

On August 20, 2008, bounty hunter Leonard Padilla, from Sacramento, California, arranged for a bond of $500,200 to be posted to secure Casey Anthony's release. Padilla, a dramatic man who wore a cowboy hat and was the host of a *National Geographic* bounty hunter TV show, had also run for Governor of California in 2003.

It was probably inevitable that reality TV and Casey Anthony would find each other, but few people would have predicted that they would start a relationship so soon.

Reality TV is all about staging human relationships and behavior for dramatic effect, while asserting that nothing is staged. And while Casey wasn't going to appear on Padilla's show, flirting with the industry made perfect sense. Reality TV was made for Casey Anthony. She'd already lived like a reality TV star for many years—pretending to be someone she was not, thriving on drama and actually feeling very little for the other characters on set.

Despite the naysayers, Padilla's stated goals were quite clear. He believed that Casey was not going to yield vital information about the whereabouts of Caylee while she was imprisoned. And, whether for fame or for humanitarian reasons or both, he wanted very much to find Caylee alive.

Padilla's brother Greg (also a bounty hunter), who hadn't spoken with him for a decade, nonetheless came to his defense when critics suggested Padilla was just seeking the limelight. "I am sticking up for Leonard on this," he told

Investigation Discovery television. "Leonard can find anybody. He's the best in the business. You can't hide from him. If he can talk to Casey Anthony, he will get enough information to find out what happened to Caylee."

Casey was released on August 21, 2008, at 10:28 A.M. As a condition of bail, she agreed to allow one of Mr. Padilla's employees, Tracy McLoughlin, to shadow her at all times—literally living in the Anthonys' home with her.

Padilla's impression of the Anthony residence and the Anthony family echoed that of River Cruz. "In her universe that she runs," Padilla told me, "everything is perfect. Her home is like a magazine. Her daughter was a part of that and her granddaughter. Everything had to be letter-perfect. She knew her daughter was not normal, but she chose to gloss over it."

Human beings can't live as framed portraits of perfection. They die psychologically from a lack of emotional oxygen.

Maybe Casey was finally starting to understand what she'd been up against at 4937 Hopespring Drive. She told a friend that a song she'd been listening to in jail had moved her. The song, called "The Past," was a work by the immensely talented rock group, Sevendust:

> *Beneath the water that's fallen from my eyes*
> *lays a soul I've left behind*
> *the edge of sorrow was reached but now I'm fine*
> *I've filled the hole I had inside*
>
> *I'll pray it doesn't scream my name*
> *so I light a flame and let it breathe*
> *the air that kills the shame*
>
> *I'm up, I'm down*
> *like a roller coaster racing through my life*
> *I've erased the past again*
>
> *A risky morning, I feel like I'm alive*
> *I can't believe I've made it through this time*

the edge of sorrow I lived in for some time
(lived in for some time)
has left the hole I have inside

The burden is I try my hate
was the last thing I ever felt
or thought I could escape

I'm up, I'm down
like a roller coaster racing through my life
I've erased the past again

You left me here then broke me down
the difference is this time around
I will not let you see me drown

I'm up, I'm down
like a roller coaster racing through my life
I've erased the past again

Erased the past again now
Erased the past again

Beneath the water
that's fallen from my eyes

Sensing that you've erased the past is a step toward resurrecting it and looking at it—even if it's very ugly. Knowing that someone has broken you is a step toward resurrecting yourself.

According to Padilla, while the Anthonys wanted the house to look perfect, they routinely lied to one another.

"At one time or another," he told me, "we've all lied about something important to us. They don't have that problem. Cindy and George will lie and lie about anything and everything and not care about it."

Something about the family, according to Padilla, had resulted in Casey having "a missing part."

"I've been around fugitives and their families," he told me, "so if a mother lies for her son, I can tell. She says, 'He's surfing in Hawaii.' Well, I automatically think, Puerto Rico. But Cindy lies about everything, whether it matters or not."

Padilla also detected Casey's ability to shed one role and adopt another instantly. "Twenty minutes in Casey's life is like years for someone else," he said. "The next twenty minutes determines everything. When she was the shot girl for [Tony] Lazzaro [at Fusion Ultra Lounge], she instantly became that. Automatically. Flawlessly."

What Padilla didn't struggle with was *why* Casey was able to lie so freely and be a human chameleon. He didn't know all the times she had had to defeat her *self,* in order to avoid being known and, thereby, in my opinion exposed to the mind-shattering levels of control exercised by her mother. He didn't know how that habit of suppressing her true identity as a human being had released her from the empathetic tethers that bind the rest of us to ourselves and others and had left her "free" to leap from one incarnation of herself to another, only careful never to alight on her genuine emotions.

I believe all these mental machinations were, for Casey Anthony, entirely unconscious. She was like a bumper car bouncing off anything that presented resistance, without even registering the resistance. I doubt her lies were an effort at all. A synthesis of duplicity and distraction was her natural state.

Think of it this way: If a woman has walked with her right foot turned slightly inward her whole life, then continuing to do so probably won't be noticeable to her, nor is it likely to feel unnatural. Her pathological gait has become second nature to her. The movement that would feel strange and would take effort and thought and might cause a good deal of pain would be to walk *without* her foot turned inward—to walk *normally.*

Casey's compulsive lying was very likely the same sort of thing: a psychological gait that was automatic, triggering no guilt, no remorse, no fear and not perpetrated with any particular desire to offend anyone. Much to the contrary, her lying was likely what she considered the path of least resistance, designed to offend no one.

Tracy McLoughlin saw even more evidence of what Casey had become, but also lacked the all-important *why*—that skeleton key that unlocks every mystery of human behavior.

"She was, like, in another world," McLoughlin told me. "She wanted to have fun together. She lives for no reason at all and believes her own lies.

"After a visit from Child Protective Services, she said, 'They don't even believe I work at Universal. No one believes it. I'm the only one who knows what's going on.'"

McLoughlin noted two qualities about Casey that others—including Casey's friend Michelle Murphy—had noted, too. She couldn't be coaxed into conflict, and she wanted to make people feel good around her, maybe so they simply liked her and didn't challenge her.

"You don't try to pin her down, or she'll just turn you off," McLoughlin told me. "She wanted to make me happy. She doted on me. If you met her face-to-face, you would love her. She's really, really, really likable. And she's really, really, really sick.

"She seemed so happy. That was the strongest thing. She was like a 'cruise director.' She made me coffee every morning. She wanted for us to dress alike."

Interestingly, McLoughlin pegged her emotional age at that of a ten- or twelve-year-old, exactly the ages during which Casey later wrote about being sexually abused. And abuse of that kind can, indeed, almost "freeze" one's emotional development, locking in it in at the age when the abuse took place.

McLoughlin observed Casey's addiction to Facebook, as well. One episode she witnessed was especially telling. "Facebook is a huge part of her life," McLoughlin said. "She was in the computer room next to me. I thought I heard her crying, but when I went in, she said, 'Check out this guy on Facebook! He thinks I'm gorgeous.'"

Lots of Casey's defenses were in play while Tracy was

watching her to make sure she didn't skip bail. Another of Leonard Padilla's employees, named Rob Dick, was involved with Tracy in Casey's case. "She came on to Rob," Tracy recalled. "And she came on to me, too."

But Casey's anger wasn't entirely camouflaged. "If you call her on anything and try to bring her back to reality, she will cut you off. She can be a bitch. She'll be, like, 'Get the fuck out of my room.'"

In the end, Tracy McGloughlin came away from her time with Casey and the Anthonys with one conclusion that may have been playing at the back of Casey's mind, as well. "Maybe she's better off dead," she said.

By August 30, 2008, Leonard Padilla's confidence that he could get Casey to share important information with him about the whereabouts of Caylee Marie Anthony had run out. He said he believed Caylee was dead.

Padilla said that the Texas-based surety company that had underwritten Casey's bond was rescinding it. The company was too concerned about Casey's security—given the angry crowds outside the Anthony home—to continue being a party to keeping her in the community.

The same day that Casey Anthony entered jail again, EquuSearch, a mounted search team, joined two hundred volunteers to comb through an area of land near the Orlando International Airport, looking for Caylee or clues relating to her disappearance.

Mandy Albritton, EquuSearch's deputy director in the search for Caylee, said, "Whether we're looking for a live child or a dead child, we'd like for the community to continue to work for Caylee. Whether she's coming home to live out her life or home to rest, it's still a rescue mission."

What Albritton couldn't know was what Tracy McLoughlin had only recently learned: Were Caylee Anthony to have gone home to 4937 Hopespring Drive, she would have, in any case, met an untimely psychological end.

Casey knew that in her heart of hearts, too—even if she was consciously more focused on losing access to Facebook as she lost her freedom. She would be released on bail one more time when an anonymous source again posted bond for her on September 3, 2008.

On October 14, however, a grand jury indicted Casey on charges of first-degree murder, aggravated child abuse, aggravated manslaughter, and four counts of providing false information. She faced the death penalty.

The next day, Casey appeared in court. Bond was denied. She was placed in protective custody at the Orange County jail.

JAILED AND DEAD, BUT FREE

Remember, if you will, what Charles Mason said about going to jail:

> We're all in our own prisons, we are each all our own wardens and we do our own time. I can't judge anyone else. What other people do is not really my affair unless they approach me with it. Prison's in your mind. Can't you see I'm free?

Casey was behind bars, but that didn't stop her mind from jumping place to place, in what seemed like an unconscious strategy to continue suppressing her deep emotions and identity. She established a relationship with another inmate named Robyn Adams, who became her pen pal. The two women traded notes, which they hid for each other inside a prison library book, and also swapped via a guard. The guard was later suspended for collaborating with them.

In one of her notes to Robyn, Casey showed how quickly she could move on from a painful topic—this time, the loss of her daughter:

> I look at my pictures of Caylee so many times throughout the day and can't help but smile at my little Rock Star. I miss her, more than I can ever express in words. Somedays, the tears just won't end . . . I just sneezed my confirmation from God ☺ I've been doing that a

lot lately. Very rarely do I just "sneeze" anymore . . .
One of the few things I actually like the cold weather
for—it stifle[s] my allergy attacks. I do like wearing
cute boots and a leather jacket. And hats. Mittens. I
want a leather bomber jacket. . . . that and an awesome
pair of biker boots. Of course, the quote that comes to
mind is from Dumb and Dumber: killer boots man! . . .
Did you hear about Christian Bales outburst on the set
of the new Terminator movie?

Casey's sadness wouldn't end . . . until it turned to laughter . . . then was lost in a sneezing attack . . . then gave way to thoughts about pretty clothes and footwear . . . then yielded to a one-liner from a movie . . . then to a bit of celebrity gossip.

Elsewhere, Casey even wondered whether her attorney might be able to order a hair-removal product for her that she had seen on an infomercial, so she could use it upon her release, especially on her bikini line.

The hopscotching was likely a necessary, unconscious mental strategy. It wasn't just that she was cavalier, or flighty, or narcissistic. She was on the run from reality. After all, Casey was—according to her own writings—struggling with memories of being sexually abused by her brother and father. If that were true, and if she lacked the freedom to get online and get out of her own head and get together with one man after another, then she had to find some other path away from the truth, away from the past, and away from the self. The path had to get her lost.

It is worth noting that Casey had reportedly begun to suffer seizures. And it is not outlandish to consider the possibility that the psychology of denial had literally become a physiological disorder. Stress can precipitate seizures, so why not the stress of horrific memories beginning to surface. Her seizures had the effect of rendering her confused and disoriented. They distorted her perception of time and space. With nowhere to run and nowhere to hide from her pain, it was almost as though her brain were short-circuiting, in a last, desperate, unconscious attempt to keep the past under wraps.

Remember what Michelle Murphy had said: She and Casey had the ability to flip a switch and shut down emotionally. That strategy was failing Casey. Without access to all the strategies she used to keep her *self* under wraps, her brain could no longer contain the emotional energy surging through it.

In another note to Robyn Adams, Casey talked about plans to escape her identity for real, in the future, upon her release:

> So should I go red or blonde? I'm trying to decide how extreme I want to go with my makeover. I will get colored contacts so I can change up my look from time to time. Who is this Casey Anthony you speak of? If you could change your name, any name, what would it be? I've been thinking about that a lot lately.

Who is this Casey Anthony you speak of? That question could serve as the tag line for Casey's entire life story. Long ago, her mind had taken evasive action to avoid the dehumanizing influences at 4937 Hopespring Drive. She had confined her*self*—her exquisitely vulnerable, lacerated spirit—to a very dark place, very deep inside her. And then she had tried to forget she was even buried there, by keeping herself entertained and distracted.

It hadn't worked. It never does. The core of her had turned increasingly despondent, increasingly rageful.

Casey had been dead wrong in her myCupid.com profile when she wrote: *My motto . . . Live for the future, forget the past*.

The truth always wins. You can't outdistance the past.

Who is this Casey Anthony you speak of? George and Cindy Anthony had apparently never interacted with her in a way that encouraged her to know the answer to that question. If they were so out of touch with her as an adult not to know she was pregnant, and not express much concern that she wasn't certain who the baby's father was, and not care that she was naked and exposed in front of her own father while delivering a baby, and not (if you credit her writings at all) respond to her claims that she had been sexually abused, and not understand that it was important for her to hold her child after she was born, and not get her help when she pleaded to be placed in a psychiatric unit, and not take steps to get her any real help when she stole repeatedly and lied repeatedly, and not follow up on the fact that she had invented a fake job, and not press to meet the nanny supposedly taking care of her daughter, then it is almost certain that they were no more focused on her as a human being when she was a child.

After all, neither Cindy nor George Anthony had cared very much to proactively arm Caylee with a real and true life story, either. They both seemed more concerned that no man's name appear on Caylee's birth certificate than that her father be identified. They demonstrated no interest in the truth about her parentage, as though her life story were but a chapter of their own, as though she were their property, not her own person.

CMA (Cindy Marie Anthony), *CMA* (Casey Marie Anthony), *CMA* (Caylee Marie Anthony).

Cindy Marie Anthony had overshadowed everyone and enabled any weakness anyone in her family ever showed and inhaled every bit of emotional oxygen at 4937 Hopespring Drive, until there was no hope, and everyone around her was suffocating and light-headed and just struggling to survive—to keep their heads above water.

And, then, someone did not.

On December 11, 2008, the skeletal remains of Caylee Anthony were found in a wooded area less than a half mile from the Anthony's house. A utility worker discovered her bones wrapped in a black plastic trash bag. When he picked up the bag, a small skull rolled out.

It had come to that.

Casey would later write Robyn Adams:

> We're going to set a date for the [memorial] service sometime this coming week. I'm extremely nervous. . . .

We'll finally have a little bit of closure. Is it wrong of me though, to not really want to know the truth? I'm honestly scared of the numerous possibilities. She's safe. She's in God's loving arms. . . . she will never have to have her heart broken, or see the constant negativity our society breeds, nor will she ever be abused or taken advantage of.

The memorial service was held on February 10, 2009. Cindy Anthony addressed the gathering, thus: "It breaks my heart today that Casey isn't here today to honor her child who she loved so much. Casey, I hope you're listening to this. I wish I could comfort you. I wish I could take away your pain and wipe away your tears."

Truth: Not only was Casey not there that day; she hadn't been present—in any real way—for many years. I think Cindy had seen to that.

Now, Caylee was a memory.

On July 5, 2011, after thirty-three days of testimony by over ninety witnesses, the jury in the Casey Anthony trial found her not guilty of murdering Caylee, not guilty of aggravated child abuse, and not guilty of aggravated manslaughter of a child. She was convicted only on charges of misleading law enforcement.

Casey was released from jail on July 17, 2011. She went into hiding. Of course, she had always been in hiding.

Bella Vita.

On July 21, 2011, Cindy and George Anthony vacationed in the Bahamas at Atlantis Paradise Island and took time to swim with dolphins. They were photographed smiling while kissing and tickling the adorable creatures.

Bella Vita.

On September 12, 2011, almost two years to the day after Caylee's memorial service, the couple appeared on *Dr. Phil.* They were both dressed to kill. Cindy looked as though she'd had a makeover. She commented that she thought Casey was "an awesome mother." She has stated in the past that she hopes Casey has more children.

The Anthonys said they would not receive a dollar of the reported $500,000 to $1 million the program paid for their interviews. The money was donated to a controversial newly formed charitable fund called Caylee's Fund. One of the missions of the fund, according to the Anthonys' attorney, was to protect grandparents' rights.

The prior fund operated by George and Cindy Anthony is called the Caylee Marie Anthony Foundation. It generated allegations of misuse of the monies donated to it. Eighty percent of the foundation's profits were purportedly used to pay administrative costs.

Bella Vita.

After all, Cindy did need to get back that ten dollars that she wasted parking at Universal Studios on July 3, 2008, while searching for Casey and Caylee. I don't think she'll ever forget about that loss.

IDENTITY SUPPRESSION SYNDROME

What affliction could Casey Anthony have suffered that would lead her to invent so much of her life story, almost entirely lose sight of her real self, and end up as a central character in a drama that extinguished the life of her two-year-old daughter? What psychopathology could explain the short-circuiting of her empathy so completely that she would write in jail of grieving her daughter's death, then, within a sentence, write about fancy shoes she wanted to buy? How could she be facing execution and wonder how to order a product to remove hair from her bikini line that she'd seen on an infomercial? What shall we call the set of signs and symptoms that included her being seemingly oblivious of her own pregnancy, being "able" to let her father watch her spread-legged in the delivery suite, being "able" to invent a nanny and maintain the ruse for years, being "able" to tell so many men that she was theirs and theirs alone, being "able" to compete in—and win—a hot-body contest while her daughter's body was decomposing, being "able" to get a tattoo that read *Bella Vita*—"Beautiful Life"—when her daughter's life had ended at two years old, being "able" to bring detectives to her nonexistent office at Universal Studios, being "able" to sit for hours in a conference room with three detectives who had cracked cold-blooded murderers and leave them with nothing to show for their efforts, as though they had been in that room all that time alone?

Some have theorized that Casey Anthony suffers from

antisocial personality disorder—that she is a psychopath without conscience. Some people have wondered whether she might be bipolar, and, hence, often manic and euphoric. Some people have combed through the *Diagnostic and Statistical Manual of Mental Disorders* (DSM), psychiatry's "official" compendium of disorders, and concluded she has some variant of a dissociative identity disorder, of which multiple personality disorder is one.

I have not evaluated Casey Anthony face-to-face, so I will not render a diagnosis from the DSM. Nor do I believe that any disorder in that rather stilted and limiting book adequately describes her.

I suggest, instead, that Ms. Anthony is best described as demonstrating something I call *identity suppression syndrome*.

I see Casey Anthony as having responded to what I view as a depersonalizing environment at 4937 Hopespring Drive by burying her real self—her true identity—in order to keep alive a vestige of her real emotions and real thoughts and real hopes and real needs. Perpetuating this unconscious psychological strategy, however, required more and more in the way of mental gymnastics. That's why she "needed" to walk away from interpersonal conflict that would have "called her out," why she developed that emotional on/off switch, why she used men and sex to essentially drug herself, why she gravitated to Facebook and MySpace and Cupid.com as places where she could interact with others from a distance and from behind the masks of her "profiles," and why she used constant text messaging, not so much as a way to stay "in touch" with others, but rather as a way to keep them satisfied with tiny, fictional doses of her. *This is me!* all her frenetic, Internet-fueled activity was saying, when nothing could be further from the truth.

Yet, all Casey Anthony's efforts to bury her true identity and true self were not sufficient. They never are. Inside, I believe she was filled with primitive rage for having been psychologically suffocated, raw fear that the last of her would ultimately be extinguished by her oppressors, and self-loathing for having "allowed" her own destruction as an individual.

Even Casey's reported seizures may have been testimony to everything she had tried to resist thinking about—*resistance* being the operative concept. All her on/off switches failed her in the aftermath of Caylee's death. Runaway circuits in her brain were just more evidence of that.

Because I believe that Casey Anthony is best described as displaying identity suppression syndrome, I can see what trouble may lie ahead for her. Absent a protracted course of truly extraordinary insight-oriented psychotherapy, Ms. Anthony will need to continue to suppress her identity and run from reality. She risks running to alcohol, illicit drugs, sexual addiction, and all manner of other dependencies. Any one of these may create hazards in her life she can little predict at this moment. I would not be surprised were she, for example, to overdose.

It is also possible that the intense self-hatred I believe Ms. Anthony continues to run from will ultimately overtake her, leading her to suffer a paralyzing major depression and even psychotic syptoms. It would not surprise me to hear she had ended her own life.

It is also possible that what Ms. Anthony has denied about her *self*—what she has suppressed of her identity—will manifest itself as disorder in her physiology, that her seizures will literally have their equivalent in a breakdown of cellular integrity, leading to a malignancy.

It is also possible that the primitive rage I believe Ms. Anthony has attempted to compartamentalize inside her will burst forth, leading to the destruction of another human being.

I hope for none of these things. I hope Casey Anthony heals because I am, inextricably and irrevocably and without apology, a healer who prizes empathy above all things, and because I believe in my heart that the potential exists for anyone to be saved—that light sometimes miraculously enters the darkest places imaginable.

I hate—no I despise, I loathe—the sin, not the sinner.

I also see in Casey Anthony's story a cautionary tale. Poised as we are at the threshold of abandoning our own true identities and all reality, leaping in a wholesale fashion into social media and the Internet, there will be an increasing number of individuals who can remain, for longer and longer, buried alive, with their identities suppressed behind thick walls of trauma and denial—until those walls fail. When they do—and they always do—there will be more and more acts of nearly unspeakable, almost unthinkable violence that seem to come out of the blue but, in fact, have been a lifetime in the making.

POSTFACE

Dr. Ablow has made a substantial "Heroes' Circle" contribution to the National Center for Missing & Exploited Children, in memory of Caylee Marie Anthony.

AFTERWORD

Two years ago, when I wrote *Inside the Mind of Casey Anthony*, I coined the term *identity suppression syndrome* to denote someone who, like her, has seemingly lost access to her genuine self—including buried feelings of despondency, shame or rage—and is hiding behind what the great psychiatrist Hervey Cleckley called a "mask of sanity."

Two years ago, I wrote that Casey Anthony was partly a creation of depersonalizing forces at work inside her extraordinary family and partly a creation of depersonalizing forces at work in our society. I predicted more acts of horrific violence that would seem to come out of the blue, because our Facebook-friendly culture allows people to perpetuate false fronts as never before, letting toxic emotions smolder underground, then erupt into unspeakable acts, seemingly without explanation.

Well, just two years has been enough time to meet James Holmes, the 25-year-old man accused of dressing as the Joker and killing a dozen people (and injuring 58 others) at the premiere of *The Dark Knight Rises* at a theater in Aurora, Colorado. Just two years has been enough time to meet Anders Breivik, the 32-year-old Norwegian man who hid behind anabolic steroids and cosmetic surgery before killing 77 people, including 69 adolescents attending a summer camp. Just two years has been enough time to meet Adam Lanza, the 20-year-old man accused of emerging from the windowless basement of his mother's home, where he played video games several hours a day, to fatally shoot his mother in the face, then kill 20 children and six staff members at the Sandy Hook Elementary School in Newtown, Connecticut. Just two years has been enough time to meet pretty Jodi Arias, the soft-spoken, 28-year-old woman who suddenly stabbed her ex-boyfriend 27 times, slashed his neck and shot him in the head.

There have always been people who try—and fail—to keep their incendiary emotions under wraps, inaccessible even to themselves, but now the tools to do so are more numerous and more available, creating more human time bombs than ever. The pathophysiology of what I call identity suppression syndrome will continue to explain seemingly inexplicable acts of destruction that will make headlines—and more and more of them—in the coming years.

When a person is trapped behind a mask, as an actor in a made-for-YouTube version of life, then negative feedback from the real world—whether being fired from a job, jilted by a lover, or given a bad grade by a teacher—can lead him to project all his buried self-loathing onto others, not infrequently including family members. There are thousands of such people in our communities at this very moment.

No one can predict what will crack the mask and cause it to fall away.

The pathological narcissist addicted to Facebook, with 1,248 friends, and the video game junkie with Asperger's Syndrome, armed to the teeth, are close cousins—related by their lack of connection to self and others, caused, in part, by exposure to toxic technologies.

Casey Anthony herself hasn't made any new headlines for acts of violence toward others. She's gone underground and into hiding, surfacing here and there when her continuing legal entanglements—including civil suits against her—require her presence in a courtroom. In a way, her disappearing act is a predictable chapter in her life story. What she lived through as a child led her to disappear, for all intents and purposes, long before she ever made headlines.

In this regard, we do know more than we knew about Casey Anthony two years ago. We have the recently released depositions of psychiatrist Jeffrey Danziger, M.D. and psychologist William Weitz, Ph.D. regarding their official psychiatric evaluations of Ms. Anthony.

She showed no attempt to deceive Danziger on the sophisticated psychological tests he administered—the Minnesota Multiphasic Personality Inventory.

She did not qualify for any psychiatric diagnosis.

She did not qualify for antisocial (sociopathic) personality disorder.

She did not qualify for narcissistic personality disorder.

She did not qualify for borderline personality disorder.

She didn't even come close.

"Certainly," Danziger told prosecutor Jeff Ashton in his deposition, "there was no exaggeration or malingering (faking) or amplification of symptoms."

No, the real story of Casey Anthony is that of a girl who buries her inner self so deeply that she is, for all intents and purposes, absent from her own existence. Gone. A ghost. A stranger to us, and even to herself.

But there is much more to say. Because the material in Danziger and Weitz's depositions rings so true for a victim of horrific sexual abuse that it is stunning. I am making no claim here of my own that George Anthony is a pedophile and child rapist, but I challenge any other mental health professional with any experience treating victims of trauma to review the depositions Danziger and Weitz rendered and come away believing that Casey Anthony's assertion that she was abused seems entirely fabricated.

Danziger stated that the scenes of sexual abuse Casey Anthony related to him as occurring at the hands of her father George Anthony were "disgusting, demeaning, intercourse, and everything." Casey Anthony told him the abuse started when she was 8 and tapered off when she turned 11. After that, it was an occasional rape, with the last one occurring when she was 18.

"I tried to fight back when I was older," Casey Anthony told him. "I'm not a big person."

"I'm not a big person." She sounds almost apologetic. She sounds powerless. And that's the way victims of sexual abuse sound.

But there's more. "My first real sex was at age sixteen," she said. Asked by Jeffrey Ashton what she meant by that, Danziger stated, "Well, as opposed to anything that was intrafamilial."

I have listened to victims of sexual abuse by family members for over 15 years. And that is the language of a victim. Pure, and simple, and heartbreaking. Word-for-word. "My first real sex." Where on earth would Casey Anthony have learned to flawlessly mimic the lexicon of a victim of child rape?

"What would you do the next day [after being raped by your father]?" Danziger asked her.

"Well, I'd go to school. I made . . . As. I had friends. I won awards. I was a popular girl."

Casey Anthony doesn't test anything like a sociopath. And I am here to tell you, she doesn't come across as one in the Danziger or Weitz depositions, whatsoever.

"How do you handle the unspeakable?" she asked Danziger. "By putting it in a little box, hiding it deep, pretending all is well. Doing that since age eight, since elementary school, I became exceedingly perfect."

If Casey Anthony was having sex with a family member at age eight, then going to school to play four square and take arithmetic tests and do it with a smile, then you have your answer as to how her daughter could have gone missing and she could have gone dancing.

Mystery solved.

Does she hate her father? On this, too, Casey Anthony sounds like she is delivering the raw, honest truth from her gut:

"I hate the fact that I don't hate him for everything that's done, everything that happened. I hate the fact that I still love him, little girl wishing my dad could be my dad. I can't figure out why I don't hate him."

Is she full of crap? Or is she describing precisely what I told you she was suffering with: *identity suppression syndrome*—an inability to summon any true feelings from behind the dark, desperate walls of her trauma, lest they fracture her psychologically into a million tiny pieces?

The rest of the Danziger deposition is almost unreadable, so stark is Casey's telling of the story, so seemingly unadorned. You can decide for yourself if she has the acting ability of Meryl Streep, combined with the sinister mind of Charles Manson, or if she is a garden-variety victim of child rape lost in terrifying shadows of her former self.

She told Danziger that she slept with Caylee to keep the little girl away from her father, George Anthony. She locked the door "to protect her the way [she] hadn't been protected." She told him that being exposed to repeated rape without being protected by her mother is why she doesn't tend to ally with other women.

Then one early morning, when she forgot to lock the door, she said, as quoted in the deposition, George Anthony woke her up. He had Caylee Anthony soaked and dead in his arms.

"I took her from him and collapsed on the porch. He was yelling at me . . . your fault, couldn't believe you did this. . . . He left the house . . . saying, 'Daddy is going to take care of it.'"

Daddy. This is the same Daddy, you will recall, who watched his daughter give birth, from the foot of the bed, staring at her naked. This is the same Daddy who found his daughter's abandoned car, thought it smelled like a corpse, then headed off to work at a movie theater to make about 20 bucks an hour as a security guard.

This is the same Daddy who reportedly pushed his own father through a plate-glass window when the old man wouldn't turn over control of his car dealership. This is the same Daddy who boldly recounted to law enforcement officials the memory of his daughter's ultrasound when the obstetrician pointed out his granddaughter's vagina and called it a hamburger.

This is the same Daddy who reportedly neglected to ask his daughter who the father of her unborn child might be—when his daughter finally realized she was pregnant at seven months.

This is the same Daddy whose ex-wife says he was mostly interested in being a cop because he got to hide behind a uniform.

This is the same Daddy who reportedly wanted to be a character at Disney World.

Then Casey Anthony told Dr. Danziger this: "I think he held her underwater, maybe he was doing something to her and tried to cover it up. . . . I don't think it's an accident and I didn't do it."

She implied George Anthony's suicide attempt after Caylee's body was found was his way out of the grief or guilt.

Do you feel nothing but hatred now for Casey Anthony, after these two years? Do you think she is lying? Do you think that she is as gifted as Sir Laurence Olivier and as smart as Bernie Madoff, this high school dropout, club-hopping, unemployed girl from Orlando?

Is it any wonder that the jurors, having read these depositions, couldn't bring themselves to convict Casey Anthony?

Keith Ablow, MD
April 8, 2013